D0081465

RED
over BLACK

Recent Titles in
Contributions in Afro-American and African Studies
Series Adviser: *Hollis R. Lynch*

"Good Time Coming?": Black Nevadans in the Nineteenth Century
Elmer R. Rusco

Race First: Ideological and Organizational Struggles of Marcus Garvey and the Universal Negro Improvement Association
Tony Martin

Silence to the Drums: A Survey of the Literature of the Harlem Renaissance
Margaret Perry

Internal Combustion: The Races in Detroit, 1915-1926
David Allan Levine

Henry Sylvester Williams and the Origins of the Pan African Movement, 1869-1911
Owen Charles Mathurin

Periodic Markets, Urbanization, and Regional Planning: A Case Study from Western Kenya
Robert A. Obudho and *Peter P. Waller*

Frederick Douglass on Women's Rights
Philip S. Foner, editor

Travail and Triumph: Black Life and Culture in the South Since the Civil War
Arnold H. Taylor

Black Ethos: Northern Urban Negro Life and Thought, 1890-1930
David Gordon Nielson

New Rulers in the Ghetto: The Community Development Corporation and Urban Poverty
Harry Edward Berndt

The FLN in Algeria: Party Development in a Revolutionary Society
Henry F. Jackson

RED
over BLACK

Black Slavery
among the
Cherokee Indians

R. HALLIBURTON, JR.

Contributions in Afro-American and African Studies, Number 27

 GREENWOOD PRESS
WESTPORT, CONNECTICUT ● LONDON, ENGLAND

Library of Congress Cataloging in Publication Data

Halliburton, R.
Red over Black.

(Contributions in Afro-American and African studies ; no. 27)
Bibliography: p.
Includes index.
1. Cherokee Indians—Slaves, Ownership of. 2. Slavery in the United States.
3. Indians of North America—Southern States—Slaves, Ownership of.
I. Title. II. Series.
E99.C5H223   301.44'93'0975   76-15329
ISBN 0-8371-9034-7

Library of Congress Catalog Card Number: 76-15329
ISBN: 0-8371-9034-7

First published in 1977

Greenwood Press, Inc.
51 Riverside Avenue, Westport, Connecticut 06880

Printed in the United States of America

10 9 8 7 6 5 4 3 2

For my wife,
La Vonne,

and daughters,
Janet and Judith

Contents

Preface

Though it is small in size, this book has been several years in the making. Its genesis dates back to 1969 when I attended the dramatic presentation of the "Trail of Tears" at the outdoor TSA-LA-GI amphitheater in the Cherokee Cultural Complex near Tahlequah, Oklahoma. The work has grown to fruition through several research papers read at historical conventions and articles published in scholarly journals.

The Cherokee Indians are a proud and ancient people. Their history reaches far back beyond definitely calculated time to the ages when tradition fathered history. At one time the Cherokees had hoped to remain apart and aloof from the white man and his civilization. White explorers, traders, trappers, missionaries, road builders, and squatters rendered that wish impossible, however, and convinced the more progressive Cherokees that they had to adopt the white man's civilization in order to survive. This decision was not unanimous, however, and well before 1800 some tribesmen had moved to the trans-Mississippi West to escape the encroachment of the white man. The vast majority who remained in the East, however, succeeded exceedingly well in their acculturation—so well that they were visited by American and European whites curious to observe the cultural and ethnological phenomenon of the primitive "forest children" who were evolving into a civilized nation within the span of two generations.

Most Cherokees were cognizant of the efficacy of voluntary acculturation and quickly accepted the accouterments of European civilization, including the institution of black slavery. Nevertheless, as late as 1975 an adequate documented treatment of the subject had never appeared in print. Myriad volumes of monographs, textbooks, biographies, essays, anthologies, and other works treating the history of the American Indian and the Afro-American are rolling from the nation's presses in seemingly ever-increasing numbers. These works sometimes refer to the subject briefly (often obliquely) and usually provide misinformation and perpetuate long-accepted myths.

The purpose of this book is to attempt to show that black slavery existed as an institution in the Cherokee Nation, in the East and West, for more than 150 years. Furthermore, I hope to show that full-bloods, half-breeds, near-whites, and whites—but Cherokees all—possessed slaves and that slavery in the Cherokee Nation was a microcosm of the "peculiar institution" that existed in the southern United States.

Since most published works represent a collective effort, acknowledgments are in order. I shall forever be appreciative to Northeastern Oklahoma State University for providing several research grants that enabled the continuation of my research. I am indebted to the Smithsonian Institution for a short-term appointment as a visiting scholar. Help provided by the Honorable Clem McSpadden, former United States Representative from Oklahoma's Second Congressional District, and his Legislative Assistant, Don Duncan, proved indispensible. Congressman McSpadden is of Cherokee extraction and is a direct descendant of Oklahoma humorist Will Rogers. The staff members of Northeastern Oklahoma State University's John Vaughan Memorial Library and its Cherokee Collection were more than helpful—they were cheerful, encouraging, and friendly. This book could never have gone to press without the expertise and professional help of Obera Cude, Helen Wheat, Jewell Dold, and Mary Catherine James of the John Vaughan Library. The aid of archivists at the National Archives, the University of Oklahoma, the Thomas Gilcrease Institute of American History and Art, the Oklahoma Historical Society, and the Tennessee State Library and Archives is sincerely appreciated.

I am indebted to the Oklahoma College History Professors Association, the Northern Great Plains History Conference, the Southern Historical Association, the Organization of American Historians, the Association for the Study of Afro-American Life and History, and several other professional organizations, all of which spurred my research with invitations to read papers at their meetings. The University of Winnipeg served as a most gracious host while I conducted a colloquium on the subject of this book. Last, but most definitely not least, I want to acknowledge my family, colleagues, and students. Their encouragement, understanding, cameraderie, indulgence, and fellowship have been appreciated.

Any value which might subsequently be attached to this work is to a large degree attributable to those acknowledged above. However, I assume full responsibility for any errors or defects that may be contained herein.

R. Halliburton, Jr.
Tahlequah, Oklahoma

RED
over BLACK

1   The Origins of Black Slavery in the Cherokee Country

Despite the voluminous literature treating black slavery in America, significant omissions remain. Areas that have not been adequately investigated include the ownership of slaves by several tribes of American Indians, including the Cherokees. No comprehensive and documented treatment of black slavery in the Cherokee Nation has ever appeared in print, and primary source materials are now scarce, scanty, and scattered. Available information mostly concerns plantation owners who were large slaveholders. These were the men of influence who left wills, diaries, letters, and other papers and whose names appeared in newspapers, in missionaries, and Indian Agents' correspondence, and in the laws of the Cherokee Nation.

Although there are numerous works treating the tribe, a definitive history of the Cherokees is yet to be written. Existing volumes barely mention or entirely omit the institution of black slavery. Southern histories, such as the ten-volume *History of the South*, provide virtually no information about slavery among the Cherokees.[1] One of the best works on black history, John Hope Franklin's *From Slavery to Freedom,* is void of material on this topic.[2] Oklahoma history textbooks, even the multivolume compendiums, are also virtually silent about black slavery in the Cherokee Nation.

There are several works on the general topic of relations between Indians and blacks in the United States. Some have specifically treated

that subject in the Southeast and in Indian Territory. Yet, the subject
of black slavery among the Cherokees is all but omitted. Annie H. Abel's
excellent work, *The American Indian as Slaveholder and Secessionist,*
admirably treats Indians as secessionists but devotes very little attention
to slaveholding in general and barely mentions the institution among the
Cherokees.[3]

This paucity of information, however, has not hindered the growth
of unsubstantiated generalizations and numerous outright myths. From
the Europeans' first meetings with the American Indians until the present,
the Indian has been a familiar—yet unknown and sometimes unreal—
person to most whites and blacks. That which is "known" about the
Indian, including the Cherokees, is often at best superficial and distorted
or at worst, utterly false. It is often alleged that the lives of black slaves
owned by the Cherokees were considerably easier than those owned by
white masters. Moreover, it has frequently been reported that the Indians
regarded their black slaves as family members and as fellow human beings,
that their slaves enjoyed much more "freedom," that slave families were
not broken up, and that intermarriage was not uncommon. One author
maintained that Cherokee slaves were so pampered that they were not
marketable in the United States.[4] There appears to be little evidence to
support such commonly accepted conclusions.

Slavery is at least as old as recorded history and appears to have been
practiced throughout most of the world at one time or another. The
Cherokees practiced slavery, yet there are no words for "slave" and
"Negro" in their language. The Cherokee Indians belong to the greater
Iroquoian language stock and once referred to themselves as *Ani Yunwiya*
("principal people"). They were also known at one time as *Kituhwagi,*
from the name of an ancient town near the center of their country. The
name *Cherokee* may be derived from a Choctaw term that signified the
inhabitants of a cave country.[5]

The Cherokees resided in the southeastern portion of what is now the
United States and had a semi-sedentary hunting, fishing, gathering, and
agricultural economy when Europeans and Africans first appeared among
them. The tribe possessed a vast region in the southern Appalachians
where they had lived for as long as archaeological evidence can determine.
Fields of corn, squash, pumpkins, peas, gourds, beans, and tobacco were
regularly cultivated. One distinguished American historian has written:

When the first settlers came to the New World, they found the Indians not only able but also willing to aid them in the establishment of an agricultural economy. Because of the superiority of Indian crops over the European when grown in the virgin soil and environment of the New World, Indian farming became the basis of all American agriculture. Indeed, it is in this field that the American Indian has made his great contribution to white civilization.[6]

European influences modified most of the arts and practices of American Indians. Usually the first things that the Indians adopted from their white neighbors were improved weapons and tools. Slavery, however, had existed in parts of North America long before the arrival of Europeans. A form of slavery had existed among several tribes for sufficient time to become prominent in tribal mythology and to modify the habits and institutions of the people. Although slaves were usually prisoners taken in wars with other tribes, there appears to have been a regular commercial traffic in some areas, and slavery was the basis of considerable wealth. Expeditions were sometimes launched for the express purpose of capturing slaves. On the Northwest Pacific Coast many villages contained large numbers of slaves; it was said of one of them that "almost a third of the population were slaves."[7]

Unfortunately the early Spanish and French historians seem to have used the terms "slave" and "prisoner" interchangeably when referring to those in the possession of various Indian tribes. Although most of the slaves were probably prisoners, not all of the prisoners were slaves. From the time of their earliest contacts with whites, the Cherokees were one of the largest and most influential of the aboriginal tribes. They held many prisoners or captives and practiced enforced adoption. Newly obtained adult captives were usually handed over to the women for torture and death. Child prisoners and the adults who were not killed were often absorbed into Cherokee families by means of enforced adoption. Many of those adopted later became members of the tribe by an act of council; those not adopted remained in a form of quasi-slavery. This custom of adoption or slavery was later applied to whites and Negroes.[8]

Hernando de Soto's expedition of 1540 recorded that the Cherokees enslaved other Indians who had been taken as prisoners of war.[9] Never-

theless, slavery, as an institution, did not exist among the Cherokees
before the arrival of Europeans. De Soto's entourage, armored in steel
and clad in rich silks and velvets, included both West Indian and black
slaves.[10] These were probably the first *Unakas* ("white men") and black
men the Cherokees had ever seen. The tribe exhibited no moral bias against
slavery and was quick to accept numerous trappings of European civilization, including the institution of black slavery.

Although there are accounts of black slaves escaping from De Soto's
expedition, Negro slavery was introduced into the Cherokee Nation at a
much later date by English traders.[11] The English were fortunate to have
many good and adaptable traders to initiate commercial relations with
the Cherokees. These traders provided household items, agricultural tools,
weapons, and rum to the Indians. Trader Robert Bunning lived and conducted business with the tribe for thirty-seven years, Cornelius Daugherty
for thirty-two years, Ludovick Grant for twenty-six years, and James
Beamer traded with the tribe for twenty-seven years.[12] Alexander Cameron,
who was a representative of "His Majesty's Indian Agent for the Southern
District," resided in the Overhill region and became known to the
Cherokees as "Scotchie." He married an Indian woman and founded a
large estate named Locharbor.[13] These traders learned the Indians' language
and adopted much of their culture. They served as interpreters and often
worked toward cultural assimilation. They frequently camped, fought,
and hunted with their Indian customers as brothers and equals. Traders
also served as teachers of new farming and livestock-raising techniques.[14]

Some traders who married Cherokee women amassed property, and
their plantations soon rivaled those of the Carolinas in size. They purchased
black slaves and left them and other properties as an inheritance to their
half-Cherokee children. Traders brought black slaves to the Cherokee
Nation and sold them to tribal members. As early as 1673 firearms were
introduced among the Cherokees. They immediately began capturing black
slaves in order to sell them and purchase ammunition.[15] The English urged
the Cherokees to sell them all the blacks whom they seized from Indians
friendly to the French. The French in turn rewarded the Cherokees hand-
somely for blacks abducted from English plantations.[16] This allowed the
Indians at least three alternatives in the disposition of blacks who came
into their possession. They could weigh the rewards offered by the English
and the French against retaining the Negroes as slaves. Regardless of what

disposition was made of the Negroes, black slavery had become a part of Cherokee life and activity.

By 1700 the Cherokee country stretched southward from the Ohio River to the southern reaches of the Tennessee River, westward and northward along the Tennessee Valley, and eastward from the Great Kanawha to the headwaters of the Savannah. The main Cherokee settlements were the Overhill settlements on the Tellico River below the Cumberland Mountains; the Middle Towns, on the Little Tennessee and Tuskasegee rivers; the Lower Settlements, on the headwaters of the Savannah; and the communities to the west of the Middle Towns, near the Valley River, which became known as the Valley Towns. The Cherokees sometimes had their black slaves stolen and became victims of enslavement themselves. In 1693 a tribal delegation lodged an official protest to the Royal Governor of South Carolina. They charged that the Congaree, Esau (Catawba), and Savannah Indians were capturing Cherokees and selling them into slavery.[17] White farmers were periodically charged with holding Cherokees in slavery during the entire colonial period. In 1705 the Cherokees accused the governor of South Carolina of granting "commissions" to a number of people to "set upon, assault, kill, destroy, and take captive" tribal members who were then "sold into slavery for his and their profit."[18]

Being enslaved themselves allowed some Cherokees to become familiar with plantation agriculture. Upon escaping or being freed by Cherokee-colonial treaty terms, they could take advantage of their newly gained knowledge and become black slaveowners. However, black slavery seems to have been utilized on the collective town farms long before individual plantations replaced the communal system.

As the white colonization of the country progressed, the Cherokees came into possession of more runaway black slaves from the Virginia and Carolina settlements. This posed a serious economic problem for the colonists, who could ill afford the losses and subsequently contributed to the signing of the unofficial Treaty of Dover. On May 4, 1730, a delegation of seven Cherokees, accompanied by Sir Alexander Cumming and Eleazer Wiggan (the "Old Rabbit"), sailed from Charlestown aboard the man-of-war *Fox*. They arrived in London on June 5, were granted an audience with King George II at Windsor Castle on June 18, and then consummated the treaty, which was signed in Whitehall. Among the provisions of the treaty was a section relating to black slaves which stipulated

that if any Negroe Slaves shall run away into the Woods from
their English Masters, the Cherokee Indians shall endeavour to
apprehend them, and either bring them back to the Plantation
from whence they run-away, or to the Governor; and for every
Negroe so apprehended and brought back, the Indian who brings
him shall receive a Match [Watch] Coat; whereupon we give a
Box of vermillion, 10,000 Gun Flints, and six Dozen of Hatchets.[19]

The treaty terms were approved by the Cherokee delegation, but, after
two days of additional deliberations, they delivered a further statement
about the black slaves which noted:

This small Rope we show you, is all we have to bind our Slaves
with, and may be broken, but you have Iron Chains for yours;
however, if we catch your Slaves, we shall bind them as well as
we can, and deliver them to our friends again, and have no pay
for it.[20]

The wars and diplomacy conducted by Spain, England, and France
resulted in a complicated and precarious existence for the Cherokees, who
were centrally located among the three powers.

Periodically, the Cherokees under a war chief, who had visited
the King of England would raid colonial settlements riding
Spanish ponies and shooting British pellets from French guns.
On returning to their Indian village the contented Indians would
drink colonial rum in the company of captured or runaway
African slaves.[21]

The Cherokees were later to become scrupulous in the fulfillment of
treaty agreements. Their government at this early date was so informal,
however, that it is unlikely that the terms of the Treaty of Dover were
strictly followed. Nevertheless, "Slave Catcher" became a common
Cherokee name.[22]

There was little time for idleness among Cherokee women. They were
occupied with household tasks, tanning, weaving baskets, making pottery,
and numerous other duties. Therefore, Cherokee women quickly approved
black slavery, which immediately lightened their traditional task of tilling

the fields. Cherokee warriors had always considered agricultural work degrading and appropriate only for women, "useless fellows," and slaves; they could now more easily be absent for extended periods on the hunt or warpath while black slaves assisted the women, children, and the old men at home. The hunter had more time to seek peltry and expand his trade from a barter business with neighboring tribes to a more lucrative commerce with whites.[23] Therefore, black slaves were normally a great asset to the Indians.[24]

The colonists did not want the Cherokees to adopt black slavery. They correctly envisioned Indians raiding their settlements for "hair and horses" and stealing their slaves. Consequently, they enacted laws which prohibited whites from taking blacks into the Cherokee Nation and from having black slaves if they lived among the Cherokees. Traders frequently circumvented the law, however, by purchasing slaves in the names of their Indian wives or other persons. On the other hand, the British government directly encouraged black slavery among the Indians by presenting slaves to important and influential tribesmen for their personal service. These slaves were known as "King's Gifts."[25] The English also offered enticing rewards for runaway slaves. At the "Augusta Conference of 1763, the price was set at one musket and three blankets for each slave brought in."[26]

The establishment of black slavery in the Cherokee Nation, as in the United States, was an evolutionary process. Antoine Bonnefoy, a French *voyageur*, became a Cherokee captive in 1741 and was subsequently adopted into the tribe. His journal describes these events in detail. On November 15, 1741, the Bonnefoy party of eight men was ambushed by a war party of approximately eighty Cherokees. Three of the men were killed, and the other five, including Bonnefoy and a seriously wounded Negro, were captured. Each of the captives immediately became a slave of a Cherokee warrior. They were bound and slave collars were placed around their necks. During the journey back to the Cherokee village, the Negro's wounds became worse, and he was set free. "He could not be adopted into the family of a Cherokee and his wounds probably kept him from being considered desirable as a slave." Not knowing what to do or where to go, the Negro followed the party for two days. On the third day, the Cherokees "gave him over to the young people, who killed him and took his scalp."[27]

The Cherokees were exhibiting a strong color consciousness by this date. They were regularly purchasing, selling and using black slaves.

Slavery had become profitable and had evolved into an accepted institution. The only potentially serious threat to black slavery in the Cherokee Nation occurred when Christian Gottleib Priber, a European, settled at Tellico in 1736. Priber learned the Cherokee language and adopted their customs and dress. He cautioned his hosts against trading with a single country and making land concessions to anyone. Priber soon ingratiated himself with tribal leaders.

After winning the confidence of Chief Moytoy, Priber persuaded the National Council to proclaim Moytoy "Emperor of the Kingdom of Paradise." The "Emperor" subsequently appointed Priber "Prime Minister" and "His Majesty's Chief Secretary of State." Among other utopian goals, the "Empire" was to become a place where runaway slaves, oppressed peoples of Europe, and Indian tribes could obtain sanctuary and happiness. Priber was cognizant of the "continual flow of runaway slaves finding sanctuary among the Cherokees" and proposed to incorporate them into his utopian communist state. Discrimination would not be tolerated on the basis of race, color, tribal affiliation, title, or wealth. Priber's grandiose plan ended when he was captured by the Creek Indians in "the Fifth Year of the Empire" and sold to Governor Ogelthorpe of Georgia. He was imprisoned in Frederica prison and remained incarcerated until his death a few years later.[28] The antislavery sentiments of Priber never persuaded the Cherokees, proved ephimeral, and were never resurrected in the future.

Black slaves had become sufficiently valuable that on April 10, 1758, Little Carpenter (Attacullaculla), an eminent chief of the Cherokees, was willing to exchange two French prisoners of war for two black slaves in an even trade. Little Carpenter, whose diplomacy was declared by Charlestown colonist William Fyffe to be superior to that of either Richelieu or Walpole, desired the blacks as servants for his wife. His offer was refused by the South Carolina officials, however, and they cited the statutes which prohibited the giving or selling of slaves to Indians.[29]

The constant encroachments and provocations by colonial frontiersmen and squatters in defiance of the British Proclamation of 1763, which forbade settlement beyond the Appalachian divide, and the good will efforts of the British caused the Cherokees to aid England during the American Revolution. In 1775, numerous Tories flocked to the Cherokee Nation from the southern colonies. Some were black slaveowners and brought their property with them.[30] The Cherokees and Tories soon went on the attack. They scalped men, women, and children and confiscated many black slaves.[31] The Cherokee lands were invaded in 1776 by Colonel William Christian's Virginia army of 1,800 men. The Virginians took the Overhill Towns without a struggle. Colonel Samuel Jack, with a force of 200 Georgians, destroyed the Cherokee towns on the Chattahoochee and Tugaloo Rivers. Colonel Andrew Williamson, with 1,100 Carolinians, laid waste the Lower Towns and then joined General Griffith Rutherford and his 2,000 North Carolinians who had decimated the Middle Towns. The combined force then proceeded to destroy the Valley Towns. The invaders usually killed or auctioned the black slaves who fell into their hands.[32]

The destruction of Cherokee towns by the colonial forces and the subsequent ceding of almost all their hunting lands in South Carolina and large tracts in North Carolina and Tennessee provided additional incentives for establishing individual farms. More and more Indians deserted the villages and began farming on their own. The ancient custom of communalism continued to erode and slowly evolved into an individualism which gave greater impetus to the institution of black slavery.

The Treaty of Hopewell of November 28, 1785, was the first treaty between the Cherokee Nation and the United States and officially ended hostilities between the two parties. The treaty was also directly concerned with black slavery. Article I stipulated:

> The Head-Men and Warriors of all the Cherokees shall restore
> all the prisoners, citizens of the United States, or subjects of
> their allies, to their entire liberty: They shall also restore all the
> Negroes, and all other property taken during the late war from the
> citizens, to such person, and at such time and place, as the com-
> missioners shall appoint.[33]

There were among the Cherokees, as elsewhere, some conflicting thoughts about the desirability and efficacy of black slavery. Many of the large slaveowners were mixed-bloods, the so-called white Indians. However, some full-bloods were also large slaveowners. No Cherokee organization actively opposed slavery during its infancy and no abolition societies were ever organized. It is not known who the first Cherokee slaveowner was or even when. However, Nancy Ward, (*Ghi-gu-u,* "Beloved Woman of the Cherokee"), a full-blood of the Wolf clan, was one of the first women in the Nation to possess a black slave. She became the owner of a Negro as a result of the spoils of war. In the Battle of Taliwa with the Creeks in

1755, when her husband Kingfisher was killed, she retrieved his weapon and fought as a warrior. The Creeks were defeated and the spoils divided among the victors. Nancy Ward received a captured Negro and possibly became the first Cherokee female to own a black slave.[34] She soon obtained additional slaves. In 1776 a Cherokee raiding party captured a white woman named Mrs. Bean, who taught Nancy Ward's slaves to make butter and cheese.[35]

During the early colonial period the Cherokees had been a semi-sedentary hunting, gathering, and agricultural society. As they gradually lost more and more of their land, they were forced to become increasingly sedentary and agrarian. They continued to abandon the communal cultivation of land and began to operate their farms on an individual basis. Black slavery both contributed to and made possible such change. Therefore, slaves continually became more valuable. Coteatoy, Chief of Tuskeegee Island Town, captured a black female slave from the Colonel Brown party in 1788 on the Tennessee River.[36] One hundred and ten blacks were captured by the Cherokees in Georgia alone in 1789.[37]

When colonists began settling in the Kentucky and Tennessee territories, the Cherokees feared the loss of even more of their land. Therefore, they frequently raided the squatter settlements. Whites were usually killed, but black slaves were taken prisoner.[38] The infamous "Muscle Shoals Massacre" of 1794 resulted in all six white men being scalped, but the three women, four children, and twenty black slaves were taken prisoner. The prisoners were taken from a boat, descending the Tennessee River under the command of William Scott, which Cherokee warriors, led by White-Man-Killer, had intercepted.[39]

Subsequently, on December 31, 1794, Bloody Fellow, a Cherokee, and Governor William Blount met to exchange prisoners. Blount delivered thirteen Cherokee prisoners, who were received and counted by Chief John Watts (Young Tassel) of the Chickamauga Cherokees. The Indians, in turn, presented only two prisoners, a white girl and a black girl. The slave girl had been captured by the Crier of Nickajack, who wished to exchange her for his own daughter.[40] Governor Blount then read the following list of captives' names and demanded that they be returned:

Miss Thornton, taken by the Otter Lifter, Five negroes, taken
from Gen. Logan, of Kentucky, Negro girl, taken from Ziegler's

Station by Shawnee Warrior, Negro, belonging to Robertson, Negro man, in possession of John Rogers, white trader, Twenty-two negroes, taken from Scott's boat.[41]

Chief Watts charged that there were also unreturned Cherokee prisoners. Regarding the black slaves, he stipulated:

They are scattered in the Nation. Some of them have changed hands many times and will have to be bought from their present owners. We are a poor people and have no goods with which to purchase the negroes from the persons who have the possession of them. If we attempt to take them by force, they might perhaps be put to death or injured. The most proper time, I think, will be when we receive our annual allowance from the government. We can, with those goods, pay the possessors, and deliver the negroes to you. The other prisoners will be delivered as soon as possible. As to the Negro in the possession of John Rogers, he is a white man, and I have nothing to do with him.[42]

Bloody Fellow then seconded Watts's remarks, saying:

All that can be said on the subject of exchange, has been said. If I should rush down and take the negroes by force from the persons who possess them, it might endanger their lives.[43]

As more and more lands were lost on the Tennessee-North Carolina border, many Cherokees migrated southward. There, in the rich bottom lands of the Coosa, Etowah, Oostanaula, Conesauga, Coosewattee, Chattooga, and other streams, some full-scale southern-type Cherokee plantations existed by the end of the eighteenth century.[44] Farming, "especially the raising of cotton, developed more rapidly than it would have under native labor, and more leisure and opportunity for culture were given to both men and women."[45] Agriculture and trade were becoming more and more the mainsprings of the Cherokee economy. The working of black slaves on a farm brought much greater profits than hunting. Most of the well-known and influential Cherokees were becoming slaveowners. Such influential Cherokees as Ross, Vann, Foreman, Alberty, Scales,

Boudinot, Lowrey, Rogers, McNair, Ridge, Chisholm, Downing, Drew, Martin, Nave, Jolly, Hildebrand, Webber, and Adair became slaveholders.

In 1791, during the administration of President George Washington, a treaty was negotiated at White's Fort (the present site of Knoxville, Tennessee), on the Holston River. The Treaty of Holston indirectly encouraged the growth of black slavery among the Cherokees. Article 14 of the treaty stipulated:

> That the Cherokee Nation may be led to a greater degree of civilization, and to become herdsmen and cultivators instead of remaining in a state of hunters, the United States will from time to time furnish gratuitously the said nation, with useful implements of husbandry and . . . will send . . . persons . . . not exceeding four in number, who shall qualify themselves to act as interpreters. These persons shall have lands assigned by the Cherokees for cultivation for themselves and their successors in office; but they shall be precluded exercising any kind of traffic.[46]

During the following year, Chief Bloody Fellow notified the United States Secretary of War, Henry Knox, that "ploughs, hoes, cattle, looms and other things for a farm, this is what we want. . . . We must plant corn and raise cattle, and we desire you to assist us."[47] In 1793 Congress, in the Second Intercourse Act, authorized an expenditure of not more than $20,000 annually for the purchase of domestic animals and farming implements for the Indian nations. The act also provided for presidential appointment of temporary agents to live among the Indian tribes. President Washington advised the Indians to "stop warring and adopt the white man's ways."[48] In 1797, Silas Dinsmoore was appointed by President John Adams to reside among the Cherokees and instruct them "in the raising of stock, the cultivation of land, and the arts."[49] Dinsmoore induced a "considerable number" of Indians to plant cotton and taught women to spin and weave cotton fibers.[50]

Several of the leading chiefs were slaveowners and "the capture of negroes by warriors had been a frequent occurrence."[51] If the captor did not desire to retain the slave for his own use, the Negro was sold. Therefore, the slave was sometimes sold several times in a relatively short period. This made the recovery efforts of white owners most difficult. "It is useless to expect the return of slaves captured by the Indians during the wars, as they have changed hands so many times in the Nation," wrote agent Dinsmoore.[52] Moreover, the Indian who had obtained a slave by purchase usually refused, regardless of treaties, to surrender his property.

Among the captives which Colonel Whitley had carried back to Kentucky to insure the return of negroes who had been taken from him in raids by the Cherokees, were relatives of the chief Otter Lifter. . . .

The Colonel's slaves were in possession of John Taylor, a half-breed who had commanded the Indian cavalry in the attack on Buchanan's Station; he objected strenuously to giving them up. "You cannot have them!" he exclaimed, and accented the statement by beating a drum and voicing the war-whoop. Warriors gathered and assumed a threatening mien. "I thought times were squally," Whitley afterward related, "but I looked at the Otter Lifter, and his face was unchanged." "He told me that I should not be killed." When Taylor demanded that he "prove his property," Whitley retorted, "If I have to do that, I will go back to Kentucky and bring a thousand witnesses, each with a rifle to speak for him." The influence of the Little Turkey was required before they were surrendered. The fact that the captives of Colonel Whitley were blood-kin to a prominent chief rendered him more fortunate than most slave owners in such circumstances.[53]

The Cherokees continued to obtain additional black slaves by purchase and capture. The capture of blacks had become not only profitable but an acceptable form of revenge. When Colonel Evan Shelby undertook his Chickamauga Expedition back in 1799 and proceeded to destroy the Indian towns in that region, the Cherokees sought revenge. Chief Bench, determined to avenge his humiliation, boasted, "I am going back next summer and pay old Shelby a visit and take all his Negroes."[54]

During the summer of 1799, Brothers Abraham Steiner and Frederick C. De Schweinitz of the Moravian Church made a tour of the Cherokee country. They reported seeing many plantations with orchards and large fenced fields of corn, wheat, cotton, and vegetables. They also saw many cotton cards, spinning wheels, and looms along with large numbers of horses, cattle, hogs, fowl, dogs, and cats. The two clerics also reported that "our hosts had, also, negro slaves that were well clothed; bright,

lively and appeared to be happy and well cared for. These conducted
themselves toward the Indians, with all courtesy."[55]

Another missionary commented on black slavery in the Cherokee
Nation by saying:

> This institution was derived from the whites. It has all the gen-
> eral characteristics of Negro slavery in the Southern portion of
> our union. In such a state of society as we find among these
> Indians, there must of necessity be some modifications of the
> system; but in all its essential features, it remains unchanged.[56]

NOTES

1. The publisher, Louisiana State University Press, states on the dust
jacket of volume 1 that this massive work was "designed to present a
balanced history of all the complex aspects of the South's culture from
1607 to the present."

2. John Hope Franklin, *From Slavery to Freedom: A History of
Negro Americans* (New York: Alfred A. Knopf, 1967), passim.

3. A careful study of the standard, revisionist, innovative, and icono-
clastic books on slavery provides little significant information about the
institution among Indians in general and the Cherokees specifically. Works,
including Ulrich B. Phillips, *American Negro Slavery* and *Life and Labor
In The Old South,* John Hope Franklin, *From Slavery to Freedom: A
History of Negro Americans,* Kenneth M. Stampp, *The Peculiar Institution:
Slavery in the Ante-Bellum South,* and Robert W. Fogel and Stanley L.
Engerman, *Time on the Cross: The Economics of American Negro Slavery,*
and a plethora of lesser lights, all fail to cast any illumination on the subject. The efforts of authors in scholarly journals also fail to provide en-
lightenment. Some have treated the subject of relations between Indians
and blacks in the Southeast and in Indian Territory. Yet, black slavery
among the Cherokees is all but omitted in Wyatt F. Jeltz, "The Relations
of Negroes and Choctaw and Chickasaw Indians," *Journal of Negro
History* 33, no. 1 (January 1948), pp. 24-37; J. H. Johnson, "Documentary
Evidence of the Relation of Negroes and Indians," *Journal of Negro
History* 14, no. 1 (January 1929), pp. 21-43.; Kenneth W. Porter, "Negroes
on the Southern Frontier," *Journal of Negro History* 33, no. 1 (January
1948), pp. 53-78; Kenneth W. Porter, "Notes Supplementary to Relations
between Negroes and Indians," *Journal of Negro History* 18, no. 3 (July
1933), pp. 282-321; Kenneth W. Porter, "Relations between Negroes and
Indians within the Present Limits of the United States," *Journal of Negro
History* 17, no. 3 (July 1932), pp. 287-367; and William P. Willis, "Divide

and Rule: Red, White, and Black in the Southeast," *Journal of Negro History* 48, no. 3 (July 1963), pp. 157-176.

4. Wiley Britton, *The Civil War on the Border* (New York: G. P. Putnam's Sons, 1891), vol. 2, pp. 24, 25.

5. James Mooney, "Myths of the Cherokees," *Nineteenth Annual Report of the Bureau of Ethnology* (Washington, D.C: Government Printing Office, 1900), p. 15.

6. Norman Arthur Graebner, "Pioneer Indian Agriculture in Oklahoma," *Chronicles of Oklahoma* 23, no. 3 (Autumn 1945), p. 232.

7. Alvin M. Josephy, Jr., *The Indian Heritage of America* (New York: Alfred A. Knopf, 1968), p. 77.

8. Almon W. Lauber, *Indian Slavery in Colonial Times within the Present Limits of the United States* (New York: Longmans, Green and Company, 1913), pp. 49, 63, 136, 170.

9. Henry Thompson Malone, *Cherokees of the Old South: A People in Transition* (Athens: University of Georgia Press, 1956), p. 20.

10. Mooney, "Myths of the Cherokees," p. 25.

11. Ibid.

12. Beamer appears to have been a slaveowner and forebear of Oklahoma's future United States Senator Robert L. Owen. See Narcissa Owen, *Memoirs of Narcissa Owen* (Washington, D.C: privately printed, 1907), p. 10.

13. Mary U. Rothrock, "Carolina Traders among the Overhill Cherokees, 1690-1760," *East Tennessee Historical Society Publications* 1, no. 1 (1929), pp. 3-18. Also see Ludovick Grant, "Historical Relation of Facts Delivered by Ludovick Grant, Indian Trader, to His Excellency, the Governor of South Carolina," *South Carolina Historical and Genealogical Magazine* 10, no. 1 (January 1909), pp. 54, 69.

14. Malone, *Cherokees of the Old South,* p. 9.

15. Mooney, "Myths of the Cherokees," pp. 32, 33.

16. John Pitts Corry, *Indian Affairs in Georgia 1732-1756* (Philadelphia: University of Pennsylvania Press, 1936), p. 120.

17. Malone, *Cherokees of the Old South,* p. 20.

18. Mooney, "Myths of the Cherokees," p. 32.

19. *Journal of Sir Alexander Cuming,* in Samuel Cole Williams, *Early Travels in the Tennessee Country, 1540-1800* (Johnson City, Tennessee: The Watauga Press, 1928), p. 141.

20. Ibid., p. 143.

21. Michael Roethler, "Negro Slavery among the Cherokee Indians 1540-1866" (Ph.D. dissertation, Fordham University, 1964), p. 26.

22. David H. Corkran, *The Cherokee Frontier: Conflict and Survival, 1740-62* (Norman: University of Oklahoma Press, 1962), passim.

23. Charles K. Whipple, *Relations of the American Board of Commissioners for Foreign Missions to Slavery* (Boston: R. F. Wallcut, 1861), pp. 84-90.

24. However, in 1783 they reportedly brought smallpox to the Nation, which caused the deaths of half of the Cherokee population within one year. Mooney, "Myths of the Cherokees," p. 36.

25. Benjamin Hawkins, *A Sketch of Creek Country in 1788-1789* (New York: Bartlett & Welford, 1848), p. 66.

26. Douglas C. Wilms, "Cherokee Slave Ownership prior to the Removal," a paper read before the Ninth Annual Meeting of the Southern Anthropological Society, Blacksburg, Virginia, April 1974.

27. *Journal of Antoine Bonnefoy*, in Williams, *Early Travels*, p. 152.

28. Grant, "Historical Relation of Facts," p. 58.

29. Corkran, *The Cherokee Frontier*, p. 145.

30. Whipple, *Relations of the American Board*, p. 88.

31. *Colonial Records of North Carolina*, Vol. 10, p. 881.

32. Mooney, "Myths of the Cherokees," pp. 51, 53. Also see Grace Steel, Woodward, *The Cherokees* (Norman: University of Oklahoma Press, 1963), pp. 96, 97.

33. Charles J. Kappler, ed., *Indian Affairs: Laws and Treaties* (Washington, D.C.: Government Printing Office, 1904), vol. 2, p. 9.

34. J. B. Davis, "Slavery in the Cherokee Nation," *Chronicles of Oklahoma* 11, no. 4 (December 1933), p. 1057. Although she is best known in Cherokee history as Nancy Ward, at the time of the Battle of Taliwa, *Ghi-gu-u* was not known by that name. She later married Brian Ward, a trader, and then assumed the first name Nancy.

35. Woodward, *The Cherokees*, p. 96.

36. Zella Armstrong, *The History of Hamilton County and Chattanooga Tennessee* (Chattanooga: The Lookout Publishing Company, 1931), vol. 1, p. 40.

37. Marion L. Starkey, *The Cherokee Nation* (New York: Alfred A. Knopf, 1946), p. 17.

38. W. R. L. Smith, *The Story of the Cherokees* (Cleveland, Tennessee: Church of God Publishing House, 1928), p. 46.

39. Grant Foreman, *Indians and Pioneers* (Norman: University of Oklahoma Press, 1936), p. 201.

40. According to some reports, Nickajack was named for "Nigger Jack," a captured black slave. John P. Brown, *Old Frontiers: The Story of the Cherokee Indians from Earliest Times to the Date of Their Removal to the West, 1838* (Kingsport, Tennessee: Southern Publishers, 1938), p. 212.

41. Ibid., p. 437.

42. Ibid.

43. Ibid., p. 438.

44. Starkey, *The Cherokee Nation,* p. 17.

45. Rachel Carolyn Eaton, *John Ross and the Cherokee Indians* (Menasha, Wisconsin: George Banta Publishing Company, 1914), pp. 20, 21.

46. Kappler, *Indian Affairs,* p. 31.

47. *American State Papers, Indian Affairs,* I (Washington, D.C.: Government Printing Office, 1832), p. 205.

48. Henry C. Dennis, comp. and ed., *The American Indian 1492-1970: A Chronology and Fact Book* (Dobbs Ferry, New York: Oceana Publications, Inc., 1971), pp. 20, 21.

49. Woodward, *The Cherokees,* p. 41.

50. Henry Thompson Malone, "Cherokee Civilization in the Lower Appalachians, Especially in North Georgia, before 1830" (Master's thesis, Emory University, 1949), p. 47.

51. Brown, *Old Frontiers,* p. 446.

52. Ibid.

53. Ibid.

54. Ibid., p. 401.

55. "Report of the Journey of the Brethren Abraham Steiner and Frederick C. De Schweinitz to the Cherokees and the Cumberland Settlements," in Williams, *Early Travels,* p. 490.

56. Whipple, *Relations of the American Board,* p. 88.

2 Early Cherokee Planters and Plantations

When Return Jonathan Meigs, known by the Cherokees as "White Path," was appointed agent to the tribe in 1801, he reported that the spinning wheel, loom, and plow were in general use. Farming, manufacturing, and livestock raising were the principal topics of conversation among the men and women of the Nation.[1] A visitor to the Nation in 1802 reported that many of the Cherokees had large plantations worked by gangs of Negro slaves.[2] The mixed-bloods usually adopted the ways of the white man with alacrity, but not with respect to land ownership. The Indian custom of holding land in common was one tribal practice they always defended assiduously. Common ownership was advantageous to the planter and herdsman.

Ample tillable acreage was available to the prospective planter. Land was free to any Cherokee citizen. All land was owned by the Nation but any citizen could gain exclusive use of unclaimed acreage if it was not within a quarter-mile of land used by a neighbor. All improvements subsequently made on the land became the personal property of the individual and could be sold or willed to any citizen of the Nation. There was no limit of acreage which could be used by an individual. If a planter became surrounded by his neighbors and was therefore unable to expand contiguously, he could start another farming operation at another location. Large numbers of Indian planters took full advantage of this generous land policy. Consequently, in 1835, 224 Cherokee families operated two farms, 77 operated three, 33 operated four, 17 operated five, 8 operated six, 1 operated seven, 1 operated nine, and 1 family operated a total of thirteen farms.[3] Moreover, 93 percent of all Cherokee families operated at least one farm.[4]

At the dawn of the nineteenth century, the Cherokee Nation comprised approximately 43,000 square miles. Approximately one-half of the land was in northwestern Georgia, northeastern Alabama, and western North Carolina, with a small tract in South Carolina; the remaining one-half was in Tennessee. Theoretically, the Cherokees were a sovereign nation and outside the legal jurisdiction of the bordering states. Nevertheless, these states, especially Georgia, repeatedly contested Cherokee sovereignty and claimed parts of the Indian lands as their own. The Cherokees naturally opposed such actions, and their leaders were cognizant that the claims of the bordering states were considered legally untenable.

The Ridge (*Kah-nung-da-cla-geh*), later known as "Major" Ridge for his exploits in the Battle of Horseshoe Bend, became the first Cherokee plantation owner of magnitude. Sometime before 1800 he began to clear land and build a house like those he had seen while on the warpath in the Oothcaloga Valley. The full-blood Indian warrior—who remained illiterate throughout his life—and his bride, forsaking the ancient tradition of their people, began chopping, plowing, knitting, and weaving. He also began to acquire black slaves "to do the harder work about the premises."[5]

Ridge's plantation was known as "Chieftains." The house was built on a stone foundation that measured twenty-nine by fifty-four feet. The walls were constructed of hand-hewn logs stripped of bark and flattened on two sides. They were deeply notched at each end to fit closely and pegged together to prevent shifting. The walls were covered with sawed lumber. The house had two stories, with verandas in front and back and a brick fireplace at each end. There were eight rooms and thirty glass windows set in walnut casings. The ceilings, walls, and floors were all hardwood.[6]

Two kitchens of hewed logs stood close to the back door, and nearby was a smokehouse for the family's meat supply. Farther away were two stables, one with a loft and both with watering troughs and feeding racks for the horses and there were various sheds and cribs, including a lumber house. Some distance away stood cabins for the Negro slaves.[7]

Ridge's plantation grew rapidly. His orchard eventually contained 1,141 peach, 418 apple, 11 quince, 21 cherry, and a number of plum trees. Eight fields, containing nearly 300 acres, were soon under cultivation. The principal crop was corn, but cotton, tobacco, wheat, oats, indigo, and sweet and Irish potatoes were also cultivated. There were also a vineyard, a nursery, and a garden which contained a large variety of ornamental shrubs as well as vegetables. By the early 1820s Ridge had thirty black slaves. Moreover, large numbers of hogs and cattle grazed in his pastures and provided ample milk, butter, and meat for the family larder.[8]

The primary means of travel and transport in the Nation was by water. Cherokee plantation owners had wharfs constructed on the rivers and streams near their property from which they shipped cotton, corn, beef, and other products and received their own supplies. Flatboats and keel-boats were common sights on Cherokee streams. In 1802 Chief Double-head built a keelboat thirty to thirty-five feet long and seven feet wide to transport produce to New Orleans. During the same year he was accused of forcing a manumitted Negro, Paul Smith, back into slavery. Smith wrote to United States Secretary of War Henry Dearborn:

> My color unfortunately incapacitates me from applying personally to your honour.. . . . In 1802 my former master, W. Smith, on his death ordered me to be liberated from bondage by paying his son $400., the greater part of which I paid and was then liberated. Doublehead (a chief of the Cherokee Nation) seized my property with myself, the cattle he retained for his own use, myself he sold to Capt. John Cambell of the 2nd U.S. Regiment of Infantry to the value of $400. . . . I trust your honour will be so good as to interfere in my cause and obtain my freedom.[9]

In 1817 the American Board of Foreign Missions opened a school "to educate the male aborigines of all nations" at Cornwall, Connecticut. Students from Hawaii, the Azores, and other foreign places matriculated at the school, but by far the greatest number of students came from American Indian tribes. Students appeared at Cornwall from the Tus-carora, Iroquois, Narrangansett, Oneida, Seneca, Chippewa, Osage, Choctaw, Cherokee, and other tribes.[10]

Ridge sent his son, John, to the Cornwall school. In 1819 he visited his son and caused considerable comment. He arrived in Cornwall "in the most splendid carriage that had ever entered the town," wearing a coat trimmed in "gold lace," and he enjoyed "waiters in great style."[11] During his years at Cornwall, John met and courted Sarah Bird Northup,

the daughter of a prominent local family. When John later asked for
Sarah's hand in matrimony, her parents refused. They objected strongly
to the proposed union, ostensibly because "John suffered [from] a hip
disease," or "scrofulous complaint."[12] Finally, it was agreed that if John
would go home and return after one year without his crutches—entirely
well—her parents would consent to the marriage. John agreed to the
stipulated conditions and returned home to the Cherokee Nation. After
the lapse of a year, John Ridge reappeared in Cornwall, entirely well and
without his crutches. Moreover, he was riding in a magnificent coach
drawn by four beautiful white horses and driven by a black coachman
in livery.[13]

The school and the town were shocked by the interracial marriage.
Sarah's father was a trustee of the school and the townspeople knew that
the marriage was approved by the bride's mother. Isaiah Bunce, editor of
the *American Eagle,* had opposed the opening of the mission school and
he now editorialized against the marriage. He castigated "the girl who
had married a savage, and departed for the wilds to live as a 'squaw.' "
Bunce "suggested that the girl should be whipped, her husband hanged
and her mother drowned."[14]

John took his young bride to Chieftains in 1824. He became "a gentleman of the green bag," a lawyer, and "set up for himself." He soon left
Chieftains with his wife and eighteen black slaves and settled six miles
away where he built a large two-story house on a high hill. He established
a fine plantation which he named *Tantatanara* ("Running Waters"). The
house measured nineteen by fifty-one feet for the first floor and twenty
by thirty-one feet for the second story. There were six fireplaces and a
spacious front porch. Twenty-four glass windows provided light and
ventilation. The kitchen was detached and there were two smokehouses.
Other buildings included a corncrib, a two-story stable, sheds, and
quarters for his slaves. His blacks labored in seven fields, containing 419
acres of farmland. Running Waters had a fine orchard with 493 peach,
100 apple, 6 quince, and 7 pear trees.[15]

Before the furor over John Ridge's marriage had abated at Cornwall,
Harriet Ruggles Gold, the nineteen-year-old daughter of Benjamin and
Eleanor Gold, asked permission to marry Elias Boudinot (*Gul-la-gee-nah*).
Benjamin Gold was a graduate of Yale and a wealthy land owner. The
family lived in a large Georgian home at Cornwall and was highly respected.
The request of their daughter saddened the Gold family. "Firmly, but

sorrowfully, they delayed their answer to her plea."[16] Elias Boudinot
was the son of David Watie (*Oo-Watie*). He was born in about 1800 and
named *Gah-la-gee-nah.* His name meant "young stag deer," and he was
therefore called "Buck." The Watie family had large land holdings and
were probably among the earliest black slaveowners. They lived in a comfortable home. It was through the influence of Elias Boudinot, a states-
man from New Jersey and a supporter of the Cornwall Mission School,
that Buck Watie was sent to Cornwall. Thus, according to Cherokee
custom, young Buck Watie took the surname of his benefactor.[17]

After being refused parental permission to marry Boudinot, Harriet
became ill and did not respond to treatment. As a result of the illness,
the Golds informed their daughter that they would no longer oppose the
marriage. There was an immediate "flood of righteous indignation" from
other members of the family, however. Harriet's brother, Stephen, swore
that he would kill Boudinot. When the Board of Agents of Cornwall Mission School heard of the wedding announcement, they were angry and
dismayed. They pleaded with Harriet to abandon her wedding plans. They
threatened to "publish their ban on the marriage in a manner they deemed
fitting." Harriet remained firm in her decision and the ban was published.
The agents declared their disapproval of the marriage and accused all of
those involved of "offering insults to the Christian Community." This
caused the townspeople to take up the cudgels. Crowds of angry citizens
gathered, denouncing the marriage and demanding that action be taken
against the union. Harriet, hiding behind the curtains of a window, saw
herself, her fiancé, and her mother burned in effigy. Her brother, Stephen,
lighted the fire. Nevertheless, on March 28, 1826, Harriet Gold and Elias
Boudinot were married in the Gold home and immediately departed for
the Cherokee Nation. The Cornwall Mission School could not survive
the shock and closed its doors.[18]

James Vann was another early Cherokee planter. He was a rich man
by any standard and operated a trading post near Spring Place, Georgia.
In 1803 or 1804 he built the finest plantation house in the Cherokee
Nation. It was a two-story red brick mansion with fireplaces at each end
and elegant "porticoes" at the front and rear. The Georgian structure was
noted for its carved mantlepieces and "floating" stairway. The bricks
were fired on the site, and the structure, planned by a Philadelphia architect, was the first "solid architectural creation to appear in Indian country."[19]

Vann was far-famed, little loved, and greatly feared. He owned many cattle and farmed many acres of rich land. His black slaves labored under the supervision of a white overseer, Joseph Crutchfield. Vann enjoyed the luxury of two Cherokee wives and was extremely fond of strong drink. He maintained his own private distilling apparatus and kept "gargantuan supplies of brandy and whisky and dealt drinks like a lord to his followers." But, "drunk or sober, he ruled his slaves with a rod of iron. He shot one whom he caught plotting against his life; another who had robbed him he burned at the stake." When the newly arrived Moravian missionaries began planting their first crops at Spring Place in 1801, Vann loaned them six teams and slaves to complete the task. Slaves also constructed at least three of the mission buildings. Later, in 1805, Brother John Gambold and his wife, Sister Anna, enjoyed the services of a black cook named Pleasant at the mission.[20] From the time of the earliest arrivals of missionaries in the Cherokee Nation, they continuously owned, borrowed, hired, or accepted the services of black slaves.

Some of Vann's blacks usually remained at the Spring Place Mission at night. The Brethren soon stopped going to Vann's plantation to preach to his slaves, however. They came to the conclusion that "there was little interest among the blacks there."[21] (The first religious service ever performed expressly for black slaves in the Cherokee Nation had been held by Rev. Abraham Steiner on May 10, 1801, at the Vann plantation.[22])

In 1808 James Vann killed his brother-in-law in a pistol duel. "He hogtied the next man who presumed to live with his sister and gave him seventy lashes." Vann became the victim of a revenge killing in 1809. His epitaph purportedly read:

Here lies the body of James Vann
He killed many a white man
At last by a rifle ball he fell
And devils dragged him off to hell.[23]

Vann's last will and testament stipulated that his son, Joseph, should receive the majority of his estate. His widow contested the will and the National Council eventually decided the disposition of Vann's holdings. The Council granted Joseph Vann the bulk of the estate, but his mother was awarded a portion, including some black slaves. The decree of the National Council stipulated:

Whereas the National Council at Willstown on the 11th day of
October in the year 1810 had Decreed that James Brown and
David McNair Administrators of the Estate of James Vann
Shall Deliver unto Peggy Scott widow of the Said Deceased,
among other things as appears on the record, one negro man
and one negro wench from the Said Estate and whereas in the
month of October 26th 1810 the Said Administrators have
Delivered unto the Said Peggy Scott in pursuant of the Said
Decree, a certain negro man named Will and his wife Hanah both
African—we the Chiefs in Council assembled Thereby certify
that the Said two negroes are hence forward the law full [*sic*]
property of the Said Peggy Scott—to have and to Hold to herself and her heirs as Slaves for life, and as such we will Warrant
and defend the Said negroe Slaves and their future Issue to her
the Said Peggy Scott and her heirs Against all other Claim or
Claims whatsoever given under our hands in Council at
Oosteanaleh this fifth day of May one thousand Eight Hundred and Eleven.[24]

John Ross (*Cooweescoowee*) was a wealthy man and a large slaveholder.
He was a merchant and a planter and owned a fine two-story home where
black slaves waited upon him and his full-blood wife, Quatie.[25] Peacocks
"strutted about the grounds" and the house contained a small but well-
organized library.[26] Ross operated "a supply depot and warehouse" at
Ross's Landing (Chattanooga) and a large farm between Poplar Springs
(Rossville) and the Tennessee River which was cultivated by black slaves.[27]
In 1826 Ross moved his family to the "Head of Coosa," where the
Oostanaula and Etowah Rivers merge to form the Coosa. He built a comfortable and commodious two-story house that measured seventy by
twenty feet. The weather-boarded house included a basement and had
an ash-shingle roof. A high porch ran the entire length of the front and
there were brick chimneys at each end of the structure. Twenty glass
windows admitted light and ventilation, and four fireplaces provided heat.
A detached kitchen stood a short distance away. Farther away were work-
houses, smokehouses, slave quarters, stables, corn cribs, a blacksmith shop,
and a wagon house. Soon the Ross slaves were working five fields, which
ranged in size from fourteen to seventy-five acres and totaled nearly 170
acres. The plantation fruit orchard contained more than 200 trees. By the

early 1830s, Ross possessed nearly twenty black slaves who labored under an overseer.[28]

Lewis Ross, brother of John Ross, also owned about twenty slaves. A letter from Benjamin Gold, the father of Mrs. Elias Boudinot, to a relative in 1829 described the home of Lewis Ross as "an elegant white house near the bank of a river, as neatly furnished as almost any house . . . [which] has Negroes enough to wait on us." Gold also reported that David McNair had "a beautiful white house, and about six or seven hundred acres of the best land you ever saw and Negroes enough to tend it and clear as much more as he pleases."[29]

John Martin, who served as treasurer and the first chief justice of the Supreme Court of the Cherokee Nation, reportedly owned 100 black slaves.[30] Martin had two wives and maintained separate residences for them. He owned an "elegant" home known for its marble mantels and hand-carved stairways. One of his plantations was on the Federal Road near the Coosawattee River.[31]

There were still other large Cherokee slaveowners. Chief Peter Hildebrand farmed a large plantation with many black slaves. He employed an architect and constructed a magnificent mansion that took seven years to build. Hildebrand never wore a hat, coat, or shoes. After his house was finished, he decided that it was too handsome to use and built a log cabin nearby to live in so that he could really enjoy life.[32] Michael Hildebrand owned "a large boundary of land, and many slaves."[33] Joseph Brown lived near Ooltewah and owned several slaves.[34]

In 1810 the *Christian Observer* reported that there were 538 black slaves in the Cherokee Nation.[35] In 1811 the total population of the Nation was reported to be 12,395, excluding 341 whites living within its boundaries. Cherokees reportedly possessed 583 slaves at that date.[36]

The Reverend Cyrus Kingsbury of Brainerd Mission in Tennessee recorded an entry in his journal six years later, dated April 23, 1818, which stated:

At Springplace, Reverend [David S.] Butrick observed many black people in bondage to the Cherokees, and they all speak English. Their masters, so far as come to our knowledge, are willing to have them instructed, and are generally very indulgent to giving them time to attend [religious] meetings.[37]

During a visit to "Major" Ridge's home, the Reverend Butrick preached
to eight or ten slaves at Ridge's request. One elderly black woman was
especially attentive and captured the preacher's attention. He learned
that "she raised her family with the natives, & yet as a pious mother has
them all repeat their prayers morning and evening & learns them some
beautiful lines of the crucifixion of our Savior."[38] Some Cherokee slaves
traveled as far as twenty miles to attend church services. As mission work
progressed, many slaves found it possible to arrive on Saturday night and
remain until after Sunday services.[39]

Slaveholders were among the earliest converts, staunchest supporters,
and closest friends of the missionaries and the churches. This relationship
continued throughout the era of black slavery. The Cherokees called
Moravians "the ravens" because of their black dress. The Methodists were
called "loud talkers," and the Baptists were known as "the baptizers."[40]

Missionaries appear usually to have selected from the following texts
for sermons preached before audiences containing slaves: Titus 2:9-10;
1st Timothy 6:1-5; Ephesians 6:5-8; Colossians 3:22-24; and 1st Peter
2:17-20. The message of all these texts is essentially the same, as shown
by two examples:

> Bid slaves to be submissive to their masters and give satisfaction
> in every respect; they are not to be refractory, nor to pilfer, but
> to show entire and true fidelity, so that in everything they may
> adorn the doctrine of God our Saviour.   Titus 2:9-10

> Let all who are under the yoke of slavery regard their masters
> as worthy of all honor, so that the name of God and the teaching
> may not be defamed. Those who have believing masters must
> not be disrespectful on the ground that they are brethren; rather
> they must serve all the better since those who benefit by their
> service are believers and beloved. Teach and urge these duties.
> If anyone teaches otherwise and does not agree with the sound
> words of our Lord Jesus Christ and the teaching which accords
> with Godliness, he is puffed up with conceit, he knows nothing,
> he has a morbid craving for controversy and for disputes about
> words, which produce envy, dissension, slander, base suspicions,
> and wrangling among men who are depraved in mind and bereft
> of the truth, imagining that Godliness is a means of gain.
>   1st Timothy 6:1-5

It is easily understood why Cherokee owners were indulgent in giving their slaves time to attend religious services. Moreover, some slaves attended church to interpret for masters who did not speak English.

Some Cherokees, even slaveowners, resisted the efforts of the missionaries, however. One was Drowning Bear (*Yonaguska*), a chief who resisted every persuasion to emigrate west and was suspicious of Christianity. He refused to allow the Scriptures to be read to his people until he had first heard them. After hearing one or two chapters of the Book of Matthew, the chief remarked, "Well, it seems to be a good book—strange that the white people are not better, after having had it so long."[41]

The Methodists made the last large-scale mission effort among the Cherokees and they experienced the quickest success. In one year's time they converted 189 Indians and 63 black slaves.[42] John Ross was one of that number.

NOTES

1. James Mooney, "Myths of the Cherokees," Nineteenth Annual Report of the Bureau of Ethnology (Washington, D.C.: Government Printing Office, 1900), p. 214.

2. F. A. Michaux, "Travels to the West of the Allegheny Mountains in the States of Ohio, Kentucky and Tennessee," in Ruben Gold Thwaites, *Early Western Travels* (Cleveland: The Arthur H. Clark Company, 1904-1907), vol. 18, p. 28.

3. Henry Thompson Malone, *Cherokees of the Old South: A People in Transition* (Athens: University of Georgia Press, 1956), p. 138.

4. Ibid.

5. Thurman Wilkins, *Cherokee Tragedy: The Story of the Ridge Family and the Decimation of a People* (London: The Macmillan Company, 1970), p. 30.

6. Ibid., p. 181.

7. Ibid., p. 182.

8. Ibid., pp. 182-183.

9. National Archives, Paul Smith to Henry Dearborn, Secretary of War Files, Indian Division, No. 1484 (1805).

10. Lillian Delly, "Episode at Cornwall," *Chronicles of Oklahoma* 51, no. 4 (Winter 1973-74), pp. 444-445.

11. "The Foreign Mission School at Cornwall, Connecticut," *Chronicles of Oklahoma* 7, no. 3 (September 1929), p. 247.

12. Edward Everett Dale and Gaston Litton, *Cherokee Cavaliers* (Norman: University of Oklahoma Press, 1939), p. 7.

13. Ibid.

14. Delly, "Episode at Cornwall," p. 446.

15. Wilkins, *Cherokee Tragedy*, p. 184.

16. Delly, "Episode at Cornwall," p. 447.

17. Ibid., p. 446.

18. Ibid., pp. 448-449.

19. Clemens de Baillow, "The Chief Vann House at Spring Place Georgia," *Early Georgia* 2, no. 2 (Spring 1957), pp. 3-11.

20. Ralph Henry Gabriel, *Elias Boudinot Cherokee & His America* (Norman: University of Oklahoma Press, 1941), pp. 24-29.

21. Edmund Schwarze, *History of the Moravian Missions among Southern Indian Tribes of the United States* (Bethlehem, Pennsylvania: Times Publishing Company, 1923), p. 74.

22. Ibid., pp. 63, 64.

23. Grace Steel Woodward, *The Cherokees,* (Norman: University of Oklahoma Press, 1963), p. 5.

24. Cherokee Documents, Thomas Gilcrease Institute of American History and Art, Tulsa, Oklahoma.

25. Gabriel, *Elias Boudinot,* pp. 60, 134-135.

26. Richard M. Ketchum, *Will Rogers: His Life and Times* (New York: American Heritage Publishing Company, Inc., 1973), pp. 15, 16.

27. Gabriel, *Elias Boudinot,* pp. 60, 134-135.

28. Gary Evan Moulton, "John Ross, Cherokee Chief" (Ph.D. dissertation, Oklahoma State University, 1974), pp. 53, 54.

29. Emmet Starr, *Early History of the Cherokees* (n.p., 1917), p. 109.

30. In 1824 the newly organized Cherokee Supreme Court heard one of its earliest cases involving black slavery. The Court ordered Richard and John Rattliff to pay Lewis Ross $92.50 for harboring one of his blacks for a year. Malone, *Cherokees of the Old South,* p. 83.

31. Leola Selman Beeson, "Homes of Distinguished Cherokee Indians," *Chronicles of Oklahoma* 11, no. 3 (September 1933), p. 934.

32. Ibid., p. 940.

33. "Report of the Journey of the Brethren Abraham Steiner and Frederick C. De Schweinitz to the Cherokees and the Cumberland Settlements," in Samuel Cole Williams, ed., *Early Travels in the Tennessee Country, 1540-1800* (Johnson City, Tennessee: Watauga Press, 1928), p. 460.

34. Zella Armstrong, *The History of Hamilton County and Chattanooga Tennessee* vol. 1 (Chattanooga: The Lookout Publishing Company, 1931), p. 39.

35. *Christian Observer* (London), November 1811, p. 723.

36. Ibid.

37. Robert Sparks Walker, *Torchlight to the Cherokees* (New York: The Macmillan Company, 1931), pp. 86, 87.

38. Malone, *Cherokees of the Old South,* p. 141.

39. Ibid.

40. Walker, *Torchlight to the Cherokees,* pp. 86, 87.

41. Douglas L. Right, *The American Indian in North Carolina* (Winston-Salem: John F. Blair, 1957), pp. 204-205.

42. Anson West, *A History of Methodism in Alabama* (Nashville: M. E. Publishing House, South, 1893), pp. 384-397.

3 Maturity and Westward Movement

The Cherokees were not the only Indians who had experienced the loss of their lands, nor were they the only tribe capable of sophisticated political organization. Tecumseh, the great Shawnee leader, won several tribes to his grandiose plan for an Indian confederacy which would attempt to arrest the constant encroachment upon Indian lands. Tecumseh spent the years 1788 and 1789 with the Cherokees, and his mother had resided among the tribe for many years. It is possible that his association with Dragging Canoe during this time influenced Tecumseh's political life and helped fashion his concept of the great Indian confederacy that became his life work. In 1811, Tecumseh journeyed back to the South to enlist the aid of the southern tribes. All were asked to send representatives to hear Tecumseh speak in the square at Tukabatchie, the principal Creek town. In his speech, Tecumseh made the Indians' claim to territorial rights clear:

> The white people have no right to take the land from the Indians, for it is ours. The Great Spirit gave it to us. Let all the redmen unite in claiming a common and equal right in the land, as it was at first, and should yet be, for it never was divided, but belongs to all, for the use of each of us.[1]

"Prophets" who preached the return to the old ways of life then began to appear in Cherokee towns. A Cherokee prophet from Coosawatie spoke before a great council at Ustanali and explained:

We have taken the white man's clothes and trinkets. We have
beds, tables, and mills. Some even have books and cats. All
this is bad, and because of it the Great Spirit is angry, and the
game is leaving the country. If the Cherokees would live and be
happy as before, they must put off the white man's dress,
throw away the mills and looms, kill the cats, put on paint and
buckskins, and be Indians again. Otherwise, swift destruction will
overtake them.[2]

Whether by design or otherwise, there was no mention of black slavery
although the bulk of the most influential Cherokees were slaveowners.
Seeing that most of the audience was receiving the prophet's message
eagerly, "Major" Ridge shouted that "such talk will lead to war with the
United States, and mean ruin for the Cherokees."[3] Ridge's statement was
so resented that he probably would have been killed had his friends not
spirited him away. The prophet then declared a day of reckoning for all
who failed to accept the new doctrine. He declared, "On that day, the
Great Spirit will send a hailstorm and destroy all but the faithful, who
must assemble on the highest peak of the Smoky Mountains."[4]

Many Cherokees were severely agitated and in a state of uncertainty
when the issue was decided by a party of Red Stick Creeks who killed a
Cherokee woman near Etowah, in Georgia. The Lower Creeks then invited
the Cherokees to join them and the Americans in putting down the Red
Sticks.[5]

The dramatic change in the Indian's life-style was demonstrated by an
admonition of Chief Doublehead in 1818. When the Cherokees began
"war talk," the chief counseled, "We must not war; I have seen more
white men in one town [Philadelphia] than would be sufficient to eat
all the Indians, if made into a pie."[6] Doublehead was not the first to
counsel peace and industry, however. As early as 1794, Little Turkey,
himself a war chief, exclaimed, "We have long wished to live so that we
might have gray hairs on our heads."[7]

The Moravian missionary Abraham Steiner made an official visit to
Spring Place in 1819 and reported, "The Upper Cherokees had made the
greatest advance in civilization and were no longer hunters and trappers
but agriculturalists and manufacturers."[8] (The Upper Cherokees were
slaveowners to a much larger degree than the Lower.) By 1820 the number
of black slaves in the Nation had increased, and the political, social, and

cultural leadership of the tribe was gravitating toward the mixed-bloods. These men were Cherokees in every respect, however. They were busy developing a legal code to regulate taxes, internal improvements, payment of debts, the liquor traffic, marriage, voting, crime, and black slavery.

The advent of slavery on a larger scale had been accompanied by unique problems concerning the conduct and legal status of slaves. This condition was partially alleviated by the enactment of a series of slave codes. Since the Cherokees were in the process of accepting the white man's civilization, it is not surprising that they also adopted his slave codes. The first of these acts was apparently passed in 1819 as the result of a runaway black's trading a stolen horse to a Cherokee. The act read:

New Town, Cherokee Nation, November 1st, 1819.
In Committee
The National Committee have taken up the case submitted to
them by the Council relating to the exchange of horses between Otter Lifter and a runaway negro man, belonging to Wm.
Thompson. The horse delivered to Otter Lifter by said negro
man was proven away from him, and the question submitted to
the Committee was, whether or not, the master of the negro
man, Wm Thompson, should be accountable to the Otter Lifter
for the horse so proved away from him on account of the trans-
gression of his said negro man; the Committee therefore have
decided that Wm. Thompson ought not to be accountable for
the contract entered into with his runaway negro man by any
person contrary to his approbation, and, *Resolved by the Committee,* that no contract or bargain entered into with any slave
or slaves, without the approbation of their masters shall be binding on them.

                                          Jno. Ross, Pres't N. Com.

                         Path   his mark   Killer[9]

Subsequently, the National Committee and Council passed the following act on October 28, 1820:

That any person or persons whatsoever, who shall trade with
any negro slave without permission from the proper owner of
such slaves, and the property so traded for be proven to have

been stolen, the purchaser shall be held and bound to the legal proprietor for the same, or the value there of; and be it further *Resolved,* That any person who shall permit their negro or negroes to purchase spirituous liquors and vend the same, the master or owner of such negro or negroes shall forfeit and pay a fine of fifteen dollars for every such offense, to be collected by the Marshalls within their respective Districts for the National use; and should any negro be found vending spirituous liquors without permission from their respective owners, such negro or negroes, so offending, shall receive fifteen cobbs or paddles for every such offense, from the hands of the patrolers of the settlement or neighborhood in which the offense was committed, and every settlement or neighborhood shall be privileged to organize a patroling company.[10]

It is doubtful that many Indian masters would admit that their slaves were bootlegging with their approval when it would mean the confiscation of the liquor, the slave, and a fifteen-dollar fine. If a master pleaded ignorance of his slave's bootlegging activity, he would suffer loss of the liquor only and the slave could take the beating. The closing clause of the act was permissive legislation for the organizing of patrols to regulate the activity of slaves. Such patrol companies were organized and operated during the entire period of black slavery within the Cherokee Nation.

During the 1820s the Cherokees continued to abandon village life and establish individual farming units. This brought a concurrent increase in the number of black slaves. The mass of the people lived in cabins, some of which were constructed of hewn logs and had plank floors and chimneys. The more affluent slaveowners continued to build comfortable two-story brick and frame houses—some of them very elaborate—and lived in much the same style as white planters of the same economic standing in the southern states. Most families cultivated corn, rye, oats, wheat, cotton, and tobacco. They engaged in livestock raising, planted apple and peach orchards and vegetable gardens. Cotton was raised in sufficient quantities to supply the Cherokees' own needs fully and leave a considerable surplus to be shipped on boats of their own making to New Orleans. Hides and livestock were also sold in neighboring states. These commodities brought sufficient quantities of currency into the Nation.[11]

In 1820 President James Monroe appointed Jedidiah Morse to survey Indian removal problems and to furnish Secretary of War John Calhoun with a report. Morse wrote:

> To remove these Indians from their homes . . . into a wilderness among strangers, possibly hostile, to live as their neighbors live, by hunting, a state to which they have not been lately accoustomed, and which is incompatible with civilization, can hardly be reconciled with the professed object of civilizing them.[12]

Spring Place was visited by the Reverend Theodore Schultz in April 1826, and he reported that "plantations were in better shape and industries, looms, mills, etc., were increasing."[13] About this same time the Reverend Samuel A. Worcester wrote:

> Agriculture is the principal employment and support of the people. It is the dependence of almost every family. As to the wandering part of the people, who live by the chase, if they are to be found in the nation, I certainly have not found them, nor ever heard of them, except from the floor of Congress, and other distant sources of information. I do not know of a single family who depend, in any considerable degree, on game for a support.[14]

The increased numbers of black slaves in the Nation brought about a rash of legislation. In 1825 David Brown, a half-breed preacher, wrote in the *Richmond Family Visitor:*

> The slaves have been from time to time brought in and sold by white men. They are, however, generally well treated, and they much prefer living in the Nation to residence in the United States. There is hardly any intermixture of Cherokee and African blood.[15]

Miscegenation and intermarriage had been repugnant to the Indians from their earliest contacts with Negroes. The first known marriage of a Cherokee to a Negro was that of Chief Shoe Boot. Shoe Boot was a friend of Andrew Jackson and had been instrumental in winning the Battle of Horseshoe

Bend. After his white wife left him, he married her black servant, Lucy, who was his property. Lucy bore him two children. The chief petitioned the Council for free status for his children who were his black slave property according to common law. The request was granted, but the Council warned Shoe Boot that interracial marriages between Cherokees and blacks were not sociallyacceptable.[16] The Council made its position unequivocally clear with the passage of the following act on November 11, 1824:

That intermarriages between negro slaves and Indians, or whites, shall not be lawful, and any person or persons, permitting and approbating his, her or their negro slaves, to intermarry with Indians or whites, he, she or they, so offending, shall pay a fine of fifty dollars, one half for the benefit of the Cherokee Nation; and

Be it further resolved, That any male Indian or white man marrying a negro woman slave, he or they shall be punished with fifty-nine stripes on the bare back, and any Indian or white woman, marrying a negro man slave, shall be punished with twenty-five stripes on her or their bare back.[17]

Legislation against miscegenation demonstrates the real position of blacks. The Cherokees may have displayed the strongest color prejudice of all American Indians. It has been stated that the Cherokees once had a death penalty for marrying a Negro.[18] Even the Spaniards were not considered "white" by some. In 1793 Little Turkey, a prominent chief, declared that the Spaniards were not "real white people, and what few I have seen of them looked like mulattoes, and I would never have anything to say to them."[19] The Cherokees were adamant in their determination not to become racially identified with a subject people whom they regarded—as did their white neighbors—as their servants and inferiors. Some miscegenation did occur, just as it did in the white South, but a Cherokee Negro was always regarded as a Negro.[20]

The sale of stolen feed and livestock by black slaves continued to prove troublesome and the following act (November 11, 1824) was expected to solve the problem:

Resolved . . . That it shall not be lawful for negro slaves to possess
property in horses, cattle or hogs, and that those slaves now possess-
ing property of that description, be required to dispose of the
same in twelve months from this date, under the penalty of confiscation, and any property so confiscated, shall be sold for the
benefit of the Cherokee Nation.[21]

The Cherokees did not experience the inner conflict between the practice of slavery and conscience that permeated much of the United States.
They never felt the need to justify slavery and never expressed the opinion
that slavery was in the best interest of the black. Neither did they give
voice to the "positive benefits" of Christianizing and civilizing their slaves.
Slavery was justified solely on the basis of the benefits that accrued to
masters. Yet, unlike the white community, there appears to be little or
no feeling of guilt among the Cherokees today.

During the early part of the nineteenth century, the Cherokee Nation
was considered a separate and independent government. The jurisdiction
of the United States was not considered to extend over the Cherokee
Nation. Therefore, fugitives began to seek sanctuary there. Runaway black
slaves and some free blacks sought refuge within the Nation. They were
not welcome, and the General Council attempted to remedy the situation
with the following act (November 11, 1824):

Resolved . . . That all free negroes coming into the Cherokee
Nation under any pretense whatsoever, shall be viewed and
treated in every respect, as intruders, and shall not be allowed
to reside in the Cherokee Nation without a permit from the
National Committee and Council.[22]

Two days later the following augmenting act was declared law.

Resolved . . . That no citizen or citizens of the Cherokee Nation
shall receive in their employment, any citizen or citizens of the
United States, without first obtaining a permit agreeably to law,
for the person or persons so employed; and any person or persons violating this resolution, upon conviction before any of the
District Courts, shall pay a fine for every offense at the discretion
of the Court, not exceding ten dollars; and the person employed
to be removed.[23]

The *Cherokee Phoenix* reported the numbers of known black slaves in each district of the Nation in 1824. It also stated that there were 20 grist mills, 14 sawmills, 56 blacksmith shops, and 6 cotton gins in operation at that time.[24]

	Slaves	Male	Female
Coosewaytee District	295	168	127
Tahquoa District	24	7	17
Chickamauga District	187	90	97
Hickory Log District	—	—	—
Aquohee District	19	10	9
Chattooga District	292	122	170
Higher Tower District	79	43	36
Amohee District	142	73	69
Total	1038	513	525

In 1825 it was reported that a total of 13,563 native Cherokees still resided in the East. They possessed 1,217 black slaves.[25] Elias Boudinot conducted a survey in 1825 and determined that Cherokees owned 22,531 black cattle, 7,683 horses, 46,732 hogs, 2,566 sheep, 330 goats, 172 wagons, 2,843 plows, 762 looms, 2,486 spinning wheels, 10 sawmills, 31 grist mills, 1 powder mill, 62 blacksmith shops, 2 tanneries, and 8 cotton gins.[26]

All numbers of blacks, including census figures, should be construed as a bare minimum. Even census takers could easily have missed slaves in the more remote areas. Moreover, Cherokees who owned slaves who had previously escaped from white owners in the United States may not have wanted them reported.

The number of slaves held by the Cherokees in the trans-Mississippi West is not known. Many of them were slaveowners, however, and had taken their slaves with them when they emigrated. Others had purchased slaves both within and outside their country.

The idea of Indian removal appears to have originated with President Thomas Jefferson. As early as 1790, however, small bands of Cherokees were moving westward into Arkansas and Texas to escape the encroachment of white men. In 1794 The Bowl, a Cherokee war chief, led a band of warriors and their families across the Mississippi River into Spanish territory. They settled in what later became Arkansas Territory. This community became the nucleus for additional migrations. By 1811 there were nearly 2,000 Cherokees in Arkansas.[27] In 1817 a group of Western Cherokees, who were to become known as "Old Settlers," were led to Tennessee by John Jolly and signed a removal treaty exchanging some of their ancient homeland for territory in northwestern Arkansas. By 1820 there were approximately 6,000 Western Cherokees. In 1828 these Old Settlers signed a treaty with the United States, exchanging their Arkansas lands for territory farther west in the northeastern section of present-day Oklahoma. Most of the Old Settlers moved to their new home within a year and began clearing fields, establishing settlements, and opening the wilderness.

This region, which was to become the Cherokee Nation in the West, had experienced or at least sanctioned black slavery since the arrival of the first Europeans. Whether the area was Spanish, French, or American and was known as Louisiana, Indiana Territory, Louisiana Territory, Missouri Territory, Arkansas Territory, or Indian Territory, black slavery had always been tolerated there. Louisiana Territory contained "a considerable number of Negro slaves . . . before the arrival of the Cherokees."[28] Some had been brought by early traders who had ascended the Arkansas River and established trading posts at strategic points. There are numerous accounts about the "luxury" in which Colonel Auguste Pierre Chouteau indulged himself at Grand Saline, his trading post on the Neosho (Grand) River forty miles north of the present Fort Gibson. His father, Jean Pierre Chouteau, and his father's brothers had amassed great wealth in the fur trade, and his son was well-qualified to add new luster to the family name. He was both fair and just with the Indians, but stern when occasion demanded. It was a combination of virtues that the Indians understood and respected. Chouteau's wife was a comely Osage woman about whom travelers spoke highly, which further guaranteed him the loyalty of the Osage Indians.

Commissioner Henry R. Ellsworth, together with Washington Irving, Count Albert de Portales, and Charles Latrobe, visited Chouteau at Grand Saline in 1832 and found the trader "surrounded by a retinue of colored . . . retainers. . . . Negro girls ran about giggling, while others took and tethered the horses."[29] With black slaves to serve him and perform manual labor and Indian hunters to provide his table with wild turkey, venison, and other gustatory delights of the prairie and forest, Chouteau lived the life of "a wilderness potentate."[30]

Thomas Nuttall traveled through the Arkansas country in 1819 and visited Walter Webber, a Cherokee who had removed to that area. Nuttall described Webber as being

> a metif, who acts as an Indian trader, is also a chief of the nation, and lives in ease and affluence, possessing a decently furnished and well provided house, several negro slaves, a large, well cleared, and well fenced farm; and both himself and his nephew read, write and speak English. Yesterday, while passing along the bank of the river, I observed with pleasure the fine farms and comfortable cabins occupied by the Indians.[31]

Nutall continued his description of the Cherokee countryside:

> Both banks of the river, as we proceeded, were lined with the houses and farms of the Cherokees, and though their dress was a mixture of indigenous and European taste, yet in their houses, which are decently furnished, and in their farms, which were well fenced and stocked with cattle, we perceive a happy approach towards civilization. Their numerous families, also, well fed and clothed, argue a propitious progress in their population. Their superior industry, either as hunters or farmers, proves the value of property among them, and they are no longer strangers to avarice, and the distinctions created by wealth; some of them are possessed of property to the amount of many thousands of dollars, have houses handsomely and conveniently furnished, and their tables spread with our dainties and luxuries.[32]

Chief Tom Graves was a Cherokee slaveowner in Arkansas at this early date. Edwin James, a botanist and geologist with the expedition of Major Stephen H. Long in 1819 and 1820, described a visit to the Graves' home. He reported that Graves, a full-blood, lived with his full-blood wife in a "substantial house" surrounded by lesser buildings. He possessed large enclosed fields of corn, cotton, and sweet potatoes and also owned droves of swine and flocks of geese. Graves did not speak English but owned a black female slave who served as an interpreter. Other slaves tilled his fields and waited his table.[33]

Charles Labrobe, an English naturalist and author, later mentioned
the presence of many black slaves in his writings about the Cherokee
country.[34] Black slavery had become an established institution after the
arrival of the Old Settler Cherokees. From the beginning, they practiced
slavery in the West, and black labor helped to create farms and plantations
in the wilderness.[35] Moreover, it was considered an indication of wealth
and status to own Negroes; consequently, "everyone who could afford to
do so owned one or more."[36]

Black slaves in the West were sometimes the recipients of harsh and
brutal treatment. The following letter from the Cherokee agent in Arkansas
to the secretary of war graphically illustrates such conditions.

Reuben Lewis To The Secretary of War
    Cherokee Agency Arkansas August 15th 1819

. . . A circumstance happened sometime since in this Nation,
and which I am told is not the only one of the kind which has
happened among the Cherokees, which in my opinion calls upon
the humanity of our Government to put an end to. A Negro
Man belonging to a Cherokee woman had fallen under the dis-
pleasure of her husband, (from what cause I have not been
able to ascertain sirtainly,) the Negroes Mistress desired her
husband to kill him, which he d'clined, she then desired him
to tye the Negroe, which he did, she then with an axe nocked
him in the head; cut it off, and threw the body into the River.
There is no Law or custom among the Cherokees to protect
the lives of that poor unfortunate part of the human Species,
and as among Savages particularly, passion often gets the
ascendency of reason, they hold there lives by a feble tenure,
calling imperiously for protection. . . .

                                    R. Lewis
The Honbl The Secretary   Cherokee Agt at Arkansas[37]
        of War

Chief John Jolly (*Oo-loo-te-ka*), Walter Webber, Captain John Rogers,
and John Drew were among the more affluent and inflential Cherokee
slaveowners in the West. They engaged in commercial farming and hastened
to claim large tracts of fertile land. They cultivated cotton and corn that

were tended by blacks under the supervision of overseers. The rich bottomland was ideal for growing crops that were transported to market by
Arkansas River steamers. "At one time in the Cherokee Nation there was
more than one slave for every ten Indians, and several Indians owned as
many as one hundred slaves."[38] The poorer and less educated Cherokees
usually sought the back country hills that reminded them of their eastern
home. They usually tilled only small garden plots, lived in simple structures,
and had little need for large numbers of slaves. Before moving west, Jolly
had operated a trading establishment at the mouth of the Hiwassee River
in Tennessee that had helped make him wealthy. He had also been a planter
there and had owned a large number of slaves to till his many acres. Jolly
had been a leader of the "plantation element" of the Cherokees in the
East and continued to be so in the West.[39]

Western Cherokees often found their slaves to be troublesome. In 1823
Celia, a black slave woman of Arkansas, broke out of the Pulaski County
jail, where she had been placed under an attachment, and supposedly departed for the Cherokee Nation with two other slaves belonging to her
former owner, Walter Webber.[40] Such isolated incidents are sometimes
quoted as proof of leniency on the part of Cherokee masters. It was not
uncommon, however, for slaves to run away from new masters or new
geographic locations to return to their former homes or home areas. There
were myriad reasons for such behavior, including the rejoining of family
and friends, nostalgia, and fear. When Cherokees moved to the West, a
number of black slaves fled from their Indian masters and made their way
back to the East.

The Old Settlers experienced numerous legal problems with their black
property. The following illustrative notice appeared in the *Arkansas Gazette*
in 1826.

Cherokee Nation

Spadrie Bluff, Sept 28th, 1826

Whereas, it has been represented to the undersigned, that sundry
persons in Arkansas Territory, and others within the Cherokee
Nation, have been endeavoring to perchase, traffic for, or procure
under color of legal process, certain NEGRO SLAVES, the
rightful property of the heirs and legates of a Cherokee called
CONNETOO, deceased; and whereas, the undersigned has been
duly appointed Agent and attorney in fact of said heirs, now

this is to forewarn all persons, whatsoever, from purchasing, trafficing for, receiving, or procuring in any manner, or under any pretence, any of said negro slaves. They are now, or recently were with, or in possession of, the following named persons, to wit:—

With *Thomas Graves.* (a Cherokee) James, Teany, Silvey, and two children (names unknown):—with a Cherokee called *John Leak,* Anney and three children (names unknown):—with the *widow Otter,* (a Cherokee woman), Easter and two children (names unknown):—with *Major Jolly,* principal chief of the [Western] Cherokees, one man named Frank: with *Samuel Baggs,* (a Cherokee) one girl (name unknown); and with *William Marshall,* an Indian trader, near the Delaware Village, one man, named Jacob.

> JOHN DREW, Agent
> and Attorney in fact for the heirs of
> Connetoo, deceased.[41]

The following notice is an example of proposed litigation involving black slaves with regard to inheritance. The adjudicatory problems involving estates were frequently complicated by slavery.

> Know all men by these presents that I Aky Victory of the C. Nation have this day made nominated and appointed . . . John Drew . . . my true and lawful attorney . . . to ask demand and sue for my part of the Negroes formerly owned by my father John Rogers . . . and all such as may be coming to me from that Estate. . . .
>
> | Witness | Given from under my hand | Aky | her
Victory |
> |---|---|---|---|
> | Aaron Hicks | This Oct 22, 1826[42] | | mark |

Most of the early slaves were bilingual in English and Cherokee and frequently served as interpreters. These interpreters were usually called "linksters." This term was probably a corruption of the word "linguist."[43]

In the Cherokee Nation, as in the United States, a class distinction developed within the black slave caste system. "Those around the house look[ed] down on those who worked in the fields." Another elite group included the trusted bilingual messengers, bodyguards, and blacks who aided their Indian masters in business transactions.[44]

The growth of slavery in the West presented concomitant problems as it had in the East. Intruders continued to pose a constant menace, as they had in the East.

Cherokee Agency A. T. Dec. 24th 1828.

Sir About the 20th of this month a person by the name of Jessee Burton of Crawford County at the head of an armed party, went within the boundary of the Cherokee Indians in this Territory, in violation of the intercourse law, between the United States and Indian tribes, within its limits and took by force Eight Negro Servants from the Cherokees, valued in all at Thirty three hundred dollars, which they [Cherokees] will claim of the General government, if the property is not restored immediately, therefore I have to request you will cause justice done to both parties as soon as possible.

Very Respectfully Your Ob[t] Serv[t]
P. Brearly, U.S. Sub Ag[t] Ind Aff[s]

Robert Crittenden Esq[r]   Act. Governor of Arkansas[45]

One month later the following article appeared in the *Arkansas Gazette:*

The Cherokees.—We understand that considerable excitement and alarm exists at this time among the Cherokees, in this Territory, which has been caused by a late forcible wresting of property from them by some of their white neighbors. It appears, that a number of negroes were found in the possession of some of the Cherokees, who are alleged to have belonged to a man who was murdered and robbed by a party of that nation, on the Tennessee River, upwards of 30 years ago. Some of the identical negroes who were stolen, it is alleged, are among them, and the others claimed are said to be the descendants of those who were stolen. A citizen of Crawford county has set up a claim to them, either by purchase, or otherwise: and recently, without any legal process, proceeded with a party of men, to the nation, and forcibly seized and carried off eight of them.—This arbitrary proceeding has produced

great sensation among the Indians, who are apprehensive that
it is only a prelude to other similar aggressions. Some of
them, we understand, keep a close watch over their property,
and declare their intention of protecting it with their lives;
but we have not heard of their making any threats of endeavoring to retake the property which has been forcibly wrested
from them.—They will demand its restitution of the government
and if their claim is a just one, we hope and trust that the property will be restored to them. We know nothing of the validity of
the adverse claim which has been set up to it but we are clearly
of opinion, that whether it be valid or invalid, the step taken to
get possession of it, is irregular and illegal. Measures, we understand, are in a train, for placing the property in safe hands, until
such time as legal investigation shall adjudge it to its rightful
owners.[46]

One week later the *Gazette* announced the final disposition of the
matter: "We learn, by a gentleman who returned a few days since from
Cantonment Gibson, that the Negroes who were recently forcibly taken
from the Cherokee Indians . . . by a citizen of Crawford county, have been
surrendered, and returned to the Cherokee nation."[47] Nevertheless,
Cherokees continued to be apprehensive about the security of their property and intruders remained a serious problem.

The numbers of black slaves constantly increased by natural prolifera-
tion, purchase, and immigration. On January 28, 1830, about two hundred emigrating Cherokees passed Little Rock on the steamboat *Industry*
on their way up the Arkansas River. The party contained both Indians
and slaves. The next day the steamboat *Waverly* passed carrying nearly
the same number of immigrants and slaves.[48]

NOTES

1. John P. Brown, *Old Frontiers: The Story of the Cherokee Indians
from Earliest Times to the Date of Their Removal to the West, 1838*
(Kingsport, Tennessee: Southern Publishers, 1938), p. 460.
2. Ibid.
3. Ibid.

4. Ibid.

5. Ibid.

6. William Faux, *Faux's Memorable Days in America, November 27, 1818-July 21, 1820,* in Reuben Gold Thwaites, *Early Western Travels* (Cleveland: Arthur H. Clark Co., 1904-1907), vol. 11, p. 247.

7. Brown, *Old Frontiers,* p. 445.

8. Edmund Schwarze, *History of the Moravian Missions Among Southern Indian Tribes of the United States* (Bethlehem, Pennsylvania: Times Publishing Company, 1923), p. 135.

9. *Laws of the Cherokee Nation: Adopted by the Council at Various Periods* (Tahlequah: Cherokee Nation, Cherokee Advocate Office, 1852), pp. 8, 9. Hereafter cited as *Laws of the Cherokee Nation,* 1852.

10. Ibid., pp. 24, 25.

11. Rachel Caroline Eaton, *John Ross and the Cherokee Indians* (Menasha, Wisconsin: George Banta Publishing Company, 1914), pp. 34, 52.

12. Henry C. Dennis, comp. and ed., *The American Indian 1492-1970: A Chronology and Fact Book* (Dobbs Ferry, New York: Oceana Publications, Inc., 1971), p. 24.

13. Schwarze, *Moravian Missions,* p. 178.

14. Althea Bass, *Cherokee Messenger* (Norman: University of Oklahoma Press, 1936), pp. 100-101.

15. Andrew V. Cain, *History of Lumpkin County for the First Hundred Years 1832-1932* (Atlanta: Stein Printing Company, 1932), p. 10.

16. Henry Thompson Malone, *Cherokees of the Old South: A People in Transition* (Athens: University of Georgia Press, 1956), p. 142.

17. *Laws of the Cherokee Nation,* 1852, p. 38.

18. Frank Cunningham, *General Stand Watie's Confederate Indians* (San Antonio: The Naylor Company, 1959), p. 11.

19. *American State Papers, Indian Affairs,* vol. 1, (Washington, D.C.: Government Printing Office, 1832), p. 461.

20. Chapman J. Milling, *Red Carolinians* (Chapel Hill: University of North Carolina Press, 1940), pp. 341, 359. Melville J. Herskovits, an eminent anthropologist, estimates that more than 27 percent of American blacks possess Indian blood. Melville Jean Herskovits, *The American Negro* (Bloomington: The University of Indiana Press, 1928), p. 10.

21. *Laws of the Cherokee Nation,* 1852, p. 39.

22. Ibid., p. 37.

23. Ibid., p. 34.

24. *Cherokee Phoenix,* June 18, 1828. The *Phoenix* was America's first aboriginal newspaper and had subscribers in the states and in foreign countries. Spellings of Cherokee districts vary widely with time and sources.

25. Thurman Wilkins, *Cherokee Tragedy: The Story of the Ridge Family and the Decimation of a People* (London: The Macmillan Company, 1970), p. 186.

26. Oliver Knight, "History of the Cherokees, 1830-1846," *Chronicles of Oklahoma* 34, no. 2 (Summer 1956), p. 160.

27. Thomas L. McKenney, *History of the Indian Tribes of North America with Biographical Sketches and Anecdotes of the Principal Chiefs,* 3 vols. (Philadelphia: Rice, Rutler and Company, 1870), vol. 2, p. 294.

28. Edwin C. McReynolds, *Oklahoma: A History of the Sooner State* (Norman: University of Oklahoma Press, 1954), p. 49.

29. Harriette Johnson Westbrook, "The Chouteaus," *Chronicles of Oklahoma* 11, no. 3 (September 1933), p. 961.

30. Harry Sinclair Drago, *The Steamboaters* (New York: Bramhall House, 1968), p. 55.

31. Thomas Nuttall, *Journals of Travels Into the Arkansas Territory During The Year 1819, With Occasional Observations On The Manners Of The Aborigines* (Philadelphia: Thos. W. Palmer, 1821), reprinted in Reuben Gold Thwaites, ed., *Early Western Travels 1748-1846* (Cleveland: The Arthur H. Clark Company, 1905), XIII, p. 181.

32. Ibid., p. 174.

33. Reuben Gold Thwaites, ed., *Account of an Expedition From Pittsburg to the Rocky Mountains, Compiled From the Notes of Major Long and Other Gentlemen of the Party by Edwin James* (Cleveland: Arthur H. Clark Company, 1905), vol. 4, p. 17.

34. Charles Joseph Latrobe, *The Rambler in North America* (London: R. B. Seeley and W. Burnside, 1836), passim.

35. Gaston Litton, *History of Oklahoma* (New York: Lewis Historical Publishing Company, Inc., 1957), vol. 1, p. 183.

36. Eaton, *John Ross*, p. 165.

37. Clarence Edwin Carter, comp. and ed., *The Territorial Papers of the United States,* vol. 19, *Territory of Arkansas* (Washington, D.C.: Government Printing Office, 1954), p. 97.

38. Jack Gregory and Rennard Strickland, *Sam Houston with The Cherokees 1829-1833* (Austin: University of Texas Press, 1967), pp. 12, 13.

39. Ibid., p. 13.

40. *Arkansas Gazette,* October 14, 1823. Also see Orville W. Taylor, *Negro Slavery in Arkansas* (Durham: Duke University Press, 1958), p. 217.

41. *Arkansas Gazette,* November 24, 1826.

42. Gregory and Strickland, *Sam Houston,* pp. 12, 13.

43. T. L. Ballenger, "The Andrew Nave Letters: New Cherokee Source Material at Northeastern State College," *Chronicles of Oklahoma* 30, no. 1 (Spring 1952), pp. 4 f.f.

44. Carter, *Territorial Papers,* vol. 20, p. 821.

45. Ibid., p. 82.

46. *Arkansas Gazette,* January 20, 1829.

47. *Ibid.,* January 27, 1829.

48. Grant Foreman, *Indian Removal: The Emigration of the Five Civilized Tribes of Indians* (Norman: University of Oklahoma Press, 1932), p. 231.

4   The Last Decade in the East

In 1809 the Cherokees began to enact laws by the National Council. In 1819 they adopted a commission form of government with legislative powers vested in a committee of thirteen elected members. Then in 1820 the Nation was apportioned into eight districts, each represented in the council by four salaried members chosen by popular election every two years. As the tribe became increasingly sedentary and agrarian, its institutions grew more complex and sophisticated. The people placed additional demands upon their leaders and government for equity, protection, and services. Therefore, on July 26, 1827, a convention of delegates duly authorized by the Cherokee people met in assembly at New Echota and ratified and adopted a constitution closely patterned after that of the United States. The National Council then became a legislative body composed of two houses, comparable to the United States Congress. The principal chief and the second chief, at first chosen by the National Committee and then by the National Council, were now to be elected by popular vote. Consequently, in order to provide responsive government more adequately, the Cherokees became the first Indian tribe to adopt a written constitution.

The new constitution contained the following sections directly related to black slavery.

Article III, Section 4: No person shall be elegible to a seat in the General Council, but a free Cherokee male citizen, who shall have attained to the age of twenty-five years. The descendants of Cherokee men by all free women, except the

African race, whose parents may have been living together
as man and wife, according to the customs and laws of this
Nation, shall be entitled to all the rights and privileges of
this Nation, as well as the posterity of Cherokee women by
all free men. No person who is of Negro or Mulatto parentage,
either by the father or mother side, shall be eligible to hold
any office of profit, honor or trust under this Government.

Article III, Section 7: All free male citizens, (excepting negroes
and descendants of white and Indian men by negro women
who may have been set free,) who shall have attained to the age
of eighteen years, shall be equally entitled to a vote at all public
elections.[1]

There were other significant events of 1828 and 1829 which profoundly
affected the destiny of the Cherokee people: John Ross was elected principal chief; Andrew Jackson was elected president of the United States;
The *Cherokee Phoenix,* a national newspaper, was created; Georgia enacted
laws confiscating Cherokee lands; and gold was discovered in the Nation.
The Georgia legislature declared its jurisdiction over all Cherokee lands
within the state's boundaries, ruled Cherokee laws null and void, and conducted a statewide lottery for distributing the Indians' land and homes to
whites. The temper of the time was reflected in the following lyrics of
a song popular among many Georgians:

All I want in this cre-a-tion
Is a pretty little girl
and a big plan-ta-tion
'Way up yonder in the Cherokee
Nation.[2]

One account gives a black slave credit for finding the first gold nugget
some fifty miles from the Cherokee national capital of New Echota. The
news spread rapidly and caused a gold rush into the Nation. The illegal
intrusion of white prospectors caused additional pressures on the Eastern
Cherokees to remove west and leave their ancestral home.[3]

The State of Georgia intensified its harassment of the Cherokees.
It confiscated Cherokee national property (school buildings,

council houses, printing plant), also the property of certain
chiefs who opposed removal. It sent surveyors into the Nation,
and instituted lotteries to distribute Cherokee property. Unofficial 'pony clubs' were permitted, exempt from prosecution,
to raid Cherokee plantations and drive off livestock, to kidnap
slaves in the fields, and to destroy crops.[4]

In 1829 about 1,500 Cherokees with more than 100 black slaves emigrated west.[5] One intermarried Cherokee who continually refused to
abandon his home and property was John Rogers ("Nolichucky Jack").
For more than fifty years he had lived on the Chattahoochee River where
he cultivated wheat and corn and raised hogs, cattle, and sheep. He lived
in a large two-story, hand-hewn log house and had amassed a small fortune.
At his death in 1851, he possessed fifteen slaves and a plantation in excess
of 600 acres.[6]

The problems of intruders and tribal disagreement on the question of
removal did not slow the growth of black slavery. The *Cherokee Phoenix*
frequently contained entries indicating its growing importance. Notices
of slave sales, rewards for runaways, and announcements of marshall's
sales were published regularly. An advertisement proclaimed:

MARSHALL'S SALE

Will be sold to the highest bidder on the 17th of July next at
New Echota, one Negro named Peter, levied on as the property
of Edward Hicks to satisfy a bond given by said E. Hicks to the
National Treasuror.

> June 24th 1829
> Joseph Lynch
> Marshall[7]

The *Cherokee Phoenix* also published news of the international slave
trade and abolitionist activities in the United States, including the trial
of William Lloyd Garrison. The paper carried slave stories—including
anecdotes—which indicates that there was widespread interest in the institution.[8] By the 1830s an Indian without a farm was an exception rather
than the rule. Spinning wheels and weaving paraphernalia became common-
place articles among household possessions, and thousands of cotton cards
were distributed throughout the Nation. A marked increase in black slavery

accompanied this agrarian progress.[9] A public slave auction was announced in the issue of the *Phoenix* of October 1, 1831.

NOTICE

Will be sold to the highest bidder on a credit of twelve months at the place of holding court in Amohee District, on the first day of October next, two negro boys, sixteen and seventeen years old . . . property of Julius S. Marshall deceased. . . .

J. M. Lynch
Administrator[10]

Less than two weeks later, the following reward was offered for the return of a runaway slave.

$40 REWARD

Will be paid by the subscriber to any person who will secure a mulatto woman named Eliza who on the second day of this month absconded with a white man by the name of Michael Doudy, a shoemaker by profession. . . .

Moses Downing

Six's Cherokee Nation Nov. 5, 1831[11]

Two months later the following reward notice appeared in the *Phoenix.*

$20 Reward

RUNAWAY from the subscriber about the last of October a Negro Woman by the name of Lucy about 35 years of age— tall slim-built and tolerable likely two of her upper front teeth out—speaks very broken English—having been raised in the Cherokee Nation—speaks the Cherokee language. She formerly belonged to Moses Paris a resident of the Nation and it is probable that she is now somewhere in that section of the Country. I will give the above reward of $20. for her delivery to me in Lawrenceville Gwinnett County and all reasonable expenses paid, if she is found in the limits of the nation and if found in the county of Gwinnett or any adjoining County half that sum.

7 Jan. 1832.   Thomas Hollingsworth[12]

As slavery continued to mature as an institution, it became virtually identical with that of the southern states. The practice of "hiring out" was an important aspect of black slavery in the Cherokee Nation. The following is a receipt for such services.

RECEIPT FOR THE SERVICES OF A NEGRO SLAVE

July 28, 1832—Received of Elias Boudinot forty nine dollars and twelve and a half cents in full for the hire of a negro man [named] July, for one year, commencing March 1st 1831.

George Lowrey[13]

Elias Boudinot was the brilliant editor of the *Cherokee Phoenix*. George Lowrey (*I-gili*), was a large slaveowner and one of the most respected men in the Indian country. Lowrey was born at Tahskeegoe on the Tennessee River near Tellico Blockhouse about 1770. About 1796 he married Lucy Benge, who was reportedly the half-sister of Sequoyah. Lowrey entered Cherokee politics in his youth and was a member of the delegation that visited President George Washington at Philadelphia in 1791. He served as a major in Colonel Gideon Morgan's regiment of Cherokee volunteers during the War of 1812 and rendered distinctive service in the Battle of Horseshoe Bend. He later was a member of the delegation that negotiated the treaties of 1817 and 1819.

During this period Lowrey was amassing considerable wealth. On March 29, 1824, Secretary of State John Quincy Adams made the following entry in his diary:

Ridge, Hicks and Lowry *[sic]*, now here, are principal chiefs, and Ross. They write their own state papers, and reason as logically as most white diplomats. Each of the chiefs here named possesses from fifty to a hundred thousand dollars property.[14]

Lowrey was then living in northeastern Alabama in much the same style as the white planters of the cotton-growing South. The census of 1835 credited Lowrey with owning twenty black slaves. On September 29, 1838, he left his comfortable estate in Wills Valley and, with his wife, their family slaves, and transportable possessions, joined a wagon train which he and his father-in-law jointly commanded along the infamous

"Trail of Tears." They arrived in the Cherokee Nation West in early
January 1839. Lowrey discovered two excellent springs of water approximately eight miles south of Tahlequah and decided to settle there. He
constructed shelters for his family and slaves and eventually had several
hundred acres under cultivation. In time, a "substantial house" was
erected and the plantation was named "Greenleaf." Greenleaf Plantation
has lent its name to the present Greenleaf Creek, Greenleaf Lake, and
Greenleaf State Park.[15]

Many Cherokees had taken their slaves to the West in 1832. Three
hundred and eighty Cherokee immigrants, including 108 black slaves, left
the Cherokee Agency at Calhoun, Tennessee, on April 10, 1832. They
traveled aboard nine flatboats down the Tennessee River to Waterloo
where they transferred to the steamer *Thomas Yeatman.* They proceeded
down the Tennessee, Ohio, and Mississippi rivers and then up the Arkansas.
They passed Little Rock on the 30th of the month and proceeded to the
Cherokee Agency just above Fort Smith. Some disembarked at the agency
while the remainder were transported farther upstream to the mouth of
the Illinois River. After the Indians went ashore, they learned that there
was no food for them. Since they had no money, the Cherokee agent provided some rations for the Indians—but not for their slaves.[16]

The Old Settlers in the West had no written constitution and only a
few written laws. They met in council at Tahlonteskee—their capital and
Chief John Jolly's home—near the mouth of the Illinois River, twice each
year. At these councils they elected their chiefs, councilmen, judges, and
lighthorsemen. The Cherokee Nation West was divided into four districts
and was governed in a loose manner, similar to the way the Eastern Nation
had been governed a few decades previously.

The increasing number of slaves in the West caused the Old Settlers
to enact additional control legislation at Tahlonteskee in 1833.

An Act Prohibiting Negro Slaves to own Property Resolved
by the National Committee and Council, In General Council
Convened, That after the expiration of six months from and
after this date, no slave or slaves in the Cherokee Nation, shall
have the right or privilege to own any kind of property whatever. And Therefore, all slaves in the Cherokee Nation, now
owning any kind of property, are hereby required to sell or
dispose of it previous to the expiration of said six months.
And if any slave or slaves now holding property, and failing

to comply with this law, by not selling it off by the above
named time, shall thereby forfeit their property to their owners,
and the National Light-Horse are hereby required to enforce
and carry into effect this law in their respective Districts.

Resolved further, That if a slave or slaves are caught gambling
or intoxicated, or if they should in any way abuse a free person,
he she or they, (negroes) shall for either of the above offenses,
receive sixty lashes on the bare back for each and every such
offense, to be inflicted by the Lighthorse.

Tah-lon-tees-kee, Dec. 3d, 1833

> Approved—John Jolly
> Black Coat, Chiefs
> W. Webber[17]

The above statute prohibited slaves from owning any kind of property
whatsoever, not just livestock as previously. Moreover, failure to dispose
of property previous to the stated time resulted in its confiscation by the
slave's master rather than in its sale for the benefit of the Nation. Cherokees
who were guilty of misdemeanors were usually fined or lashed. The punishment for black slaves was stripes. (The *Cherokee Phoenix* printed news of
the enactment of laws in the United States to control blacks and probably
was instrumental in influencing the opinions which led to similar laws in
the Nation.[18])

Whisky and other strong drink always posed a problem for Cherokee
authorities. Liquor was prohibited by law, and the Cherokee authorities
encouraged abstinence. Intruders, citizens, and others continually defied
the law, however. As the following letter indicates, slaves were sometimes
used as bootleggers and entered the Indian country from Arkansas.

Washington Seawell to James M. Bowman
    Headquarters South Western Frontier
    Fort Gibson *December* 27th 1834

. . . In the event you should find a slave belonging to a citizen
of Arkansas Territory in the Indian Country in the possession
of ardent spirits, you will, after destroying the Spirits, bring

to this Post such slave, with the wagon, cart or other property
in his possession. . . .

W. Seawell
Aid de Camp & Actg Ass Adjt Genl

TO, LIEUT BOWMAN U.S. Dragoons Present.[19]

Later, soon after he settled at Park Hill, Samuel Worchester, a missionary
to the Cherokees, attempted to alleviate this problem by forming a temper-
ance society. The society soon included 248 members, including "a few
blacks," who had taken the following pledge:

We hereby solemnly pledge ourselves, that we will never use,
nor buy, nor sell, nor give, nor receive, as a drink, any whiskey,
brandy, gin, rum, wine, fermented cider, strong beer, or any
kind of intoxicating liquor.[20]

Although piecemeal removal was progressing slowly by immigration,
many large slaveowners still remained in the East. Joseph Vann, the son
of James Vann, was a prosperous Cherokee whose plantation at Spring
Place, Georgia, contained about 800 acres in cultivation. He lived in a
commodious brick mansion that cost $10,000 and employed a white over-
seer to work his 110 slaves and manage his properties.[21]

An official census which was conducted in the Eastern Cherokee Nation
in December 1835 showed an increased number of black slaves. George
Waters possessed 100, John Martin owned 69, Lewis Ross had 41, and
many other Cherokees had more than 20 slaves.[22] There were 16,542
Cherokees living in Georgia, North Carolina, Alabama, and Tennessee,
and they owned a total of 1,592 slaves. The distribution by state was as
follows:[23]

State	Cherokees	Slaves
Georgia	8,946	776
North Carolina	3,644	37
Tennessee	2,528	480
Alabama	1,424	299
Total	16,542	1,592

This number did not include the slaves in the West, those who had been confiscated by Georgians, or those who had run away during the upheaval of preparation for removal. Many blacks had already been shipped west by those who purchased them cheaply and sent them at their own expense by boat to kinsmen. These entrepreneurs intended to sell the slaves to newly arrived immigrants at a handsome profit.[24]

Cherokees willed their slave property just as other southern planters in the states did. David McNair, a plantation owner and "one of the prominent and useful citizens of the Cherokee Nation," died August 15, 1836. He had owned a fine plantation with a brick home, brick smokehouse, brick slave quarters and "numerous" black slaves. To his wife Delilah, daughter of James Vann, he bequeathed "Davy and his wife Minty and their children (to wit) George, Betsy, Davy, Lewis and Maria; also another Negro woman named Phoebe, all Slaves for Life"; to his son Clement Vann McNair he left "the Negro Slaves for life named Moses, Amy and Riley"; and to his daughter Betsy he willed "a negro girl slave for life now in her possession named Haggar during the life of my said daughter Betsy with a reversion at her death, together with her increase, to her children."[25] McNair's will indicates that the Cherokees also followed the custom of a slaveowning father's giving or loaning slaves to his daughter when she married.

The harassment, indignation, and shame visited upon the Cherokees caused some to view removal to the West as the lesser of two evils. Commissioners representing the United States government attempted to persuade the National Council to accept a treaty of removal. Inducements were offered to influential Cherokees, and factions were encouraged to oppose their government. The nearest thing to a dissident party was composed of the Ridge family and their adherents. The Ridges believed that the Cherokees would eventually be forced to move; therefore, they desired to obtain the best terms possible and emigrate. After repeated attempts to negotiate with Principal Chief John Ross, United States commissioners, headed by John Schermerhorn, turned to the Ridge faction, called the Treaty Party. Subsequently, on December 29, 1835, a removal treaty was negotiated with this small minority at New Echota. The Ross faction boycotted the council and warned Ridge's followers that if they signed the Treaty of New Echota, they signed their death warrants. On March 3 a group of 466 Cherokees, including Ridge and his son John and their families and adherents, left Ross's Landing on the Tennessee River in a flotilla of eleven flatboats lashed to two steamers. They were the first party to emigrate under the "Schermerhorn treaty." Ridge was accompanied by eighteen slaves. After arriving in the West, he settled on the north side of Honey Creek and put his blacks to work clearing land. Ridge's son John sent his slaves West but kept three with him—a woman to cook, a man to drive the carriage, and a governess for the children. Upon arrival at Honey Creek he built "a good double log house" and put his slaves to clearing, fencing, and breaking land. He owned twenty-four blacks at that time.[26]

Believing that total removal was inevitable, the John Martin and George Washington Adair families left Georgia for the West in 1837. They traveled in covered wagons and took their livestock and black slaves with them. These families had black nurses for the children, maids for the kitchen and household chores, and many field hands. Adair settled on Saline Creek near the present town of Salina, and Martin made his home on Grand River near the present Locust Grove, two miles south of the Adair family.[27] About 2,000 Cherokees, mostly members of the Ridge faction, migrated under the terms of the Treaty of New Echota.

By this time there were about 8,000 people in the West and more than 1,000 farms had been established. Missionaries' correspondence indicates that it was an exceptional case to find a family of Cherokees without at least one slave to do the more arduous work.[28]

NOTES

1. *Laws of the Cherokee Nation: Adopted by the Council at Various Periods* (Tahlequah, Cherokee Nation: Cherokee Advocate Office, 1852), pp. 242-243.

2. *Chattanooga Times,* April 27, 1948.

3. Althea Bass, *Cherokee Messenger* (Norman: University of Oklahoma Press, 1936), p. 108.

4. Glen Fleischmann, *The Cherokee Removal, 1838* (New York: Franklin Watts, Inc., 1971), p. 22.

5. *Report of the Commissioner of Indian Affairs* (Washington, D.C.: Government Printing Office, 1836), p. 391.

6. Don L. Shadburn, "Cherokee Statesmen: The John Rogers Family of Chattahoochee," *Chronicles of Oklahoma* 50, no. 1 (Spring 1972), p. 16.

7. *Cherokee Phoenix,* June 24, 1829.

8. Ibid., July 15, 1829; October 14, 1829.

9. Henery Thompson Malone, *Cherokees of the Old South: A People in Transition* (Athens: University of Georgia Press, 1956), pp. 140-141.

10. *Cherokee Phoenix,* October 1, 1831.

11. Ibid., October 12, 1831.

12. Ibid., February 4, 1832.

13. A copy of the receipt is in the Cherokee Collection of Northeastern Oklahoma State University's John Vaughan Memorial Library at Tahlequah, Oklahoma. Hereafter cited as NEOSU Cherokee Collection.

14. Phil Harris, "Lucy Benge Lowrey's Remains Reburied," *Muskogee Sunday Phoenix & Times-Democrat,* December 30, 1973.

15. Ibid.

16. Grant Foreman, *Indian Removal: The Emigration of the Five Civilized Tribes of Indians* (Norman: University of Oklahoma Press, 1932), pp. 242-243.

17. *Laws of the Cherokee Nation,* 1852, p. 174.

18. *Cherokee Phoenix,* June 5, 1830.

19. Clarence Edwin Carter, comp. and ed., *The Territorial Papers of the United States,* Vol. 20, *Territory of Arkansas* (Washington, D.C.: Government Printing Office, 1954), pp. 1110-1111.

20. Bass, *Cherokee Messenger,* p. 226.

21. Foreman, *Indian Removal,* p. 12.

22. Fleischmann, *The Cherokee Removal, 1838,* p. 12.

23. Foreman, *Indian Removal,* p. 250. See also Henry Thompson Malone, *Cherokees of the Old South: A People in Transition* (Athens: University of Georgia Press, 1956), p. 118.

24. Foreman Papers, Indian Archives of the Oklahoma Historical Society, vol. 63, pp. 360, 366. Hereafter cited as Foreman Papers.

25. Carolyn Thomas Foreman, "Captain David McNair and His Descendants," *Chronicles of Oklahoma* 36, no. 1 (Autumn 1958), pp. 270, 273-274.

26. Thurman Wilkins, *Cherokee Tragedy: The Story of the Ridge Family and the Decimation of a People* (London: The Macmillan Company, 1970), pp. 152, 288, 296, 298.

27. Cherrie Adair Moore, "William Penn Adair," *Chronicles of Oklahoma* 29, no. 1 (Spring 1951), pp. 33, 34.

28. Poor Indians who had only one slave or slave family sometimes allowed them to live in their own houses. Norman Arthur Graebner, "Pioneer Indian Agriculture in Oklahoma," *Chronicles of Oklahoma,* Vol. 23, No. 3 (Autumn 1945), p. 241.

5 ———————The New Nation in the West

Despite the heroic efforts of such champions of their cause as Henry Clay, Davy Crockett, Ralph Waldo Emerson, Edward Everett, Theodore Frelinghuysen, Sam Houston, John Howard Payne, and Daniel Webster, the Cherokees were forced to emigrate en masse to the West. The Georgia legislature had authorized the survey of Cherokee lands and disposal of the choice properties by a state lottery. The estates of John Ross and other wealthy Cherokees were confiscated. Spring Place Mission, long a center of learning and culture, was included in the lottery. The individual who drew this ticket was a bartender, and he immediately converted the mission into a saloon. Although many slaveowners, especially the larger ones, had already removed to the West, "hundreds" of owners remained "just previous to removal."[1]

The Treaty of New Echota, ceding all Cherokee lands east of the Mississippi River, had been signed in December 1835. It gave the Cherokees approximately six million acres in present-day northeastern Oklahoma and allowed two years for the removal. The bulk of the Eastern Indians did not migrate until 1838 and 1839, however. The hardships suffered during that migration are well known. Principal Chief John Ross's wife, Quatie, died at Little Rock, Arkansas, during the journey. The Cherokees refer to the trek as *Nuna-da-ut-sun'y,* "The Trail Where They Cried," which is commonly known as the Trail of Tears. It is not commonly known that many black slaves also tramped that trail and that 125 to 175 of them perished during the journey.

Andrew Ross, a brother of Principal Chief John Ross, brought slaves with him from the East and settled in the valley of Sallisaw Creek.[2]

Lewis Ross, another brother, reportedly shipped 500 slaves from Georgia. He evidently purchased most of these slaves for resale in the West. Lewis Ross and his wife, Fannie Holt Ross, settled south of Park Hill, only a quarter of a mile from his brother John, where he established Prairie Lea Plantation. Later he moved near the present Spavinaw, Oklahoma, where he built an "ornate Victorian" home and established Grand Saline Plantation, which was tended by black slaves. He also worked a "big bunch" of slaves at a salt well at present Salina, Oklahoma.[3]

The Lewis Ross family lived in grand style. Their Victorian mansion had carpeted floors, Boston rocking chairs, mahogany tables, and a "superior" Chickering piano. The Cherokee plantation aristocracy continued to emulate the manners, dress, mode of living, and general lifestyle of the South.[4]

In 1841 Lewis Ross wrote to his son, who was attending Princeton, that "[my] blacks all say they will *die* for me if it becomes necessary."[5] But five years later, in 1846, we learn that

> Lewis Rossess negroes had been collecting amunition & guns and a few days since he discovered it and found several fine guns & considerable quantity of powder & lead. He could not make them confess what they intended doing.[6]

For several decades the hunter and warrior had constantly been giving way to the farmer and mechanic. The forced expatriation of the Nation to the West made that evolution complete and irrevocable.

During the general upheaval of the arrival of the Eastern Cherokees, a federal order was issued that prohibited traders at federal posts from purchasing from or selling to Indians. The Cherokees vigorously protested the order, which denied them the benefit of a convenient market for their surplus cattle, pigs, lambs, poultry, eggs, venison, bear meat, butter, melons, and fruit. Most of the Indians with such surpluses were slaveowners. They had limited means of disposing of such commodities and suspected that the United States government had purposely issued the order for that reason. Moreover, this meant that the Cherokees would have to travel much greater distances to do their own marketing.[7]

Many Old Settlers resented the Eastern Cherokees, who outnumbered them. Some thought of themselves as a separate nation and viewed the newly arrived immigrants as intruders. The Old Settlers had their own government in operation under the direction of their own chiefs. Simultaneously, some of the Eastern Cherokees expressed animosity toward the Old Settlers, who were accused of deserting their historic homeland without resistance. The Eastern Indians considered their own government the only legitimate government and John Ross the only principal chief.

"Major" Ridge had been primarily responsible for the enactment of a law in 1808 which provided the death penalty for anyone signing away Cherokee land without authorization from the people. The law had been enacted after Doublehead and other chiefs had ceded a large tract north of the Tennessee River. The executioners were Ridge and John Rogers. Ridge became a victim of this law himself. In 1835, he signed the treaty of New Echota, in violation of the law, and as a result, on Saturday morning, June 22, 1839, Ridge was assassinated, along with his son John Ridge and Elias Boudinot. Ridge had hired out one of his black slaves to John Latta, who lived across the border in Arkansas where he operated a plantation and an "industrial plant" that manufactured furniture, cabinets, wagons, plows, and other farm and household implements. The slave had become ill and Ridge was on his way to investigate the situation when he was murdered.[8]

Following the assassinations, several Treaty Party families fled to Texas for safety. A list of their names includes Bell, Starr, Candy, Adair, Harnage, Duncan, Watie, Mayfield, and Beams. They settled immediately south of Kilgore and named their community Mt. Taber. Most of these families were slaveowners and took their property with them. There are still black families in that area who are descendants of those Cherokee slaves. There are several black families with the names of Mayfield, Bell, and Starr.[9]

After considerable manuevering, debate, and bloodshed, a semblance of unity was established between the Old Settlers and the newly arrived immigrants. The united tribe then adopted a new constitution, the Tahlequah Constitution of 1839, which supplanted the New Echota Constitution of 1827. There were approximately 1,200 slaves in the Nation at that time and the new constitution contained sections pertinent to black slavery.[10]

Article III, Section 5. No person shall be eligible to a seat in the National Council but a free Cherokee male citizen who shall have attained to the age of twenty-five years.

The descendants of Cherokee men by all free women except the
African race, whose parents may have been living together as man
and wife, according to the customs and laws of this Nation,
shall be entitled to all the rights and privileges of this Nation,
as well as the posterity of Cherokee women by all free men.
No person who is of negro or mulatto parentage, either by the
father or mother's side, shall be eligible to hold any office of
profit, honor, or trust under this Government.

Article III, Section 7. In all elections by the people, the
electors shall vote viva voce.

All free male citizens, who shall have attained to the age of
eighteen years shall be equally entitled to vote at all public
elections.[11]

The first three laws enacted under the Tahlequah Constitution concerned
black slavery. The first law was entitled: "An Act for the Punishment of
Criminal Offenses." Section 3 stipulated:

Be it further enacted, That upon trial and conviction of any
person charged with the offense of having committed a rape
on any female, he shall be punished with one hundred lashes
on the bare back; and upon the conviction of any negro for the
aforesaid offense against any free female, not of negro blood, he
shall suffer death by hanging.[12]

The second measure was entitled: "An Act for the Punishment of
Thefts and Other Crimes." Section 2 read:

Be it further enacted, That if any person shall enslave, or sell, or
dispose of in any manner, any free person, for the purpose of
enslaving the same, such person so offending shall, upon conviction thereof, be punished with corporeal infliction, as provided
in the section above, and compelled to make ample remuneration
by such compensation as the court may determine.[13]

The third law was entitled, "An Act to Prevent Amalgamation with
Colored Persons."

Be it enacted by the National Council, That intermarriage
shall not be lawful between a free male or female citizen
with any slave or person of color not entitled to the rights
of citizenship under the laws of this Nation, and the same is
hereby prohibited, under the penalty of such corporeal
punishment as the courts may deem it necessary and proper
to inflict, and which shall not exceed fifty stripes for
every such offense;—but any colored male who may be convicted under this act shall receive one hundred lashes.[14]

Some Cherokees were accused of illegally taking slave property belonging to others when they immigrated. The following letters illustrate one
such instance.

To the Hon. Wm. L. Fulton,
Little Rock

Dear Sir,

I have received your letter of the 10th inst. in relation to
two negroes, claimed by Gen. Wilborn of Alabama, which I
have not been able to obtain in the way I was required to
proceed, and which will not be given up unless they are obtained
by force, and any attempt to obtain them in that way would
probably lead to serious consequences, as the friends of the
woman that claims the negroes are very numerous, and are of
the opinion that she is the proper owner of them. . . .

M Arbuckle Brvt Brig. Gen. U.S.A.
Fort Gibson, June 26, 1839[15]

Catherine Vaught of the Cherokee Nation had the slaves and fully intended to keep them. Meanwhile, as the following letter attests, the United
States Army was busy devising strategy and tactics to obtain them.

Head Quarters 2nd Dept. W Division,
Fort Gibson March 15, 1840

Sir,

The Commg. Genl. Directs that you will proceed with your Command to the house of one Leip or Lype, a white man with an

Indian wife formerly Mrs. Catherine Vaught. Should you find
on your arrival there, two negro men, one named Auddy, about
25 years of age, and the other Jack, about the same age, you
will seize them and bring them to this post, in accordance with
instructions received from the War Depart. under date of the
11th Feb. 1840, these negroes being claimed by Col. Wilborne
of Alabama as his property.

The greatest precaution must be used to prevent the object
of your visit from being known, as the slightest suspicion on
their part would cause the negroes to fly or be secreted. Therefore, I should advise you, when in the vicinity of the house,
to halt your Command out of view of it, to send your sub-
altern with four or six men to inquire after deserters in order
to lull suspicion, and should he be able to seize them, if not
let him join you and wait a favorable oportunity of doing
so. Should you suceed in taking them, I wish you to say to
Mr. and Mrs. Lype that I should be pleased to see them as
soon as possible on the subject of these negroes.

	I am, Sir, Respectfully,
To Capt. Moore	Your Obt. Servt.
1st. Dragoons	L. G. Simmons
	AD. C & A. A. Adj. Gen.[16]

The dragoons visited the Lype home on at least two occasions. The
slaves had been hired out and were not there, however. The following
letter seems to have ended the matter as far as the army was concerned.

| To the Sec of War | Fort Gibson Mar. 17, 1840 |
| Sir, | |

. . . It is the intention of Mrs. Lype, as I understand, to collect
at an early period, Such testimony as She believes will satisfy
the Govert. that she is justly entitled to the negroes . . . claimed
by Gen. Welborne, and to eight others sold by her former husband,
Vaught, to some other citizen of Alabama.

M. Arbuckle[17]

Josiah Gregg reported that "most of the labor among the wealthier classes of Cherokees, Choctaws, Chickasaws, Creeks, and Seminoles is done by negro slaves; for they have all adopted substantially the Southern system of slavery."[18] The United States government had continually encouraged the Cherokees to engage in agriculture since the administration of President George Washington. Annual gifts of hoes, plows, rakes, and other farm implements along with cotton cards, spinning wheels, and looms had been received. Cultivation of the land and herding continued to grow in importance as the principal means of livelihood. The plantation became a more important unit of production, as it had long been in the southern United States. Plantation agriculture demanded an abundant labor supply for "gang system" cultivation. Capital was borrowed from banks in neighboring states to develop plantations and cattle ranches. Range cattle were purchased in Texas. Dairy cattle were purchased in Wisconsin and transported to the Nation by water. Cotton, wheat, and other seed-grains were obtained at New Orleans. Additional black slaves were purchased in slave markets as far away as Mobile and New Orleans.[19] The numbers of slaves purchased in these and other markets are unknown. After 1838 the United States Indian commissioners failed to list the number of blacks owned by Cherokees. This was probably a conscious omission since the commissioners were Southerners and proslavery and did not desire to see abolitionism gain a foothold in the Cherokee Nation.

Communities such as Fort Gibson, Sallisaw, Salina, Vinita, and Webbers Falls became trading centers. Park Hill and Tahlequah became small cities. Park Hill was the cultural mother of the Cherokee Nation and would soon be known as the Athens of the Indian Territory. A regular steamboat trade was developed from St. Louis and New Orleans and all points in between. The principal landings in the new Nation were Fort Gibson and Webbers Falls. There were at least twenty-two landings, however, between Fort Smith and Fort Gibson, including Sallisaw, Vian, Illinois River, Cabin Creek, Green Leaf, and Bayou Menard. Black slaves were used extensively in this trade. When boats arrived at settlements along the river they blew their whistles or fired a swivel gun.

Then the negro roustabouts on deck would swing their hats
and sing lustily in praise of their boat. . . .
Come shake de ash, my bully boys
    and make de fires burn,

De engineer am coming round
  To give her another turn
  Ranjo, oh, oh, o, o!
De captain on de boiler deck,
  Ise sure I herr'd him say,
He beat the Daniel Webster
  And pass her on her way,
  Ranjo, oh, oh, oh, o,o!
De ladies in de cabin
  are troubled in der mind,
Because de took der passage
  on de Bully Brandywine
  Ranjo, oh, oh, oh, o, o![20]

Be it enacted by the National Council, That if any person or
persons shall interrupt by misbehavior any congregation of
Cherokee or white citizens, assembled at any place for divine
worship, within the Cherokee Nation, such person or persons,
so offending, shall upon conviction thereof before any of the
courts, be fined in a sum not exceeding twenty nor less than five
dollars, for every such offence, to be adjudged by the court of
the District in which such offence may be commited; and if any
negro slave shall be convicted of the above offence, he shall be
punished with thirty-nine stripes on the bare back. And all
moneys so collected shall be paid over to the National Treasury.[21]

The slave population was both larger and more concentrated after tribal
removal. Therefore, immediately after adoption of the Tahlequah Constitution, the National Council adopted a series of slave codes. The following
untitled act was signed into law early in October 1839.

Free blacks and slaves continued to pose problems, however. The Cherokees suspected the free blacks of attempting to foment unrest among their
slaves. Also, the Old Settlers had prohibited slaves to own property of any
kind since 1833. The Eastern Cherokees, however, had only prohibited
the ownership of livestock. The following act of 1840 was an attempt to
rectify both problems.

Be it enacted by the National Council, That it shall not be
lawful for any free negro or mulatto, not of Cherokee blood, to

hold or own any improvements within the limits of this Nation; neither shall it be lawful for slaves to own any property of the following description, viz: horses, cattle, hogs, or firearms. And it is hereby made the duty of the Sheriffs of the several Districts, from and after the first day of June next, (1841) to sell, at public sale, to the highest bidder, after ten days notice, all such property as may be found owned by slaves, in violation of this prohibition: after deducting eight per cent for the Sheriff's fee.

And if any slave, free negro, or mulatto, not of Cherokee blood, shall introduce into the Nation, or sell, any spiritous liquors, it shall be the duty of the Sheriff of the District, upon being notified thereof, to waste or destroy such spiritous liquors, and to inflict thirty-nine lashes on the bare back of any such person, as above named, for so offending.[22]

Black slavery continued to flourish in the unified Nation and slave buyers from the United States made trips through the Indian country to purchase and sell slaves.[23] Cherokees purchased and sold slaves among themselves, other tribes, white traders, and commercial firms as far away as New Orleans. The hiring out of slaves continued to be common practive. Missionaries—even anti-slavery missionaries—were sometimes obliged to hire slaves from their parishioners for domestic help, nursing duties, and other work.[24]

The Cherokee slave code became comprehensive and comparable in its harshness to the laws of the southern states. The motive for these laws was the same also. They were designed to preserve the slave mentality, protect against insurrection, control free blacks, prevent miscegenation, and control virtually all personal and group activities of slaves.

Principal Chief John Ross settled at Park Hill when he arrived in the West. He erected a house, which he called "Rose Cottage," about two miles from the mission station. In 1840, John Howard Payne (the composer of "Home Sweet Home") visited Ross at Park Hill for several months. Payne related that there were numerous black slaves at Rose Cottage at that time. One black cleaned Payne's boots every Saturday and earned the sobriquet "my man Saturday."[25] As Ross's economic circumstances improved, the modest house was replaced by a magnificent mansion. The furniture was reportedly valued at $10,000. The house was furnished with rosewood and mahogany, silver plate, and imported china. The mansion, situated on a hillside and surrounded by native oaks and elms, was approached by a half-mile-long driveway bordered with exotic roses. Rose Cottage could

accomodate forty guests in comfort. The ample interior included guest
rooms, family rooms, a library, and a parlor. The spacious grounds surrounding the house were enhanced by shrubbery and flowers. The orchards (the
apple orchard contained a thousand trees) and vegetable garden supplied the
family table, which usually included guests, and a retinue of house and
field servants.[26]

Rose Cottage grew to a thousand acres or more by 1844 and had its
own blacksmith shop, brick kiln, laundry, smokehouse, dairy and "negro
cabins galore." Ross married Mary Bryan Stapler of Wilmington, Delaware,
in September 1844, and he and his wife lived and entertained in opulent
style. His wealth was reported to be $500,000 at that time. He and his
beautifully gowned young wife traveled in a handsome Victorian carriage
with a black driver and footman in livery. His stables were as large as the
public stables of a city and his hitching posts provided ample space for
fifty horses. Rose Cottage was operated in the same manner as any large
southern plantation and was immensely profitable. All food, clothing, and
implements were grown or manufactured on the premises. Only the luxuries
of the great house were imported.[27] In 1852, a visitor to Ross's plantation
reported seeing about forty black slaves at work in the fields.[28]

The work performed by Cherokee slaves varied little from that done by
slaves in the southern states. Agriculture consumed the time and energy
of most slaves. Blacks cleared and improved land, split rails, built fences,
plowed ground, planted, cultivated, and harvested crops of cotton, corn,
and other commodities. They also tended livestock, milked, and provided
domestic service by cooking meals, waiting tables, cleaning, washing,
gardening, and grooming horses. Female slaves sometimes served as
"mammies" and taught their mistresses the operation of the card and
spinning wheel. Some slaves were highly skilled artisans, including wheelwrights, blacksmiths, midwives, millwrights, millers, carpenters, tanners,
cobblers, physicians, and masons. These were a small minority, however.
Domestic manufacture was frequently an important slave activity. Beginning with raw materials, blacks produced tools, cotton and woolen cloth,
knitted stockings, gloves, and scarves. Some industrial slavery existed, with
slaves operating several salt works, mills, and tanneries. Old slaves were
given the customary titles "Uncle" and "Aunt."[29]

"Hunters Home" was the Park Hill plantation of George Michael Murrell,
who married the niece of Principal Chief John Ross and the daughter of
Lewis Ross, treasurer of the Cherokee Nation. It was a spacious two-story

frame mansion built with slave labor and with furnishings imported from
France and Italy. The furniture was mahogany and "red plush," and imported curtains surrounded the beds. Hunters Home, built during 1844
and 1845, was architecturally typical antebellum southern style. The
mansion contained a parlor, library, dining room, entrance hall, kitchen,
four spacious bedrooms, and large porches at the front and rear. There
were also barns, a smokehouse, springhouse, mill, and slave quarters. It is
reported that Robert E. Lee was once a guest at Hunters Home when he was
at Fort Gibson in November 1855.[30] Murrell, who had assisted in the removal
from Tennessee, also owned a large plantation in Louisiana, and he and his
family usually lived there for a part of each year. The wealth of the Murrell
family impressed the children of the poor missionaries. Alice Robertson,
a future member of the United States House of Representatives from
Oklahoma, said that it was always a thrill to see the Murrell coach with
its black coachman and footman in livery "with a high cocked hat" arrive
at her grandfather Samuel A. Worchester's church at Park Hill.[31]

Elaborate gatherings were held frequently at Hunters Home. The Murrells'
guests sat on handsome furniture and drank from heavy silver goblets en-
graved with the letter "M." Black servants served from tables laden with
chicken in paste, beef a la mode, pickled walnuts, and Maryland biscuits.
For dessert, guests had their choice of floating islands, macaroons, or
dumplings that floated in a sea of delicious blueberry or blackberry juice.
Mrs. Murrell, a gracious hostess, was the author of a cookbook published
in 1846 in Maryland. The volume reflected both the white and Indian
cultures, with recipes for American and French dishes along with recipes
for Indian bread and other delicacies.[32]

Cherokee slaves frequently reacted to their status by running away,
exhibiting defiance, stealing, and malingering. Runaway slaves, who frequently
headed back East, were sometimes hunted with dogs. In order to identify
their property, some Cherokee masters branded their slaves. Many slaves
had no last names, others took their masters' names. Some never knew
their parents; others were sired by their masters or members of their
master's family. Black women were sometimes sold for refusing to become
pregnant. Some masters sought obedience by regularly taking one or more
of their slaves to witness hangings. Black women were usually expected
to do the same work as men. They were lashed and ran away just as the
men did. Some slaves became drivers and overseers. Mothers were sometimes sold away from their children. A few slaves purchased their freedom.

Slavery in the Nation was different in one respect—Cherokee slaves did not always enjoy the holidays and laying-by time that slaves in the United States did.[33]

The slaves' quarters usually consisted of windowless log huts with dirt floors. A stone fireplace supplied warmth and heat for cooking. Slaves usually did their own cooking from rations periodically issued by the master or overseer.[34]

George Murrell owned many slaves who toiled on his plantation under the direction of a manager and overseer. Murrell's coachman and butler once ran away. Murrell promptly inserted an advertisement in the *Cherokee Advocate* offering fifty dollars' reward for the capture and return of his property, whom he had purchased in New Orleans. Murrell described Spencer, the butler, as being "clothed in a pair of Janes pants, a brown Janes dress coat, three-forths worn, a silk hat, brim lined with Bombazin— also a black dress coat and two blankets."[35] Hunters Home is one of the few antebellum residences of the Cherokee Nation still standing in the West. The old mansion with a part of its grounds, including the sites of its slave quarters, is now a state park. John Ross, George Murrell, and other slaveowners of the Park Hill area had sufficient numbers of slaves to establish a Cherokee slave cemetery near the famous Park Hill cemetery where many of the greatest Cherokees are interred.

Joseph Vann (*Teaultle*), the son of James Vann, became the largest slaveowner in the Cherokee Nation. He had inherited the bulk of his father's estate and was considered to be the wealthiest man in the Nation. Known throughout the Indian country as "Rich Joe" Vann, he was one of the most colorful Cherokees. He stood 6'6" tall, was fond of blooded horses, racing, and strong drink. One historian has written that Rich Joe Vann, like other progressive Cherokees, was the personification of the peculiar red-white culture that characterized his people in the early nineteenth century.

It is not hard to imagine Vann in his home, seated in a comfortable chair near one of the large windows which overlooked the rolling countryside. He could watch some of his many Negro slaves toiling in the cotton and corn fields. Perhaps he read the latest Indian news and opinion in the bi-lingual pages of the *Cherokee Phoenix,* published at New Echota.[36]

Fearing confiscation of his property by the state of Georgia, he sold his plantation improvements for $28,179 in 1834. He took 100 black slaves and moved to the Tennessee area of the Cherokee Nation. One year later he owned "35 various buildings, 110 slaves, a mill, a ferry, and 300 acres in cultivation."[37] After removal, he settled a few miles downstream from Muskogee where he lived in a three-story brick mansion at Webbers Falls on the Arkansas River. He operated a plantation of five or six hundred acres and reportedly owned three to four hundred slaves. In addition to his plantation, Vann possessed other interests, including the steamboat *Lucy Walker*. He operated the sidewheeler on the Arkansas, Mississippi, Ohio, and Tennessee rivers. Louisville, Memphis, and New Orleans were regular ports of call. Slaves constituted the majority of the *Lucy Walker*'s crew. Vann was also a horse fancier and owned a famous racing animal named Lucy Walker. It has been reported that the mare's foals were sold for $5,000 each.[38]

Avery Vann, the great-grandfather of humorist Will Rogers, was a large slaveowner who emigrated from Georgia in 1832 with "his many slaves." He settled in Saline District in present Mayes County. His slaves built a pine-log house of seven rooms, each of which was 20' square. The flooring was sawed, tongued and grooved, and planed by hand. Vann had a brick kiln constructed, and his slaves burned brick to build four large brick chimneys.[39] Will Rogers's grandmother, Sallie Vann, was born in this house.[40]

They [Avery Vann family] were kind to their slaves and gave orders that they were not to be whipped or abused. John Naw, a son-in-law, disregarded these orders and tried to whip an old slave named Uncle Joe, who cut John Naw in two with a bowie-knife. Naw died and Uncle Joe was mobbed by a gang of men and beheaded and his head stuck on a pole.[41]

Upon Vann's death, his daughter, Katie Williams, inherited his property, including the slaves. She freed the slaves during the Civil War.[42] Robert Rogers, grandfather of Will Rogers, was a slaveowner who settled in Going Snake District in 1835 or 1836, approximately five miles northwest of the present town of Westville, Oklahoma.[43] He built a five-room log house, established a ranch, and prospered almost immediately in the fertile bottomland.

Clement Vann Rogers, the father of Will Rogers, was a slaveowner in Cooweescoowee District.[44] He was born in 1839, only one year before the death of his father, Robert Rogers. When Clem was five years old, his mother married William Musgrove. Clem disapproved, refused to attend the ceremony, and hurled stones at the newlyweds as they drove away on their honeymoon. Clem grew up on his father's ranch and attended a Baptist mission school and the Cherokee National Male Seminary at Tahlequah. He left home at the age of seventeen to start a new life in the Cooweescoowee country along the Verdigris River. His mother and stepfather presented him with twenty-five longhorn cows, a bull, four horses, supplies for the ranch and trading post he intended to establish, and two black slave brothers named Rabb and Huse, who had belonged to his father. Upon reaching Cooweescoowee, Clem carefully selected the tract of land for his ranch and put his two slaves to work farming, planting corn to feed the livestock. The cattle were turned out on the rich bluestem grass that stretched unbroken for miles.

Rogers built a two-room log house on his new property and quickly became financially successful. Several years later he married a tall, dark-haired girl whom he had met at Tahlequah, Mary America Schrimsher. Rogers's range was soon to include approximately 60,000 acres of excellent bluestem grassland.[45]

When the Civil War began, Clem sent his wife to his mother's home. She later went to her family in Tahlequah and finally fled with her parents and sisters to Texas. Meanwhile, Clem had enlisted in the Cherokee Mounted Rifle Regiment and served as a captain under Stand Watie.[46] The divisiveness of the conflict in the Cherokee Nation is clearly demonstrated by Rogers's two black slave brothers, Rabb and Huse, who fought on opposite sides during the conflict.[47]

George Sanders, who had owned a large plantation in Georgia, emigrated and settled near Tahlequah on a "large plantation" with a "large number" of slaves.[48] Dave Downing "was one of the largest slaveowners before the Civil War." Upon arrival in the West in 1837, he settled in the northern part of present Adair County on "a plantation just north of the town of Westville."[49] Joseph M. Lynch, a prominent Cherokee attorney, settled near the present town of Spavinaw where he owned a mill, salt works, plantation, and tannery.[50] Lynch owned a valuable black slave tanner named Boston and once remarked jocosely that he was also a tanner: "I would tan Boston's hide and then Boston would tan the cows."[51] Israel G. Vore and his wife Sallie Vann Vore were slaveowners. Sallie Vann, the daughter of Rich Joe Vann, emigrated to the West with her family and thirty slaves by boat, arriving at Webbers Falls in 1836.[52]

Martin Vann purchased more than 100 slaves at New Orleans and shipped them west by steamboat. He settled north of the present town of Muskogee near Vann's Lake and put his slaves to clearing land and splitting rails. He eventually had "several hundred acres under cultivation in corn and cotton."[53] Vann owned a black slave named Mollie Glasscut by whom he fathered a slave son, Henry Henderson, who later fought with the Pin Indians in the 82nd Infantry during the Civil War.[54] One former slave related many years afterward that the Vanns were relatively good to their slaves because they believed that the slaves "had to be fed well, clothed well and properly housed to get the best labor obtainable from them."[55] (Some authors have erroneously stated that since there were no cotton gins in the Cherokee Nation West at an early date, there was no cotton. The cotton seeds were picked out by hand, then the lint was spun into thread and woven into cloth.[56])

Dick Ratcliff operated a farm southeast of Tahlequah where his slaves raised wheat, corn, and Hungarian millet.[57] "Granny Wolfe" of Park Hill spoke no English but owned "several slaves," including a female interpreter who always accompanied her.[58] The Whitmire family were wealthy Cherokees. Johnson Whitmire owned a plantation known as the "Whitmire Plantation" on Peavine Creek. It was north of the present town of Stillwell and was worked by numerous slaves.[59] George Whitmire operated the Whitmire Plantation on Barren Fork Creek.[60] The grandparents and parents of W. W. Harnage owned "many" slaves, and the John Harnage family were big slaveowners.[61] Judge David Carter lived south of Tahlequah and "owned lots of slaves."[62] Return Jonathan Meigs and his wife Jane Ross Meigs, daughter of John Ross, were slaveowners.[63]

Ben Johnson lived on the north bank of the Arkansas River midway between Fort Smith and Fort Coffee and the Skullyville boat landing. He brought "a whole passel of slaves" to the Nation from Tennessee. He was known as a tough master and employed an overseer.[64] Mrs. J. A. Lawrence later recalled that her parents possessed approximately thirty-five "slave houses located east and west of the plantation."[65] The families of Mary Scott Gordon, Ellen Howard Miller, and Mrs. S. S. Cobb were all slaveowners.[66] John N. Riley and his wife Betsie emigrated in 1838 and settled at Park Hill. After Riley's death, his widow and children moved to the vicinity of Fort Gibson where they operated a "good farm" with "numerous" black slaves.[67] Margaret Bean married John Gott and the couple established a farm near Stillwell. Mrs. Gott's dowry had included four female slaves whom her mother had brought from Georgia.[68] Richard Wyley King of Flint District was also a slaveowner.[69] John Lynch Adair's "aunts and uncles owned over four hundred slaves."[70] It is reported that while John Lynch Adair attended the Moravian Mission, "he learned more how to endure pain than from the speller and catechism, as he was daily whipped for idleness and disposition to mischief." He "was quick, active and swift of foot, and fond of rough and tumble exercises and coon-hunting with the 'niggers' at night, of whom his uncles and aunts had hundreds." In 1849 when the gold fever in California reached the Nation, John and a cousin, William Buffington, headed west in a wagon drawn by four yoke of oxen and driven by a black slave.[71]

John R. Price of Park Hill possessed slaves, as did Joe Sheppard and John Agnew of the Peavine area.[72] A Cherokee known as Greenbriar Joe was an "extensive slaveholder."[73] David Rowe, who once served as assistant chief, was a "large slave owner" in the Saline District.[74] The Tyners, Meltons, Landrums, and Keys families were all slaveowners.[75] Caleb Starr was a man of great wealth and reportedly possessed "hundreds" of slaves when he arrived in the West.[76] James Starr and his family had emigrated westward to Fort Gibson in December 1833 with three male slaves.[77]

The Starrs were members of the Ridge Party. At the time of the murders of the Ridges and Elias Boudinot, James Starr's life was threatened also. His son Tom Starr was nineteen years of age at that time. Shortly thereafter, Tom's notorious career of violence commenced as he and a number of others assembled to witness a footrace between a white man and a black slave who belonged to another Cherokee. Tom Starr exchanged words with David Buffington and the disagreement ended in a duel in which young Starr stabbed Buffington to death. From that time forward Tom Starr was an outlaw. His father was murdered soon afterward and Starr determined to slay every man he met who harbored any enmity toward his father or had any share in his death. Starr was not a common highwayman or brigand, and he reportedly never killed for plunder, only for revenge. At least once, however, he did steal some black slaves and sell them to the first bidder he met.

Tom Starr remained a fugitive from justice until after the Civil War and the death of Principal Chief John Ross. The election of Louis Downing as principal chief brought a Ridge Party administration to power. Subsequently, the Cherokee government entered into a unique arrangement with Starr. It made a treaty with him whereby all outstanding warrants were canceled and Starr agreed to return home and live the life of a peaceful and law-abiding citizen. Starr accepted the provisions of the agreement and settled along the Canadian River near Briartown where he lived quietly until his death some twenty-five years later.[78]

NOTES

1. Zella Armstrong, *The History of Hamilton County and Chattanooga Tennessee,* vol. 1, p. 33. The majority of the captains who headed immigrant companies along the "Trail of Tears" were slaveowners.

2. Carolyn Thomas Foreman, *Park Hill* (Muskogee, Oklahoma: Star Printery, Inc., 1948), p. 131.

3. John L. Springston, "Lynch's Mill Was Spavinaw's Name in Early Day History," *Chronicles of Oklahoma* 5, no. 3 (September 1972), p. 326. Also see Phil Harris, *This Is Three Forks Country* (Muskogee, Oklahoma: Hoffman Printing Co., 1965), p. 38, and Foreman Papers, vol. 62, p. 366, found in the Indian Archives of the Oklahoma Historical Society, Oklahoma City, Oklahoma, and hereafter cited as Foreman Papers.

4. Norman Arthur Graebner, "Provincial Indian Society in Eastern Oklahoma," *Chronicles of Oklahoma* 23, no. 4 (Winter 1945-1946), p. 326.

5. Foreman, *Park Hill,* p. 23.

6. Edward Everett Dale and Gaston Litton, *Cherokee Cavaliers* (Norman: University of Oklahoma Press, 1939), p. 30.

7. Grant Foreman, *Advancing the Frontier 1830-1860* (Norman: University of Oklahoma Press, 1933), pp. 53, 54.

8. T. L. Ballenger, "The Death and Burial of Major Ridge," *Chronicles of Oklahoma* 51, no. 1 (Spring 1973), p. 102.

9. George Morrison Bell, Sr., *Genealogy of "Old & New Cherokee Indian Families"* (Bartlesville, Oklahoma: Privately printed, 1972), p. 553.

10. Norman Arthur Graebner, "Pioneer Indian Agriculture in Oklahoma," *Chronicles of Oklahoma* 23, no. 3 (Autumn 1945), p. 241.

11. *Laws of the Cherokee Nation: Adopted by the Council at Various Periods* (Tahlequah, Cherokee Nation: Cherokee Advocate Office, 1852), p. 7. Many of the signatories of the new constitution were black slaveowners.

12. Ibid., pp. 17, 18. In 1845 the penalty became one hundred lashes.

13. Ibid., p. 18.

14. Ibid., p. 19.

15. National Archives, Record Group 393, Records of the US Army Continental Commands 1821-1920, 2d Military Department, Letters Sent, November 1834-June 1841, p. 218.

16. Ibid.

17. Ibid., p. 121.

18. Josiah Gregg, *Commerce Of The Prairies,* edited by Max L. Moorehead (Norman: University of Oklahoma Press, 1954), pp. 400-401.

19. *Report of the Commissioner of Indian Affairs,* 1842, p. 255.

20. Muriel H. Wright, "Early Navigation and Commerce along the Arkansas and Red Rivers in Oklahoma," *Chronicles of Oklahoma* 8, no. 1 (March 1930), p. 74.

21. *Laws of the Cherokee Nation,* 1852, p. 37.

22. Ibid., p. 44.

23. Nave Letters of the NEOSU Cherokee Collection in the John Vaughan Library, Tahlequah, Oklahoma.

24. Grant Foreman, "Notes of a Missionary among the Cherokees," *Chronicles of Oklahoma* 16, no. 2 (June 1938), pp. 177-178.

25. Foreman, *Park Hill,* p. 18.

26. Rachel Carolyn Eaton, *John Ross and the Cherokee Indians* (Menasha, Wisconsin: George Banta Publishing Company, 1914), p. 164.

27. Ibid., p. 165. Also see Foreman, *Park Hill,* p. 90.

28. Foreman, *Park Hill,* p. 90.

29. Foreman Papers, vol. 4, pp. 403-413; vol. 54, pp. 27-36; vol. 24, p. 497.

30. Harris, *Three Forks Country,* p. 37.

31. Foreman, *Park Hill,* pp. 104-105.

32. Grace Steel Woodward, *The Cherokees* (Norman: University of Oklahoma Press, 1963), p. 248.

33. Transcribed interviews with Rochelle Allred Ward, Victoria Taylor Thompson, Charlotte Johnson White, and Sarah Wilson, all former slaves, are in the "Ex-Slaves File" of the Oklahoma Historical Society.

34. Foreman Papers, vol. 112, pp. 179-189.

35. Foreman, *Park Hill,* pp. 51-53.

36. Henry Thompson Malone, *Cherokees of the Old South: A People in Transition* (Athens: University of Georgia Press, 1956), p. 1.

37. University of Oklahoma, Western History Collection, Claims Book No. 25, p. 60. Leola Selman Beeson, "Homes of Distinguished Cherokee Indians," *Chronicles of Oklahoma* 11, no. 3 (September 1933), pp. 927-941.

38. Carolyn Thomas Foreman, "Early History of Webbers Falls," *Chronicles of Oklahoma* 29, no. 4 (Winter 1951-1952), p. 460n.

39. Foreman Papers, vol. 104, pp. 236, 443.

40. Ibid., p. 238.

41. Ibid., vol. 2, p. 65.

42. Ibid., p. 66.

43. Phil Harris, "The Roundup," *Muskogee Sunday Phoenix & Times-Democrat,* August 5, 1973.

44. Foreman Papers, vol. 75, p. 34.

45. Richard M. Ketchum, *Will Rogers: His Life and Times* (New York, American Heritage Publishing Company, Inc., 1973), p. 21.

46. Ibid., p. 23.

47. Ibid., p. 22. Rogers County in northeastern Oklahoma is named in honor of Clement Vann Rogers.

48. Foreman Papers, vol. 75, pp. 249-250.

49. Ibid., vol. 56, p. 523.

50. Ibid., vol. 54, p. 30.

51. *Tulsa Daily World,* November 11, 1925.

52. Foreman Papers, vol. 43, p. 400.

53. Ibid., vol. 28, p. 395.

54. Ibid.

55. Ibid., vol. 43, p. 408.

56. Ibid., p. 407.

57. Ibid., vol. 106, p. 442.

58. Ibid., vol. 108, p. 213.

59. Ibid., vol. 4, p. 503.

60. Ibid., vol. 103, p. 462.

61. Ibid., vol. 4, p. 338.

62. Foreman, *Park Hill,* p. 31.

63. Ibid., p. 74.

64. Sarah Wilson Interview, Ex-Slaves File, Oklahoma Historical Society, Oklahoma City, Oklahoma.

65. Foreman Papers, vol. 74, p. 539.

66. Ibid., vol. 4, p. 102; vol. 80, p. 17; vol. 3, p. 100.

67. Ibid., vol. 4, p. 122.

68. Ibid., vol. 5, p. 54.

69. Ibid., vol. 6, p. 101.

70. Ibid., vol. 61, p. 386.

71. H. F. O'Beirne and E. S. O'Beirne, *The Indian Territory: Its Chiefs, Legislators and Leading Men* (Saint Louis: C. B. Woodward Company, 1892), p. 465.

72. Foreman Papers, vol. 8, p. 403; vol. 9, p. 254; vol. 53, p. 104.

73. Ibid., vol. 81, p. 422.

74. Ibid., p. 443.

75. Ibid., vol. 109, p. 180; vol. 95, p. 368; vol. 98, p. 219.

76. Bell, Sr., *Genealogy of "Old & New Cherokee Indian Families,"* p. 561.

77. Charles E. Farris to author, February 15, 1973.

78. O'Beirne and O'Beirne, *The Indian Territory,* pp. 93-96.

6   The Great Runaway and Stricter Controls

The National Council found it necessary to enact another series of control laws in 1841. The first again authorized slave patrols and charged them with the responsibility of arresting slaves absent from their homes without passes and of administering punishment to those found carrying weapons. The act read:

> *Be it enacted by the National Council,* That from and after the passage of this act, it shall be lawful to organize patrol companies in any neighborhood, where the people of such neighborhood shall deem it necessary; and such company, when organized, shall take up and bring to punishment any negro or negroes, that may be strolling about, not on their owner's or owners' premises, without a pass from their owner or owners.
>
> *Be it further enacted,* That any negro not entitled to Cherokee privileges, that may be found or seen carrying weapons of any kind, such as guns, pistols, Bowie-knives, butcher-knives or dirks, such patrol company may take, and inflict as many stripes as they think proper, not exceeding thirty-nine lashes.[1]

The above law was soon supplemented by the following:

> *Be It Further Enacted:* That all masters or owners of slaves, who may suffer or allow their negro or negroes to carry or own firearms of any description, Bowie or butcher knives, dirks

or any unlawful instrument shall be subject to be fined in a
sum not less than twenty-five dollars.

Be It Further Enacted: That any negro whether free or slave,
that may be found or seen carrying weapons of any kind in
violation of the section of this act, such patrol company or
companies may take up and inflict as many stripes on the
bare back as they think proper.[2]

The above supplemental act placed a penalty on the master as well as
the slave for weapons infractions. Also, free blacks were placed in the
same prohibitive category as slaves, and the maximum limit of lashes
was omitted.

The Cherokees became America's first literate Indian tribe. In 1821,
Sequoyah, the American Cadmus, presented his people with an eighty-six
letter syllabary or phonetic alphabet which facilitated literacy and provided
an impetus for education among the population. During the early decades
of black slavery, some Cherokee masters sometimes permitted slave children
to attend the mission schools if they lived nearby. As late as 1832, Miss
Sophia Sawyer, a missionary teacher, was ordered to cease teaching two
slave children. Georgia authorities had appeared at her school in the
Cherokee Nation in the East and informed her that she was violating the
law and was subject to a $1,000 to $5,000 fine. "Miss Sophia's pupils
included the Ridge and Boudinot children and two slaves named Sam
and Peter. Peter had been attending class regularly. Sam, who was eight
years old, had been attending only when he could be spared from his
kitchen duties."[3]

The National Council enacted legislation in 1841 that created a public
school system. The Cherokee Nation was probably the first nation in the
world to provide free compulsory tax-supported education for all of its
citizens. It was not considered desirable for slaves to become literate, however. In the same year that the public school system was created, the following act was also passed.

Be it enacted by the National Council, That from and after
the passage of this act, it shall not be lawful for any person or
persons whatever, to teach any free negro or negroes not of
Cherokee blood, or any slave belonging to any citizen or citizens
of the Nation, to read or write.

Be it further enacted, That any person or persons violating this
act, and sufficient proof being made thereof, before any of the
Courts, in this Nation, such person or persons, upon conviction,
shall pay a fine for every such offense in a sum not less than
one, nor over five hundred dollars, at the discretion of the
Court, the same to be applied to National purposes.[4]

In 1842 there was a major black slave uprising in the Cherokee Nation.[5]
Some two hundred or more slaves belonging to Joseph Vann, Lewis Ross,
and other Cherokees in the Canadian District (that section of the Nation
lying between the Canadian and Arkansas Rivers) were joined in the revolt
by slaves from the Creek Nation. Webbers Falls was the center of the
plot, but slaves from a wide area along the lower valleys of the Grand and
Verdigris rivers appear to have been involved. One of Benjamin Franklin
Landrum's slaves reportedly composed and sang a song entitled "I'll Tell
You, Marsa Ben, Yo Niggers Gwine to Leave Yo," just previous to the
escape.[6] The uprising apparently began about 4:00 A.M. when blacks
locked their overseers in their cabins while they slept. The slaves then took
horses, guns and other weapons, food, and supplies, and fled. They were reportedly headed west for Mexican territory where they thought there was
a settlement of free blacks along the Rio Grande. The slaves had supposedly
heard that somewhere in the Rio Grande Valley there was a free town, a
place of refuge from which runaway slaves could not be reclaimed.[7]

Fifty-five years later a Fort Smith, Arkansas, newspaper described the
slave rebellion as follows:

The people of Webber's Falls, Cherokee Nation, awoke one
Spring morning in the year of 1842 to find themselves abandoned
by their slaves. Not a negro could be found on any of the
farms in the bottom or in the surrounding neighborhood. At
that time there were several hundred of them there or there-
abouts. Joe Vann alone had brought out from Tennessee, two
years before, more than two hundred of them and settled
on the rich alluvial lands of that section of the nation. The
owners were for a time in a state of consternation. Men rode
about the adjacent country to ascertain what had become of
the runaways. In a short time it became apparent that they had
abandoned their owners and when the trail was found the
conclusion arrived at was that they were seeking to escape

from bondage by making a desperate effort to reach New Mexico.

How these ignorant people came to learn of such a country was never known. The presumption was that some renegade Mexican had imparted the information that far away over the setting sun was a country where slavery did not exist and was not tolerated by law.

The plot of the fugitives seemed to have been closely kept, as no one had heard or entertained the least suspicion of its existence.

When it was definitely known the courts [course] the runaways were pursuing, Jown [John] Ross, then Principal Chief, was informed of the fact and national assistance asked for. Chief Ross acted at once by comissioning and authorizing Capt. John Drew to raise a sufficient force to pursue, overtake and bring back the fugitive negroes, but as it required several days to gather his force and secure transportation for necessary supplies, the Captain found himself a long way behind the runaways, who were making all the speed they could to reach their haven of refuge and freedom. In this they were not destined to succeed.

In [it] appeared that in their ignorance of the direct and most practicable route to New Mexico from the point of their departure, they had directed their flight too much to the north, and when overtaken were found wandering on the Salt Plains on the south side of the Arkansas River, in a state of bewilderment, and starving. Men, women, and children were scarcely able to drag themselves along and were overjoyed on the approach of their pursuers, whom they regarded rather as friends come to rescue them from death from starvation than as task masters certain to drag them back to bondage. Capt. Drew gave them liberally from his supplies, and allowing them a day or so for rest and recuperation, brought them back safely to the Falls.[8]

Ninety years after the slave uprising, a writer for the *Daily Oklahoman* theorized about its origin, stating:

Cause of the uprising, unquestionably, was secret agitation on
the part of Congregational-Presbyterian and other missionaries
sent from Boston to look after the spiritual welfare of the
Cherokees. Prior to the uprising Cherokees repeatedly com-
plained that the missionaries from Boston and other abolition
centers were devoting far more effort to inculcate among the
slaves the doctrine of freedom than to that of salvation.[9]

Principal Chief John Ross and the National Council did take immediate
action when apprised of the slave insurrection. The following act was passed
on November 17, 1842:

Whereas, the National Council have this day been informed,
by good authority, that certain Negroes, belonging to Joseph
Vann of Canadian District, and other citizens of the Nation,
have plundered their owners, bid defiance to the laws of the
country, and absconded: thereby making their way to the
Creek Nation.

Be it therefore resolved by the National Council, That Captain
John Drew be, and he is, hereby appointed to command a company, which shall consist of *One Hundred* effective men, to pursue, arrest, and deliver over said negroes, to the commanding
officer at Fort [Gibson] for safe keeping.

Be it further resolved, That if any or all of the said Negroes
so pursued, shall resist the company, and one or all of them
be killed, neither the Nation, the said company, nor any member thereof, shall be accountable for such act.

Be it further resolved, That the commandant and privates
of said company, shall receive from the National Treasury
such compensation as may be allowed by the National Council.

Be it further resolved, That the Principal Chief do communicate
to the United States' Agent for the Cherokee Nation, and through
him to the commanding officer at Fort Gibson. Also to communicate the same to the Chiefs of the Creek and Choctaw
Nations.

Be it further resolved, That the Captain of said company be,
and he is hereby authorized to purchase ammunition and

supplies for the expedition, and to render his accounts to the
National Council for payment, which shall be made out of the
National Treasury:—Provided that the expedition be not un-
necessarily protracted, and no needless expenses thereby
incurred.[10]

On the following day the National Council appropriated the money for
the expedition. The act read:

Be it enacted by the National Council, That the sum of Five
Hundred dollars be, and is, hereby appropriated, for the purpose
of defraying the expenses of Captain John Drew and Company,
in pursuing certain runaway negroes specified in the act of
Council of the 17th instant: and the Principal Chief is hereby
authorized to draw a warrant for the same.[11]

Cherokees frequently offered slaves as collateral in business transactions.
The slave labor performed by the blacks was considered just interest. The
slaves worked for the lender until the principal was repaid, then they were
returned to their master.[12] Slaves were also used as portable capital.[13]
John Drew once accepted a black male slave about sixteen years old
named Jack in payment for legal services rendered in 1847, and during
the following year he accepted slaves as collateral on a mortgage.[14] This
policy sometimes separated slave families. John Rollin Ridge wrote Stand
Watie: "I need money to go to California . . . . I might sell the Negroes
as I need money or I might hire them out as it seems feasible to me."[15]
Net Thompson, the son of a Cherokee slave, described the practice:

When some of the slaveowners were without money and needed
supplies, two or three of them would take a load of negroes
to Fort Smith and sell them to buy the supplies they needed.
Some of the slave owners took the negroes to Paris, Texas.[16]

The exchange of blacks for real estate improvements was common.
Houston Ratcliff recalled that when his father arrived in Indian Territory
from Tennessee, "my father traded old Jack Cockson, a negro boy, for
the place on which I was born and reared."[17]
It has been claimed that Cherokee treatment of slaves was so lenient
that it rendered them undesirable in neighboring slave states because of

resulting discipline problems.[18] Nevertheless, slave buyers from neighboring slave regions made regular trips through the Nation to purchase and sell slaves. Moreover, slave stealing also posed a serious problem. Stolen slaves were usually taken to a neighboring slave state. It is more likely that slaves who did not speak English were considered undesirable, and after 1830 the number of nonbilingual black slaves owned by Cherokees increased. The following letter, addressed to John Drew, is just one example of numerous inquiries concerning the possible purchase of black slaves in the Cherokee Nation.

Memphis Teness 6th July 1859

Mr John Drew

Dear Friend in haste i Drop you a Few Lines to [k]now what negroes is wirth in your nation. Say good men and 15 to 18 year old girles and if aney can Bee bought in your cuntry as i want to by From *100* to *200* Likely young negroes in wich i will pay the hig[h]est cash pryces pleas make inqury for me and oblige yours this is from your old Friend in haste and Friend and Obedient Servt

John Staples

N.. B.. Pleas to right with out Delay give my best respects to all my Old Friend i have a negro mart in Memphis

Yours

J Staples[19]

John Drew, a lawyer and captain of the Cherokee Light Horse, was a slaveowner who frequently bought and sold blacks. He accepted slaves in payment for his legal services and as collateral for mortgages. When he sold the Drew Salt Works on Duty Creek, the mortgage stipulated:

One Black Boy named John, about twenty years old, one Black girl named Iam, about twenty four years old, one Mulatto Boy about Eight Years Old, named John, and two girls one four, and the other three years old, one named Cynthia and the other Georgiana, . . . all of which described property is to be and remain the property of John Drew, until the above amount of Two thousand dollars, shall be finally paid.[20]

After the runaway slaves had been returned to the Cherokee Nation, the National Council appropriated compensation for Captain John Drew and his company of Light Horse in the following act:

> *Be it resolved by the National Council,* That Captain John Drew
> be allowed four dollars per day—and his company each two dollars
> per day, for their services in pursuing, capturing and guarding,
> certain runaway negroes, who absconded from their owners in
> Canadian District.[21]

In an attempt to avoid future runaways and insurrections, the Cherokees placed further restrictions on free blacks, who were constantly viewed suspiciously as fomentors of unrest and discontent among the slaves. On December 2 the National Council passed the following legislation, which ordered sheriffs to oust all free Negroes from the Nation:

> Sec. 1. Be it enacted by the National Council That it be made
> the duty of the sheriffs of the several districts of this nation
> to notify all free Negroes who may be in this nation, excepting
> such as have been freed by our citizens, that they must leave the
> limits of this nation by the first day of January, 1843, or as soon
> thereafter as may be practical.
>
> Sec. 2. Be it further enacted, That should any free Negroes, as
> aforesaid, refuse to obey the order of the sheriffs, it shall be
> the duty of such sheriffs to report such Negro or Negroes to
> the United States agent for the Cherokees, for immediate expul-
> sion from this nation.
>
> Sec. 3. Be it further enacted, That should any citizen or citizens
> of this Nation, free any Negro or Negroes, the said citizen shall
> be held responsible for the conduct of the Negro or Negroes
> so freed; and in case the citizen or citizens so freeing any Negro
> or Negroes, shall die or remove from the limits of the Nation,
> it shall be required of such Negro or Negroes, that he, she or
> they give satisfactory security to any one of the circuit judges,
> for their conduct, or herein failing, he, she or they shall be
> subject to removal as above specified.
>
> Sec. 4. Be it further enacted, That should any free Negro or
> Negroes be found guilty of aiding, abetting or decoying any

slave or slaves, to leave his or their owner or employer, such
free Negro or Negroes, shall receive for each and every offense,
100 lashes on the bare back and be immediately removed from
the Nation.[22]

Section 3 of the above act was the only restriction placed upon emancipation. Although some free blacks were black slaveowners in all American
slave states throughout the entire period of slavery, there is no evidence
that free blacks of the Cherokee Nation ever possessed slaves.

Since many drastic slave codes and laws that affected free blacks adversely
had been enacted, some Cherokees apparently thought that there was no
penalty for killing a slave. This attitude became so prevalent that it brought
the following legislation for the protection of slaves:

BE IT ENACTED BY THE NATIONAL COUNCIL: That if
any person shall wilfully or maliciously, with malice aforethought
kill any negro or mulatto slave, on due and legal conviction thereof
such person shall be deemed guilty of murder, as if such person
so killed had been a free man and shall suffer death by hanging.
If the slave so killed shall be the property of another, and not
of the offender, his estate on conviction thereof shall be liable
to the payment of such slave so killed.

PROVIDED, This act shall not be extended to any person killing
any slave in the act of resistance to his lawful owner or master;
or any slave dying under moderate correction.[23]

Any humane intention of this legislation was almost totally negated by
the concluding sentence of the act.

In 1844 Rich Joe Vann loaded his and Lewis Ross's cotton crops aboard
the *Lucy Walker* and headed for market. The sidewheeler was under the
command of Captain Halderman of Louisville, Kentucky. Vann's black
slaves served as crew members. They traveled down the Arkansas, up the
Mississippi, and into the Ohio River. When the boat reached Louisville,
Halderman resigned and Vann was forced to take command of his vessel.
As the steamer neared New Albany, Indiana, it exploded. Joseph Vann
and several of his slaves were killed.[24]

One account of the sinking is that:

The *Lucy Walker* had taken on Passengers along the route [on November 1, 1844]. Passengers were drinking and slave fiddlers were playing, everyone enjoying Vann's liquor and hospitality. Another steamer came alongside, a megaphone conversation resulted in a challenge to race. The *Lucy Walker* took the lead aided by frantic overstoking by the slave crew. Vann did not desire to simply win, he wanted to shame the rival boat. He went below and ordered his black "fireboys" to "throw on some side meat for a quick fire." The black engineer protested "Lordy, Master Joe, dat old biler got all she gwinter stand up to now!" "Iffen dat grease hit her she gwinter blow us all to hell!" Whereupon Vann brandished his "hog leg" pistol and threatened his engineer. The side of meat went into the boiler and the slave engineer went over the side. Then the boilers exploded and the *Lucy Walker* "sank like a stone in the center of the river." The engineer was the sole survivor. Only one body was discovered, that of Preston Mackey—who was Vann's son-in-law.[25]

The black engineer returned to the Nation and later lived at Fort Gibson.[26]

In the autumn of 1844 George W. Gunter erected the first cotton gin in the Cherokee Nation West. Located about fifteen miles above Fort Smith on the Arkansas River, it had a capacity of 4,000 to 5,000 pounds of cotton daily.[27] No longer would the Cherokees have to transport cotton out of the Nation to be ginned or have their slaves separate lint from seeds by hand.

James S. Vann (son of Joseph Vann) of Webbers Falls later advertised in the *Cherokee Advocate* that he would sell thirty or forty blacks to settle his father's estate.[28] In 1846 "Rich Joe" Vann's widow married a white man named Mitchell who had come west with them and had served as overseer of the Vann plantation. They built "a substantial house" and established a plantation, christened "Spring Place," ten miles east of Muskogee.

The Negro Cabins were a short distance from the home. They consisted of log cabins with a space for a yard and small garden. The little yards were always filled with flowers. All of the common varieties but very colorful. The old negro women always raised a few herbs for medicinal use. A fine orchard was planted from choice fruit trees and seeds brought from Kentucky.[29]

The Cherokees had adopted slavery and many of their other institutions from the South. Many were bound to the South by ties of blood, marriage, and economics. These influences tended to strengthen and solidify their sympathy for the South and the cause of black slavery. Moreover, the Indian agents and superintendents were Southerners and proslavery. Most were slaveowners themselves.

Pierce Mason Butler, for instance, the Cherokee Indian Agent in 1845, was also a planter and slaveowner, as the following letter and bill of lading from the A. T. Burnley Company of New Orleans indicate.

Gov. P. M. Butler

Fort Gibson

Dear Sir

Annexed we hand you bill of lading for 7 slaves received on yesterday from your Red River Plantation—We tried very hard to get the Captain of the *Virginian* to take the Negroes for a less price, but could not prevail upon him to do so fearing there might not be another boat shortly, we deemed it best for your interest to send them now—

We are most truely yr friends

A. T. Burnley Co.
by F. B. Standback[30]

A. T. Burnely & Co.

Commissioner & Forwarding Merchants, New Orleans. Addressed to Gov. P. M. Butler, Cherokee Agent Fort Gibson Arkansas

Shipped in good order and well condition by A. T. Burnley & Co. on Board the good Steamer called the *Virginia* . . . now lying in the Port of New Orleans and bound for Fort Gibson, Van Buren or Little Rock

Seven Slaves

Melinda & three children	4
Betsey	1
Sithey & child	2
	7

Not accountable for life health or Running away. . . .
Freight for the said slaves $50 if delivered at Fort Gibson,
$40 if delivered at Van Buren, $30 if delivered at Little
Rock

Dated at New Orleans the 24th day of June 1845

Jas. W. Martin
New Orleans 24 June 1845[31]

Such agents firmly believed that slavery was a divine institution and an economic blessing to both master and slave. They contributed to the myth of kind and lenient treatment in their reports. These authorities were intolerant of abolitionist sentiments and forbade such teachings among the Indians. Missionaries and school teachers who were especially zealous in dissemination of antislavery doctrines often found themselves threatened with banishment from the Nation.[32]

NOTES

1. *Laws of the Cherokee Nation: Adopted by the Council at Various Periods* (Tahlequah, Cherokee Nation: Cherokee Advocate Office, 1852), pp. 53-54.
2. J. B. Davis, "Slavery in the Cherokee Nation," *Chronicles of Oklahoma* 11, no. 4 (December 1933), p. 1066.
3. Carolyn Thomas Foreman, "Miss Sophia Sawyer and Her School," *Chronicles of Oklahoma* 32, no. 4 (Winter 1954-1955), pp. 397-398.
4. *Laws of the Cherokee Nation,* 1852, pp. 55, 56.
5. Some authors have incorrectly used other dates for the Cherokee slave uprising, while still others have confused it with a later and unrelated revolt in the Choctaw Nation.
6. George Morrison Bell, Sr., *Genealogy of "Old & New Cherokee Indian Families"* (Bartlesville, Oklahoma: Privately printed, 1972), p. 524.
7. Alvin Rucker, "The Story of Slave Uprising in Oklahoma," *Daily Oklahoman* (Oklahoma City), October 30, 1932.
8. Carolyn Thomas Foreman, "Early History of Webbers Falls," *Chronicles of Oklahoma* 29, no. 4 (Winter 1951-1952), pp. 458-459.
9. Rucker, "Slave Uprising."
10. *Laws of the Cherokee Nation,* 1852, pp. 62, 63.
11. Ibid., p. 63.
12. Foreman Papers, vol. 112, p. 180.

13. Edward Everett Dale, "Letters of John Rollin Ridge," *Chronicles of Oklahoma* 4, no. 4 (December 1926), pp. 314-315.

14. Foreman, "Early History of Webbers Falls," p. 467.

15. Edward Everett Dale, "Letters of John Rollin Ridge," *Chronicles of Oklahoma* 4, no. 4 (December 1926), pp. 314-315.

16. Foreman Papers, vol. 112, p. 180.

17. Ibid., vol. 8, p. 327.

18. Wiley Britton, *Civil War on the Border* (New York: G. P. Putnam's Sons, 1891-1904), pp. 24, 25. Similar statements are found in numerous works treating the Cherokees.

19. John Drew Papers, Gilcrease Institute of American History and Art, Tulsa, Oklahoma.

20. Foreman, "Early History of Webbers Falls," p. 465.

21. *Laws of the Cherokee Nation,* 1852, p. 74.

22. Ibid., pp. 71, 72.

23. Davis, "Slavery in the Cherokee Nation," p. 1067.

24. Foreman, "Early History of Webbers Falls," p. 460.

25. "The Cherokee Vann Families," a typed manuscript in the Ex-Slaves File, Oklahoma State Historical Society.

26. "Reminiscences of Mr. R. P. Vann, East of Webbers Falls, Oklahoma," *Chronicles of Oklahoma* 11, no. 2 (June 1933), p. 839.

27. Grant Foreman, *The Five Civilized Tribes* (Norman: University of Oklahoma Press, 1934), p. 378.

28. *Cherokee Advocate,* May 15, 1845.

29. Foreman Papers, vol. 8, pp. 515-516.

30. Carolyn Thomas Foreman, "Pierce Mason Butler," *Chronicles of Oklahoma* 30, no. 1 (Spring 1952), p. 22.

31. Ibid.

32. Rachel Carolyn Eaton, *John Ross and the Cherokee Indians* (Menasha, Wisconsin: George Banta Publishing Company, 1914), pp. 174-175.

Memphis Tenys 6 July 1859

Mr John Drew
                            Dear Friend in
haste i Drop you a few Lines to now
what Negroes is wirth in your Nation
say good men and 15 to 18 year old
Girles and if aney can Bee bought in
your Cuntrey as i want to by from
100 to 200 likley young negroes in wich
i will pay the higest Cash pryces pleas
maked in Querey for me and oblige you
This is from your old Friend
            in haste and friend
    and obedient Servt
                            John Staples

N..B.. pleas to right with out Delay
Give my best respects to all my old
friend i have a Negro Mart in Memphis
            your
                            J Staples

Letter from J. Staples to John Drew dated July 6, 1859, in the John Drew
Papers of Gilcrease Institute of American History and Art, Tulsa, Oklahoma.

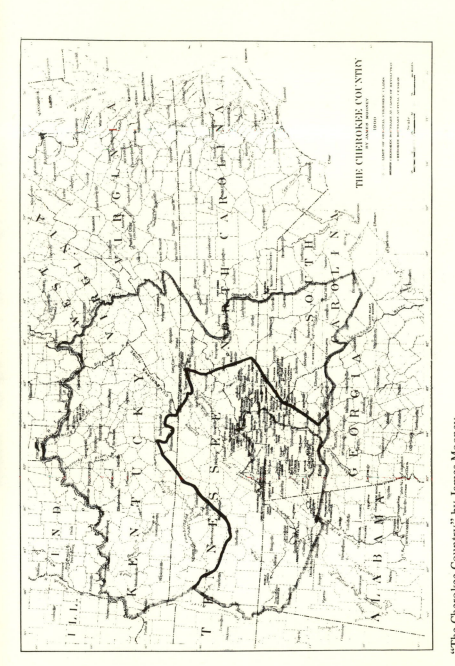

"The Cherokee Country" by James Mooney
Courtesy of Smithsonian Institution National Anthropological Archives, Bureau of American Ethnology Collection.

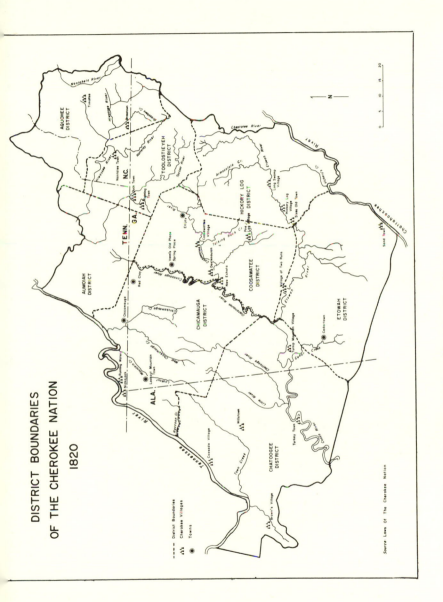

DISTRICT BOUNDARIES
OF THE CHEROKEE NATION
1820

Courtesy of Professor Douglas C. Wilms, East Carolina University.

William Penn Adair
Courtesy of NEOSU "Cherokee Collection"

Cherokee delegation in London in 1730 from an engraving in the British Museum by Isaac Basire
Courtesy of Smithsonian Institution National Anthropological Archives

John Ridge
Courtesy of the Western History Collections, University of Oklahoma Library.

John Ross
Courtesy of NEOSU "Cherokee Collection"

"Hunters Home" Plantation
Courtesy of NEOSU "Cherokee Collection"

A Cherokee slave cabin at Fort Gibson, photographed by A. L. Aylesworth, Secretary to the Dawes Commission. *Courtesy of Oklahoma Historical Society*

Major Ridge
Courtesy of NEOSU "Cherokee Collection"

Charlotte Johnson
A Cherokee Freedwoman at her home east of Tahlequah, Oklahoma, in the early 1930s.
Courtesy University of Oklahoma Archives

7   Missionaries and Abolitionism

Missionaries from the North—and most of them were from the North—sometimes viewed slavery with disapproval and occasionally gave indiscreet public expression to their opinions. These actions were usually resented and caused reprimands. The slavery issue slowly began to hamper seriously missionary work in the Nation. Ministers sometimes found the church doors locked and themselves considered *personae non gratae.*[1]

The Cherokees were already black slaveowners when the first missionaries appeared in their nation. The early missionaries had accepted slavery without serious reservations and appear to have contributed to the general belief that Indians treated their black slaves in a much more humane manner than their white counterparts in the southern United States. They periodically employed slaves, and some became slaveowners.

Missionaries were always in need of manual labor to maintain their missions. They sought help for the cooking, laundry, cleaning, nursing, and other household duties. Some did not hesitate to hire slaves to perform these tasks. They rationalized that the blacks were already slaves, present in the community, and available. Moreover, the slaves would be well-treated and not overworked while in their employment. Slaves were frequently hired to serve as interpreters, carpenters, handymen, gardeners, and in other capacities. It seemed only a small step from hiring slaves to purchasing them. A few missionaries thought it would be a charitable and benevolent act to purchase a slave—especially if the slave desired to be purchased. Furthermore, the purchase was sometimes justified with the explanation that the slave would be allowed to work out his purchase price and become free.

As slavery evolved into a moral and political issue that polarized much of the United States, it became a serious issue among the supporters of missions in the Cherokee Nation. Governing boards were usually opposed to missionaries' owning or employing slaves. Some were also opposed to the admission of Cherokee slaveowners into their churches. Since missionaries knew that to exclude slaveowners from the church and speak out against slavery would bring on expulsion from the Nation, they frequently extolled the benevolence of Cherokee masters in their reports to superiors and governing boards. They contended that slaves were treated more kindly and performed less labor than was required of domestic and industrial workers in the East. The Reverend Samuel A. Worcester was opposed to slavery, yet he had both masters and slaves in his congregation.[2] Even before his Park Hill Mission was constructed, the church had three black members. In 1836, when pressed for information to justify this situation, he wrote the board:

> My views on the subject are in some measure changed from what they once were. When I visited the Choctaw nation in company with Mr. Evarts, I agreed with him and with Mr. Kingsbury, in opposition to the views of some other Choctaw missionaries, in believing that slaves might with propriety be hired at the mission stations *with their own consent.* I could never, for a moment, so far as I remember my own feelings, have thought of employing them *without* their own consent, cheerfully given. For some time I employed at New Echota on such terms. I have since been convinced that even this will not bear scrutiny: 1st because, so far as example is concerned, the fact of the employment of slaves by missionaries will be known farther than the fact of their asking the consent of the slaves. 2nd, because hiring of slaves helps the slave market as much as buying them—slave dealers, it is said, find it much more profitable to buy slaves for the purpose of letting them out for wages, than for that of keeping them in their own employment. 3d. Because I found by a little acquaintance in Tennessee, that many justify themselves in purchasing slaves, on the ground that those who will not buy are compelled to hire, and that, for several reasons of justice and humanity, it is better to buy than to hire. This argument can be taken from only by dispensing with the services of slaves altogether. —But

my impression is that your missionaries do not all make the consent of a slave an essential prerequisite to employing him.

Aside from these considerations, is not the present state of feeling among the friends of missions such, that a general knowledge of the fact that missionaries employ slaves, in New England, would cause an excitement unpropitious to the cause? And if so, is it right to continue a practice which it is necessary to conceal from that Christian community from whom the resources of the Board are derived?[3]

The resolution of the slavery issue in the Reverend Worcester's conscience did not settle the problem for others. Individuals and organizations continued to press the American Board for a stronger position on the matter. Memorials against slavery and against employment of missionaries who admitted slaveowners into their congregations were forthcoming at each annual meeting. In 1844, in reply to a series of specific questions from the board, the Reverend Worcester wrote: "None of the Cherokee Missionaries, I think, at present, hire slaves from their masters. But it is most true that some slaveholders are members of our church."[4] The Reverend Worcester then cited "apostolic example" and said that he did not know how to exclude slaveowners or even to refuse their future admission. He related that the apostles had welcomed slaveholders without requiring them to emancipate their slaves.[5]

The board became convinced of the truth of apostolic example and in 1845 formulated a resolution addressed to the Reverend Worcester and other missionaries. They asserted:

While the strongest language of reprobation is not too strong to be applied to the system of slavery, truth and justice require this Board to say that the *relation* of a Master to one whom the constitution of society has made a slave, is not to be regarded as in all cases such a sin as to require the exclusion of the Master, without further inquiry, from Christian ordinances.[6]

During the late 1840s, abolitionist-oriented churchmen experienced increased harassment and opposition in the Cherokee Nation. Most feared the consequences of pressing abolitionism and chose to avoid the issue completely, if possible. When pressed for explanations of why they were silent, they answered that it was a political subject rather than religious and was outside their jurisdiction. Although slaveowners were a minority, they always had a very strong, even dominating, voice in government. This caused some missionaries sponsored by northern groups to turn over their responsibilities to their southern brethren who did not find slavery and Christianity incompatible.[7] The Reverend Worcester, of course, would never leave and would always minister unto all. In 1847 he wrote: "Our third daughter, Hannah, made a profession of religion, and was received to the church, Feb. 7th. A black man, a slave, was received at the same time."[8]

In 1848 the American Board, a board representing Protestant churches, operated five churches in the Cherokee Nation. They were the Park Hill, Fairfield, Dwight, Mount Zion, and Honey Creek congregations. The board sent S. B. Treat, its corresponding secretary, on an inspection tour of these missions in 1848. Treat was instructed specifically to investigate slavery in the Nation and determine whether the missionaries were conducting themselves properly with regard to the institution. After visiting the missions, Treat received a lengthy letter from Elizur Butler and Samuel Worcester which was intended to clarify their position with regard to black slavery in the Nation. They said in part:

> It is a comparatively easy task to apply the discipline of the church to evils which are *explicitly* condemned in the word of God; but a far more difficult and delicate task to apply it to such as are only *impliedly* condemned by the general law of love.

> The laws of the Nation, sustaining the system of slavery, prevailing jealousy of missionary interference with what is generally regarded as simply a political institution, and the views of church members themselves, all are difficulties in the way of any church discipline which has a direct bearing on the subject of slavery.

> It is not always wise to attempt what is manifestly impracticable to be accomplished, though in itself desirable. In our answers to questions, we must have reference sometimes to what we suppose practicable to be done, rather than to what we might be glad to do.

> In regard to the question of rejecting any person from the church *simply* because he is a slaveholder, we cannot for a moment hesi-

tate. For (1) we regard it as *certain* that the Apostles, who are our patrons, did receive slaveholders to the communion of the church; and we have not yet been able to perceive any such difference between their circumstances and ours, as to justify us in departing from this practice in this respect. And (2) our general rule is to receive all to our communion who give evidence that they love the Lord Jesus Christ in sincerity; and we cannot doubt that many slaveholders do give such evidence.[9]

The numbers of slaveholders and slaves in the congregations involved at that time are listed in the following table.[10]

Church	Total Members	Slaveholders	Slaves
Park Hill	36	4	3
Fairfield	85	12	20
Dwight	50	5	–
Mount Zion	22	2	–
Honey Creek	44	1	–
Totals	237	24	23

Upon receiving Reverend Worcester's communication, Secretary Treat prepared a lengthy and detailed report for his governing board, which stated in part:

It does not seem to have been the aim of the brethren to exert any *direct* influence, either by their public or their private teachings, upon the system of slavery. And they discovered, as they supposed, a sufficient warrant for this course in the New Testament. On looking to the example of the Saviour and his Apostles, they found what they conceived to be an infallible rule to guide them in their labors. They found that nothing was said in direct condemnation of slavery as a system, neither was its sinfulness denounced, nor its continuance prohibited. But they did find that the mutual obligations of masters and servants were repeatedly and freely discussed. "Here then," they seem to have argued, "is our course marked out for us. We must give instruction on the relative duties of the master

and his slaves, just as the Bible has enjoined. As for the rest,
we must rely on the earnest and faithful preaching of Christ
and him crucified. With the blessing of God, and in his own
time, we hope to see a great change effected. We hope to see
the evils of slavery not only diminished, but actually and finally
brought to an end. But in no other way do we regard ourselves
as commissioned to labor for the accomplishment of this object."[11]

Treat's report did not satisfy some board members who continued to think
that it was wrong to sustain missions connected with slaveholding: "It seems
impossible that special marks of approbation are bestowed upon missions
that connive at enslaving men, buying and selling human beings, and ad-
mitting, as a matter of course, slaveholders and slave-sellers, or as the Bible
describes them, 'men-stealers,' who 'give evidences of piety,' to the Lord's
table." Financial supporters of the missions were also cognizant that
slavery was continually increasing as the Indians became more enlightened
and "the predominate influence" in the Nation was "in the hands of
slaveholders."[12]

Meanwhile, a few missionaries, since they were not citizens of the
Cherokee Nation, thought that it was not forbidden to them to teach black
slaves to read and write. The Cherokee National Council made its intent
unequivocally clear on October 24, 1848, by enacting the following law:

> Be it enacted by the National Council, That an Act passed
> October 22d, 1841, prohibiting the teaching of Negroes to
> read and write, be amended so that if any white person, not
> a citizen of the Cherokee Nation, should be guilty of a viola-
> tion of this act, it shall be the duty of the Sheriff of the Dis-
> trict where such violation should take place, to notify the
> Chief of the same, and it shall be the duty of the Chief to
> notify the agent, and demand a removal of such person or
> persons from the limits of the Cherokee Nation.[13]

Word reached the Mission Board in 1851 that Reverend Stephen Foreman,
a Cherokee and a Princeton graduate in the employ of the Board, owned a
slave. The secretary wrote Reverend Worcester about the matter, stating:

> I am sure we shall be embarased if Mr. Foreman has purchased
> a slave, *to retain her as a slave.* I am sorry to find, in 1848, that

Mrs. Foreman was a slaveholder, but as this was an old matter,
& as she held her slave as separate property, I thought we could
get along with the fact. . . . If he has not done so, will he not
emancipate at once, permitting the slave to work out the purchase money? This would of course relieve the case.[14]

Hannah Worcester, daughter of Reverend Samuel Worcester, married
Alijah Hicks ("Corn Planter") in 1852. The couple lived in a two-story
frame house at Park Hill and enjoyed the services of a black cook named
Aunt Sallie whose freedom had been purchased by Hicks.[15] The Reverend
Worcester had previously aided slaves to purchase their freedom. In 1853
he had written an article in the *Missionary Herald* about Abraham and
Nancy Moore, both of whom had formerly been slaves.

I think it is more than twenty years since they were redeemed
from slavery by the mission at Brainerd, being at that time members of the church there. They afterwards, mostly by labor performed for the mission, refunded the price paid for them.

In 1839, having removed to this side of the Mississippi, they were
received into the church at this place, and they have adorned the
Christian profession. For the sake of finding a better home for
some of their children, they set out in their old age for Liberia,
with one son who was born free, one whom they had redeemed,
and a daughter whom they had helped redeem. They embarked
in the *Zebra*, at New Orleans; and they, with their daughter and
one son were among those who died of cholera on board that
vessel.[16]

In 1854 Agent George Butler maintained that slavery had been a positive
asset to the Cherokees in the development of their nation. Butler also charged
that missionaries were behaving "obnoxiously" by "fanatically pursuing a
course which, if persisted in, must lead to mischievous and pernicious consequences."[17] In the following year, Butler investigated the Reverend
Samuel Worcester, hoping to determine the extent of abolitionist sympathies among the missionaries. He discovered some evidence of antislavery
attitudes, but nothing sufficient to warrant action. Evidence was available
concerning the Baptist missionaries Evan Jones and his son, John. Evan
Jones, a native of Wales, had made the "Trail of Tears" trek and had settled

near the Cherokee boundary in Washington County, Arkansas. The Joneses
were apparently demanding that slaveholders either free their blacks or
leave the church. Butler hoped that the abolitionist problem would be
treated by the Cherokees themselves.[18]

The National Council investigated the missionaries' antislavery activities
during the 1855 annual session. The council acknowledged that the Cherokees
were a slaveholding people "in a Christian like spirit" and directed Principal
Chief Ross to correspond with the various missionary societies on the subject of slavery "as a Christian principle." The National Council then passed
an act prohibiting any missionary to advise a slave "to the detriment of
his owner . . . under the penalty of being removed" and making it illegal
for teachers known to have abolitionist views to be employed by the
Cherokee public schools. Ross vetoed the bill, probably because of his
friendship with the missionaries. The veto was subsequently overridden
in the National Committee but was sustained in the National Council
(the lower house). This action evidently did not intimidate the Joneses
because in 1858 Agent Butler again reported the dismissal of slaveowning
church members from their congregations.[19]

The activities of a few missionary abolitionists in 1854 caused Choctaw
and Chickasaw Agent Douglas Cooper to write Charles W. Dean, southern
superintendent, to warn:

> If things go on so they are now doing, in 5 years slavery will be
> abolished in the whole of your superintendency [Indian Territory].
> (Private) I am convinced that something must be done speedily to
> arrest the systematic efforts of the Missionaries to abolitionize the
> Indian Country.
>
> Otherwise we shall have a great run-away harbor, a sort of Canada—
> with "underground rail-roads" leading to and through it—adjoining
> Arkansas and Texas.
>
> It is of no use to look to the General Government—its arm is
> paralized by the abolition strength of the North.
>
> I see no way except secretly to induce the Choctaws & Cherokees
> & Creeks to allow slave holders to settle among their people &
> control the movement now going on to abolish slavery among
> them.[20]

Some missionaries continued to hire slaves, and this often caused compli-
cations. One such incident was related by the Reverend Charles Cutler
Torrey of Fairfield Mission.

> We were obliged to hire slaves from their owners if we wished
> extra help, and always gave them some money for themselves
> in addition to what we paid their masters. In July, 1856, we had
> in our employ a slave named David, a member of our church,
> and a good man and a good servant. He found that he was to
> be taken from us and hired out at another place to which he
> dreaded to go. So he determined to run away. He asked for my
> horse to go to Park Hill, and without any suspicion of his real
> purpose. I let him take the horse. He went to Park Hill, but
> instead of returning, struck out for Kansas—a foolish thing,
> for he was sure to be called to account by the first white
> man or Indian he should meet. He was arrested and brought
> back and Mr. Worcester and I were charged with instigating
> him to run away, and with furnishing him with money and a
> horse for the purpose. (My horse, incidently, was nearly ruined
> and died not long afterwards). The affair stirred up general excite-
> ment throughout the country. It was taken up in the legislature,
> and certain parties tried to get an act to request my removal. I
> made an affidavit as to the real facts, showing that I knew noth-
> ing whatever of David's purpose. They tried to pass an act requir-
> ing all missionaries to appear before the U.S. Agent an give an
> account of themselves, but this also failed. I had an opportunity
> to do this later.[21]

The Methodist Episcopal Church South operated six missions in the
Cherokee Nation in 1855 and reported 140 black members. Bilingual slaves
sometimes sat with their owners in church in order to interpret the sermon.
Other slaves usually sat in segregated areas in the back of the building.
Sehon Chapel was an exception, however. Only the second brick church
constructed in the Cherokee Nation, it was completed in 1856. The
church was built at the expense of Principal Chief John Ross, George M.
Murrell, and other public-spirited citizens and sat on a beautiful promon-
tory overlooking Park Hill. The church boasted a belfry, a special bell,
"ornate pulpit," and excellent seats. "Men attendants sat on one side of

the church and women on the opposite side, while Negro slaves occupied the gallery constructed especially for their use."[22]

Most missionaries were probably secretly opposed to slavery. A few were abolitionists, and fewer yet made little effort to conceal their sentiments. Yet, there is no evidence that the underground railroad ever extended into the Nation, either in the East or West. There was much concern expressed in neighboring states, particularly in the West, about abolitionist activity among the missionaries. Texas, especially, voiced such concern, and both Arkansas and Missouri did to a lesser degree.

The Cherokees called a council in 1857 to debate whether or not to expel the missionaries from the Nation. The Reverend Charles Cutler Torrey successfully spoke to the council and assured it that the missionaries were not abolitionists.

> We disapprove of the system of slavery; but we came here as abolitionists, not to make the blacks discontented, or to stir up strife, but to preach the gospel of Christ, and to educate your children . . . believing that whenever the spirit of Christ took possession there would be loving kindness and tender mercy.[23]

In 1858, Agent George Butler charged the Reverend Samuel Worcester with interference in the following letter:

> Sir—You have been reported to me as an abolitionist, teaching and preaching in opposition to the institution of slavery in this Nation.
>
> You will please attend immediately to the truth or falsehood of this charge.[24]

The Reverend Worcester succintly answered the charge:

> I have received your note of day before yesterday, calling upon me to answer to charges presented to you against me. I plead not guilty.[25]

Reverend Worcester was pleased that soon afterward Stand Watie, who was proslavery, came to him with a list of petitioners who were asking for a missionary to be sent to Honey Creek. Worcester interpreted this action as a vote of confidence from proslavery Cherokees.[26]

During the following year, the Reverend Evan Jones was accused of being an abolitionist and fomenting antislavery agitation.[27] In September 1860 his son John, also a Baptist missionary, was ordered by the Indian agent to leave the country within three weeks. His expulsion was the result of an article published in a northern newspaper which stated that Jones was "engaged in promulgating anti-slavery doctrines among his flock." Other missionaries were also compelled to depart, and the excitement aroused by these incidents continued to increase.[28]

In 1860 a black slave of the Park Hill area was "cruelly whipped." The Reverend Charles Cutler Torrey was accused of making "inflamatory remarks" about the affair. A mob of "disorderly men" went to the Torrey home at Park Hill and demanded that the minister appear before them. After much difficulty, Mrs. Torrey convinced the mob that her husband was not at home. She became so upset by the excitement and anxiety that she gave premature birth. The Reverend Torrey was subsequently warned by friends and neighbors not to go to Tahlequah to fill his regular preaching appointment. Nevertheless, he went and upon arrival found the building locked. The janitor informed him that he would not be allowed further use of the building because of his antislavery remarks. The Reverend Torrey denied the charges and explained that he had not heard of any cruelty to Negroes. Meanwhile, a crowd of would-be worshipers had gathered in the street. The minister asked that the building be opened in order that he might clarify the slavery position of his governing board. The doors remained locked, however.[29]

Later, Reverend Torrey went to the Cherokee agent and explained that he and his governing board disapproved of slavery. But, he emphasized, he had not come to the Cherokee Nation as an abolitionist or to stir up strife and discontent. He maintained that his sole purpose was "to preach the Gospel of Christ, and to proclaim the Golden Rule." Reverend Torrey later said, "I have no doubt the Agent was a pro-slavery man, but he seemed satisfied with my statement, and I think that he was pleased that I was willing to come to him."[30]

As one southern state after another left the Union, the American Board decided that the Reverend Torrey must close his mission. The board reasoned that the Cherokees could no longer be classified as a heathen people and subjects for foreign missions. War had become a virtual certainty and the

Cherokee Nation was sure to be involved, so it was considered prudent to abandon the field. Many missionaries left the Nation, although others remained, some becoming associated with other sponsoring groups. On February 9, 1861, the Torrey family started their journey eastward in a two-horse farm wagon while their baggage was transported in an ox wagon.[31]

NOTES

1. Grant Foreman, "Notes of a Missionary among the Cherokees," *Chronicles of Oklahoma* 16, no. 2 (June 1938), p. 186.

2. Althea Bass, *Cherokee Messenger* (Norman: University of Oklahoma Press, 1936), pp. 207, 236.

3. Ibid., pp. 235-236.

4. Ibid., p. 236.

5. Charles K. Whipple, *Relations of the American Board of Commissioners for Foreign Missions to Slavery* (Boston: R. F. Wallcut, 1861), p. 102.

6. Bass, *Cherokee Messenger,* p. 237.

7. William T. Hagan, *American Indians* (Chicago: University of Chicago Press, 1961), p. 90.

8. Bass, *Cherokee Messenger,* p. 277.

9. Whipple, *Relations of the American Board,* p. 102.

10. Ibid., p. 97.

11. Ibid., p. 96.

12. Cherokee Documents, Folder 27, "Missions 1849-1873," pp. 2, 3, 5, in NEOSU John Vaughan Library Cherokee Collection, Tahlequah, Oklahoma.

13. *Laws of the Cherokee Nation: Adopted by the Council at Various Periods* (Tahlequah, Cherokee Nation: Cherokee Advocate Office, 1852), pp. 173-174.

14. Bass, *Cherokee Messenger,* pp. ˙ ˙ -238.

15. Mary Elizabeth Good, "The Di   f Hannah Hicks," *American Scene* 13, no. 3 (n.d.), p. 3. *American S*   is published by the Gilcrease Institute of American History and Art, T   Oklahoma, and the diary is in that institution's archives.

16. *Missionary Herald* 49, (1853), p. 310.

17. Morris L. Wardell, *A Political History of the Cherokee Nation* (Norman: University of Oklahoma Press, 1938), p. 121.

18. Butler to Drew, September 27, 1854, "Report of the Commissioner of Indian Affairs, 1854," 33rd Congress, 2d Session, *Executive Document*

1, pp. 322-323; Butler to Manypenny, June 22, 1855, Cherokee Agency, Letters Received, Office of Indian Affairs, National Archives; Butler to Dean, August 11, 1855, "Report of the Commissioner of Indian Affairs, 1855," United States Senate, 34th Congress, 1st Session, *Executive Document 1* (Washington, D.C.: A.O.P. Nicholson, 1856), pp. 444-445.

19. Proposed bill in the National Council, October 24, 1855; note attached to the proposed bill, undated [October 1855?] ; Butler to Mix, October 12, 1858, Cherokee Agency Letters Received, Office of Indian Affairs, National Archives; Greenwood to Rector, June 4, 1860, Letters Sent, Office of Indian Affairs, National Archives.

20. Annie Heloise Abel, *The American Indian as Slaveholder and Secessionist* (Cleveland: The Arthur H. Clark Company, 1915), pp. 41, 42.

21. Autobiography of Charles Cutler Torrey, Foreman Papers, vol. 53, pp. 410-411, Oklahoma Historical Society, Indian Archives, Oklahoma City, Oklahoma.

22. Carolyn Thomas Foreman, *Park Hill* (Muskogee, Oklahoma: Star Printery, Inc., 1948), p. 100.

23. "Autobiography of Mr. Torrey," in Foreman, "Notes of a Missionary among the Cherokees," p. 177.

24. Bass, *Cherokee Messenger,* p. 341.

25. Ibid.

26. Ibid.

27. Abel, *The American Indian,* p. 47.

28. Rachel Carolyn Eaton, *John Ross and the Cherokee Indians* (Menasha, Wisconsin: George Banta Publishing Company, 1914), pp. 174-175.

29. Foreman, *Park Hill,* pp. 115-116.

30. Ibid.

31. Ibid., p. 116.

8   The Prewar Years

After 1850 the question of whether the fugitive slave law of the United States was operative in the Indian Territory became of prime importance. Finally, United States Attorney General Caleb Cushing, "influenced apparently by Jefferson Davis," rendered the opinion that the law was operative.[1] Nevertheless, the sparsely settled region afforded an attractive refuge for fugitive slaves, both local and from the states. Fugitives even had the opportunity to reside in settlements of free blacks. Therefore, slaveowners in the Cherokee Nation, as in the United States, experienced continual problems with their "troublesome property."

$20 REWARD

RANAWAY on the 21st September last from the subscriber, living on Grand river, near the mouth of Honey Creek, Cherokee Nation, a negro man named ALLEN, who is about 25 years old . . . very black; has very white eyes, rather a stoppage in his speech . . . also marks of the whip enflicted before he came into my possession. . . .

PETER HILDEBRAND[2]

The Cherokees became apprehensive about the increased theft or kidnapping of slaves. Therefore, late in 1846, legislation against such activity was passed.

Be it enacted by the National Council, That any person or persons, who may be convicted of stealing a negro or negroes,

shall suffer death by hanging. And any person or persons, who
may be convicted of stealing a horse, mule, jack or jinny, for
the first offence shall be punished with not less than one
hundred stripes on the bare back, and compelled to make payment as is provided for in said act, and any person or persons,
who upon conviction before any Court having jurisdiction of
the same, of stealing a horse, jack, mule or jinny, for the third
offence, shall suffer death by hanging. This Act to take effect
from and after its passage; all laws, or parts of laws, militating
against this act, are hereby repealed.[3]

The security of their slave property became of prime importance to the
Cherokees. Therefore, the kidnapping of slaves became one of the very
few capital offences in the Nation. Nevertheless, it did not stop such activity.
It did cause free blacks to become more apprehensive. Less than a year
later, the "notorious villain Mat Guerring and Gang . . . broke into a home
of some free mulatto and mixed-Cherokee-blood people at Fort Gibson
and kidnapped two girls. In the presence of the mother they tied the
girls while in bed and carried them off to the States."[4]

The kidnapping of the two free mulatto girls was the subject of an act
passed by the National Council:

Be it enacted by the National Council, That the sum of
twenty-three dollars, be, and the same is hereby allowed,
out of the National Treasury, for the benefit of Charles
Landrum and Pigeon Halfbreed. That amount having been
expended by them in pursuing into the State of Missouri,
and recovering the two grand-daughters of Shoe Boot, deceased, who had been kidnapped on the night of the 27th
of September last, from the residence of their mother in
Delaware District, Cherokee Nation, for the purpose of
being sold into slavery.[5]

The Nation Council, at every session, considered and debated questions
regarding black slavery. On October 25, 1850, it passed the following
enactment:

Be it enacted by the National Council, That from and after
the passage of this Act, it shall be unlawful for any person

to trade with a negro slave, in any way whatever, without
first having obtained permission from the owner of such
negro slave.

Be it further enacted, That any person or persons, found
guilty of a violation of this Act, before any Court of this
Nation, having jurisdiction of the same, shall be fined for
every such offence, twenty-five dollars; one half for the
benefit of the Cherokee Nation, and the other half, for
the benefit of the owner of such slave. Suits to be brought
in this case as in other civil cases.[6]

The judicial arm of the Cherokee Nation had historically meted out
three kinds of punishment for infractions of the Nation's laws: fines, whippings, and death. The custom of whipping was graphically narrated by
Josiah Gregg in his classic work *Commerce of the Prairies:*

We crossed the Arkansas river a few miles above the mouth
of the Canadian fork. We had only proceeded a short distance
beyond, when a Cherokee shopkeeper came up to us with an
attachment for debt against a free mulatto, whom we had
engaged as teamster. The poor fellow had no alternative but
to return with the importunate creditor, who committed
him at once to the care of "Judge Lynch" for trial. We ascer-
tained afterwards that he had been sentenced to "take the
benefit of the bankrupt law" after the manner of the
Cherokees of that neighborhood. This is done by stripping
and tying the victim to a tree; when each creditor, with
a good cowhide or hickory switch in his hand, scares
[scars] the amount of the bill due upon his bare back.
One stripe for every dollar due is the usual process of
"whitewashing;" and as the application of the lash is accompanied
by all sorts of quaint remarks, the exhibition affords no small
merriment to those present, with the exception, no doubt, of
the delinquent himself. After the ordeal is over, the creditors
declared themselves perfectly satisfied.[7]

On October 20, 1851, the Nation Council abolished the practice of
stripes because "the present system of corporeal punishment is contrary to
the spirit of civilization; has not diminished crime in our country; is de-

grading to the spirit of freedom; and has been long since tried and abolished by the most civilized nations of the world."[8]

Stripes were not abolished for black slaves, however. The lashing of slaves was not considered "contrary to the spirit of civilization." Yet, the myth that the slaves of Cherokees were basically contented with their condition was perpetuated by such stories as the following, from the *Fort Smith Herald* of January 17, 1852:

Something for Abolitionists to Read

About four years ago, two negro men belonging to Mrs. Ridge, now dead, and the widow of Major Ridge, of the Cherokee Nation, ran away. Nothing had been heard from them since they left until a few days ago, when one of them, a large likely fellow by the name of William, stepped into the house where he had left his mistress and voluntarily surrendered to Mr. Stand Watie, its present ocupant, and administrator of the estate of Mrs. Ridge. Mr. W. was very much surprised to see him, nor did he know that he was in the neighborhood until he had walked into the house and fell upon his knees. It appears that he had been a part of the time in Iowa, a free State, and came immediately from that place home. Here is an instance of a negro prefering slavery to freedom in a free State.[9]

During the 1850s Andrew R. Nave of Tahlequah was actively engaged in the black slave trade. Nave, the son-in-law and a business associate of Principal Chief John Ross, purchased and sold slaves and also served as a broker. Selected pieces of his correspondence during this period reveal much information about slavery in the Cherokee Nation. Elizabeth Pack, who had been a large slaveowner for decades, wrote Andrew Nave on December 30, 1852, from Chattanooga, Tennessee, and said in part:

Zan Say you would like to buy Jack, perhaps we may trade on my return, though the price for Black Smith's in the Country is very high, Say from two thousand to Twenty five hundred dollars, And of course wouldbe far above the price of common field hands in the Cherokee Nation. Blacksmith hier in this Country from thirty five to forty five Dollars per month and of corse the price of hier will rise in our country Cherokee Nation in Same degree.[10]

The following is a bill of sale dated December 19, 1853.

Know all men by these presents that I Daniel R. Nave of the
Cherokee Nation for and in consideration of the sum of Eight
Hundred Dollars to me in hand well and truly paid by Andrew
Nave of said Nation, the receipt whereof I hereby acknowledge,
have bargained, sold and conveyed, all my right to a certain
negro boy named Charles, who is now about Eighteen years old,
and is sound in body and mind, and a slave for life—To have and
to hold the said negro unto Andrew Nave himself, his heirs
Executors, or Administrators I bind myself, my Heirs, Executors
or Administrators to warrant and defend the same against all
lawful claims—In witness where of I hereby set my hand and seal
this 19th day of December—and in the year of our Lord One
Thousand Eight Hundred and Fifty Three.

witness my hand and seal . . . ."[11]

Some indication of slave prices during the 1850s might be gained from a
sale by John Drew to Charlotte G. Drew of Canadian District. On April 7,
1857, Drew sold a woman named Diana, about thirty years old, and her
five children (Lydia, aged ten years, Fanny, aged seven years, Jim, aged
five years, George, aged three years, and Joshua, aged four months) for
$2,300.[12] Prices varied with the slave's skill, age, and sex. Alex Haynes,
a former Cherokee slave, stated: "Some slaves were sold for $300. on up
to $1000. There was a classed group of some of the largest and most vigorous
of the Negro men as bucks. They sold for $1000. and were mainly for breed-
ing purposes."[13]

The John Drew Papers in the Oklahoma Historical Society Archives
contains the following list of property belonging to the estate of John
Crossland, who died in the 1850s.

one negro man, named Alfred valued at	$800
one negro man, named Harry valued at	$125
one negro woman, named Nuge valued at	$600
one negro woman, named Sarah Ann valued at	$250
one negro man, named Toad valued at	$850
one negro woman, named Mary Ann valued at	$400
one negro man, named Rodey valued at	$100[14]

Cherokee slaveowners seldom allowed their slaves to purchase their freedom. S. H. Mayes did allow his black slave, Callis, to purchase his freedom in 1852. Mayes, who had gone to the California gold fields in 1850, had returned to the Nation and was preparing to drive a herd of cattle to the Sacramento Valley of California and wanted Callis to help with the long trail drive. This would have been a violation of California law, however. Therefore, Mayes sold Callis his freedom for $1,000 and the slave agreed to work out the purchase price.[15] Robert Blackstone was a slaveowner who resided in the Webbers Falls area. His son, Washington Blackstone, decided to join the prospectors in the California gold fields. Robert Blackstone, concerned for his son's welfare and safety, promised freedom to his slave, Corbin, if the black would accompany his son and look after him. William Shorey Coody owned a slave, Rabbit, who asked permission to purchase his freedom. Coody consented and the agreed-upon price was fifty cents. Rabbit Coody later lived on the Arkansas River and earned his livelihood by selling cider and gingerbread to travelers. Rabbit Ford, located four and one-half miles east of Muskogee, Oklahoma, on the Arkansas River, is named for him.[16] There were probably far fewer instances of slaves' being allowed to purchase their freedom in the Nation than in the United States, however.

Cherokees feared kidnappers who periodically spirited their Negroes out of the Nation to be sold into slavery in the United States. The free blacks in the Cherokee Nation were not altogether secure. Five members of the "Beams family of Negroes," who had long been known as free blacks, were seized in the Creek Nation in 1854. They were subsequently sold into slavery to John B. Davis of Mississippi at a public auction in Tahlequah. One of those who was sold had previously been employed by the Reverend Samuel A. Worcester.[17]

After passage of the Kansas-Nebraska Act in 1854, violence erupted sporadically over the slavery issue in Kansas and Missouri. Afraid of possible abolitionist activity, the Nation enacted a law in 1855 which made it "unlawful for the superintendent of schools to employ any person as teacher suspected of entertaining sentiments favorable to abolitionism."[18]

Cherokee Agent George Butler wrote in his annual report for 1855 to Charles W. Deam, Superintendent of Indian Affairs, Southern Superintendency, in part:

I called the attention of your predecessor to the slavery question
in the Cherokee Nation, I again refer to it, as it is producing much

excitement in the nation. There have been causes operating silently
for some time, having a tendency to create an agitation of that
already too much agitated question, and I am sorry to say, the
cause can be traced to the anti-slavery missionaries in the nation,
who, instead of attending to the real object of their mission, have,
by the course they have been, and are now pursuing, rendered the
slave population discontented with their lot, and fostered
thoughts and feelings in their minds from which no good can
be expected, but on the other hand, much evil. It is becoming
a matter of thrilling interest, involving, as it does, some of the
most important and cherished interests of the nation. It is a
subject of daily conversation among the intelligent portion
of the community, who denounce in strong terms the movements
of the abolitionists in the country, and if the excitement is not
put down, it will lead to disastrous consequences. It is a matter
that should be left entirely with the Cherokees to settle, and I
regret to see men who were sent here to teach religion endeavoring
to stir up strife among these people.[19]

Agent Butler was probably exaggerating the amount and influence of
abolitionist activity in the Nation. He was probably correct, however,
when he assessed Cherokee resentment toward the claimed jurisdiction
of the district court of Arkansas:

There is a subject of vital importance to the Cherokees that I
would call your attention to. It is the construction placed upon
the intercourse law by the district court for the western district
of Arkansas. It will be seen by referring to the treaty of 1835,
article 5th, that the Cherokees have the power to pass laws,
binding upon, not only the Cherokees themselves, but all who
have connected themselves with them. . . . The court claims
jurisdiction over all negroes, free and slave; the right to try all
negroes who may be guilty of any criminal offense, and all
persons offending against negroes within the Indian country,
and in all such cases hold negroes to be competent witnesses,
so that a master may be carred to Van Buren and tried for an
offense against his own negro, and his own slaves may become
witnesses against him. This I conceive to be an encroachment
on the rights of the Cherokees, and is so regarded by them.[20]

The correspondence of Andrew R. Nave, a Cherokee slave dealer during the 1850s, contains numerous bills of sale, runaway notices, letters of introduction, sales notices, offers to purchase, and offers to sell slaves. Below is a bill of sale to Principal Chief John Ross.

Bill of Sale James D. Mulkey Guardian for his Brother
Lewis Andrew and Wm. P. R. Mulkey

For a Mulatto woman slave & Child—Named Harriet & Archey—

Know all men by these presents that I James Daniel Mulkey of
the Cherokee Nation on behalf of myself and as legal guardian
for my brother, Lewis Andrew and William P. R. Mulkey have
this day bargained and exchanged a certain mulatto woman
slave named Harriett about eighteen years of age and her
child Archy who is about five years old—to John Ross of the
Nation afore said and in consideration of a negro named
Toney about Twenty six years of age to me in hand delivered
and the receipt whereof I hereby acknowledge and further
bind myself heirs &c unto the said John Ross heirs &c to protect
and defend the right and tittle in the said negro woman &
child forever against the claim or demand of all person whomso-
ever. In witness whereof I hereunto set my hand and affixed by
seal at Park Hill this first day of September 1854-.

Signed sealed & delivered in Presence   J. D. Mulkey seal
of D. H. Ross and Thos. Davis.   Guardian[21]

In June of 1854, Nave received a letter from James Moosley of Van Buren, Arkansas, asking that he have handbills printed to advertise a reward for a runaway. The letter follows in its entirety.

Van Buren
June 13th

D Sir

I had a negro man to leave me on the 10th instant Which I
bought off of Picket Benge and we suppose has gone near
the Creek Agency where I understand he was raised May I
ask the favor of you to have a number of hand bills struck
30, offering a reward of fifty dollars for his apprehension

delivery to me or to Wallase Ward % of [in care of]
Buren. Any expense you may incur in the matter shall be
promptly refunded he is 21 or 22 years of age a dark mulatto
full face five feet 10 or 11 inches high would weigh 165 or 70
pounds speaks the Creek and Cherokee Languages but little
English his name John was sold some 10 months since by a man
named Williams to a Mr. Task of the nation by Task to Benge.

By attending to the above request you will confer an obligation
upon me which shall be resiprocated when ever an opportunity
offers.

Fearing this may not find you at home I have written to Johnson
Foreman on the same subject.

Your friend
James Moosley.

Distribute the hand-bills through this and the Creek nations.[22]

The following bill of sale to Stand Watie by a Mormon couple passing
through the Nation provides additional insight into prices during the 1850s.

Know all men by these presents, that for and in consideration of
One Thousand and three hundred Dollars to us in hand paid by
Stand Watie of the Cherokee Nation, the receipt of which is
hereby acknowledge[d.]

We Jacob Croft & Sebrina Croft now on our way to Salt Lake;
have this day bargained Sold & conveyed, to the above named
Stand Watie; certain Negro Slaves for life; (Namely) A woman
about thirty seven years of age named Patricia and a boy four
years old named Andrew, a boy two years old named Landy—
to the tittle of all which we guarantie to be genuine and good,
and we also will warrant the said Negroes to be sound in body
and mind—and will defend the same from all lawful claim, to
the said Stand Watie, his heirs or assign, forever.

Given from under our hand and
seal, this 7th day of June 1856
Jacob Croft
Sebrina Croft
John Hawley
George Hawley[23]

The following handbill announcing a single sale to settle an estate appeared in 1856.

NOTICE

I will send to the highest bidder, for Cash in hand—at Tahlequah
C N—on Monday at 11 O Clock A.M. the 15th day of December
next—A negro woman by the name of Judy, about 45 years
old—belonging to the estate of Richard Taylor deceased Sold
for the benefit of Creditors and an equal division among the
heirs of said Richard Taylor decd[24]

Andrew Nave received the following letter in explanation to the above notice.

Dear Sir—I have been prevented by high water, bad roads &c
from attending to the sale of the negro woman Judy at
Tahlequah on this day—I therefore request of you as a friend
to put up the advertisement enclosed marked No 2 on the back,
under the one I put on your door when there, If it is yet up. If
not—put up the one enclosed marked No 1 on the back, at top
and No 2 immediately under it—I shall be at Tahlequah certain
at the time specified in No. 2. if not providentially prevented.
I suppose you have drawn on my warrant before now—If so hold
on to it until I see you—which will be in January if nothing
happens to prevent

> Your compliance with the above
> request, will confer a great favour
> on your
>   friend

R. B. Daniel

PS If you see my friend Charley Delano tell him I want him,
if he can to be at Tahlequah on the 20th of January 1857—
to sell Judy for me[25]

Andrew Nave enjoyed the trust and respect of his clientele and they valued his judgment. The following letter from a keen bargainer and potential customer makes this evident.

D Sir. When you were here, we were Speaking about a Negro
girl & child belong to a Mr Jones which he offered at $900.
but which you tho't could be bot for $850—Now Andy if
She *is likely, Smart, Sound in body & mind & a good title to
her,* I would like to have you buy her for me—I would like to
have you get her for as much less than $900. as you can—I
Shall depend Entirely on your juggment about the girl as I
know nothing about her, Except from you—if she is a good
girl I Shall Keep her Myself as I do not wish to buy Negroes
to Speculate on; & if she is a good disposed & Kind girl &
serves me well, She will have a good home & no fear of being
sent South—its a good price to pay for a negro woman & young
Child & she Should be likely & stout—If you buy her for me &
think it will be safe to come down by the Wagon, that your
goods go up in, which Starts from here to day, why you can
send her along, but not unless you think it perfectly Safe.
As I would prefer you to Keep her until a safe opportunity
offer'd or I could send for her—I will write you by this Evgs
mail & perhaps you can have her delivd by pony at Evansville,
at which plac I could Send for her[26]

Slave buyers from the states frequently visited the Cherokee Nation.
As the following letter indicates, they usually desired to meet Andrew
Nave and other Cherokee dealers.

Van Buren Arks
August 24/59

To
Mess Hawkins & Nave
Tahlequah
C. N.

Gent permit us to introduce to your acquaintance Mr. E.
Loftin, who visits your Section of Country for the purchase
of negroes & any assistance you Can render him will be duly
acknowledged by

yours Respectfully
Ward & Southmayd[27]

Black slavery was an integral part of the Cherokee economic, social, and political systems. It had existed for three-quarters of a century and was thought to be necessary for the continued material development of the Nation. The slavery argument among the states had received relatively little attention from most Cherokees. Then, during the decade of the 1850s, when the Kansas question became of national interest, the Cherokees began seriously to consider their slave interests endangered. Consequently, the organization of the free territory of Kansas and its settlement by many abolitionists who encouraged and assisted runaway slaves became a source of considerable irritation and apprehension among Cherokee slaveowners. Nevertheless, at that time Principal Chief John Ross and the National Council did not believe that an American civil war would spill over into the Cherokee Nation.

Cherokee Agent James McKissick attempted to conduct a general census in 1847. Like later attempts, however, it was stymied by the resistance of the Cherokees. All Cherokee agents before the Civil War were Southerners. Agent George Butler, the son of former Agent William Butler and nephew of former Agent Pierce Mason Butler, served during the 1850s and was convinced that black slavery was essential to continued Cherokee advancement. He opposed all attempts to weaken or restrict Cherokee ownership of slaves.[28]

A census in 1859 reportedly revealed that 21,000 Cherokees and noncitizens resided within the Nation. There were allegedly 9,000 blacks, "mostly slaves," in addition to this figure.[29] One author has placed the number of slaves at 4,000 or more.[30] The preliminary report on the eighth census, however, stated that there were 384 Cherokee owners of 2,504 black slaves in 1860. The largest Cherokee owner possessed 57 slaves. The ten largest owners held 353 slaves, averaging 35.3 per owner. There was one black slave for each nine Cherokees in the Nation. The slave population consisted of 1,122 males and 1,282 females. Moreover, the 1860 census reported only 17 free blacks residing in the Cherokee Nation.[31] The 1860 census also showed that among the Cherokee, Choctaw, Creek, and Chickasaw Indians there were 1,154 slaveowners, who owned a total of 7,369 slaves for an average of 6.3 each. The largest owner, a Choctaw, possessed 227 slaves. Black slaves comprised approximately 12.5 percent of the total population of Indian Territory, and about one Indian in fifty owned slaves.[32]

Agent George Butler attempted to export black slavery to the "wild" Plains Indians during this time in an effort to "civilize" them. In a communication to Elias Rector, southern Superintendent of Indian Affairs, in 1859, Butler concluded that slavery had been very beneficial to all Indians.

> If every family of the wild tribes of Indians were to own a
> negro man and woman who could teach them to cultivate
> soil and to properly prepare and cook their food, stock
> cattle given them, and a schoolmaster appointed for every
> district, it would tend more to civilize them than any other
> plan . . . for it is a well established fact that all wild tribes
> have an aversion to labor and when thrown into contact with
> those who will work they gradually acquire industrious habits.[33]

In 1859 the Reverends Evan and John B. Jones organized or revived the Keetowah Society. The Keetowahs were composed primarily of full-bloods who were dedicated to the preservation of tribal traditions, not particularly sympathetic to slavery, pro-Union, and strong supporters of Principal Chief John Ross. They wore two common pins in the form of a cross on their tunic lapels and were often referred to as "Pin" Indians.

The organization was a secret society for the ostensible purpose of cultivating a spirit of nationalism among the full-bloods in opposition to the innovating tendencies of the mixed-blood element. The real purpose, however, was apparently to counteract the influence of the Blue Lodge and other secret cesessionist organizations among the wealthier slaveowners.[34]

The turbulence in the United States and within the Cherokee Nation caused John Vann to make the following request of Captain John Drew early in 1860.

> Dr Sir—permit me to call your attention to the intention of our
> Sheriff to form a patroll company in his neighborhood. I wish
> to tell you what I think and feel of the matter, because I am
> satisfied you appreciate the great importance of a well organized
> company in this or any community of negroes. The known unruly
> disposition of "Indian negroes," the convenient access, & high
> handed workings of abolitions—with Kansas contingous, makes
> it in my mind, a bounden duty of every good citizen, to bestir
> himself in compelling all negroes to know their places—and to
> form a company under the directions, of nonslaveholders, or
> young & perhaps disipated men, such cannot command proper
> respect & influence, would only lead to dissention with neigh-

bors, with complaints of particiality. The officers, should be
slave holders, & men of influence firmness & judgement, & I
think there is only two such men amongst us & to see them
Captain & Lieutenant is my desire. I have had a conversation on
the subj with the Sheriff—& he is disposed to appoint you & Mr
Vore Lieut.—will you not accept? Do not put up the excuse of
age &c. the interest of our community calls upon you, & I am
satisfied you will not disapoint it. Night riding if necessary could
be done by the younger men. This I look upon as of minor
importance to other duties of the company—and if every man
of the neighborhood, would put a veto upon other negroes
gathering about there negro quarters at night, would be in a
great measure obviate night riding.[35]

The slavery issue continued to grow to crisis proportions in the United
States. Consequently it became more intense in the Cherokee Nation.
Some Cherokees worried about the election of 1860 that brought Abraham
Lincoln to the presidency. His campaign workers, notably William H.
Seward, in an appeal to Free Soil voters,, had recommended appropriating
the land of the Five Civilized Tribes and opening it to white settlers. Also,
some Cherokees perceived Lincoln as committed to the abolition of
slavery. Thus, tribal leaders and other influential slaveowners faced the
possible loss of a substantial investment.

The war clouds that ominously shadowed the United States were, in the
language of Cherokee slaves, "too heavy to tote themselves over the Arkansas."[36]
With a few notable exceptions, including the Rosses, the proslavery element
united around Stand Watie. Watie was a nephew of Major Ridge, was a large
slaveowner from Honey Creek, and had long opposed Principal Chief
John Ross. The supporters of slavery organized a group known as the
Knights of the Golden Circle, sometimes called "Knaves of the Godless
Communion." The proslavery purposes and goals of the Knights are outlined
in portions of their constitution reproduced below.

ARTICLE I

Sec 3rd No person shall be a member of the Knights of the
Golden Circle in the Cherokee Nation who is not a proslavery
man

ARTICLE 6

Sec 1st The Captain or in case of his refusal, then the Lieutenant has power to compell each and every member of their Encampment to turn out and assist in capturing and punishing any and all abolitionist in their minds who are interfering with slavery.[37]

The Knights, who later changed their name to "The Southern Rights Party," and Keetowahs were bitter opponents and experienced numerous clashes.

The ominous slavery question evidently did not hinder the commercial activities of Andrew Nave. His correspondence indicates that the first weeks of 1861 were a period of brisk business.[38] Slaves were still selling for high prices.

NOTES

1. Annie Heloise Abel, *The American Indian as Slaveholder and Secessionist* (Cleveland: The Arthur H. Clark Company, 1915), p. 22.

2. *Cherokee Advocate,* October 23, 1845.

3. *Laws of the Cherokee Nation: Adopted by the Council at Various Periods* (Tahlequah, Cherokee Nation: Cherokee Advocate Office, 1852), p. 139.

4. *Cherokee Advocate,* October 7, 1847. Such kidnappings were a common occurrence throughout the Cherokee Nation during the two decades preceding the Civil War.

5. *Laws of the Cherokee Nation,* 1852, p. 156.

6. Ibid., p. 212.

7. Josiah Gregg, *Commerce of the Prairies,* Edited by Max L. Moorehead (Norman: University of Oklahoma Press, 1954), p. 227.

8. Ibid., pp. 221-222. The last man to be whipped at Tahlequah was Levi Keys, a black, who was convicted of horse stealing. See Thomas Lee Ballenger, "The Development of Law and Legal Institutions Among the Cherokees" (Ph.D. dissertation, University of Oklahoma, 1938), p. 181.

9. Gaston Litton, *History of Oklahoma,* vol. 1 (New York: Lewis Historical Publishing Company, Inc., 1957), p. 185.

10. Nave Letters of the NEOSU Cherokee Collection in the John Vaughan Library, Tahlequah, Oklahoma.

11. Ibid.

12. Carolyn Thomas Foreman, "Early History of Webbers Falls," *Chronicles of Oklahoma* 29, no. 4 (Winter 1951-1952), p. 467.

13. Foreman Papers, Vol. 62, p. 3, found in the Indian Archives of the Oklahoma Historical Society, Oklahoma City, Oklahoma.

14. John Drew Papers, Indian Archives, Oklahoma State Historical Society, Oklahoma City, Oklahoma.

15. "Samuel Houston Mayes," *Chronicles of Oklahoma* 6, no. 2 (June 1928), p. 230.

16. Foreman Papers, vol. 8, p. 513.

17. Grant Foreman, *Advancing The Frontier 1830-1860* (Norman: University of Oklahoma Press, 1933), p. 161.

18. *Laws of the Cherokee Nation,* 1852, p. 23.

19. George Butler, Cherokee Agent, to Doctor Charles W. Dean, Superintendent of Indian Affairs, in *Annual Report of the Commissioners of Indian Affairs, 1855* (Washington, D.C.: A.O.P. Nicholson, 1856), pp. 124-125.

20. Ibid., p. 125.

21. "Miscellaneous Letters and Manuscripts Relating to Cherokee History," a bound manuscript in the NEOSU Cherokee Collection, p. 59.

22. Nave Letters, NEOSU Cherokee Collection.

23. Cherokee Nation Collection in Western History Collections of the University of Oklahoma (Box 41, Folder 125).

24. Nave Letters, NEOSU Cherokee Collection.

25. Ibid.

26. Nave Letters, NEOSU Cherokee Collection.

27. Ibid.

28. Carol B. Broemeling, "Cherokee Indian Agents, 1830-1874," *Chronicles of Oklahoma* 50, no. 4 (Winter 1974), pp. 447-449.

29. Reid A. Holland, "Life in the Cherokee Nation," *Chronicles of Oklahoma* 48, no. 3 (Autumn 1971), p. 288.

30. Rachel Carolyn Eaton, *John Ross and the Cherokee Indians* (Menasha, Wisconsin: George Banta Publishing Company, 1914), p. 173.

31. U.S., House of Representatives, 37th Congress, 2d Session, *Executive Document No. 116,* "Preliminary Report on the Eighth Census" (Washington, D.C.: Government Printing Office, 1862), pp. 11, 136.

32. Ibid., p. 136.

33. Report of the Indian Commissioner of Indian Affairs Accompanying the Annual Report of the Secretary of the Interior, 1859 (Washington, D.C.: Government Printing Office, 1860), p. 172; Bureau of Ethnology, *Fifth Annual Report,* 1883-1884, pp. 321-322.

34. James Mooney, "Myths of the Cherokees," *Nineteenth Annual Report of the Bureau of Ethnology* (Washington, D.C.: Government Printing Office, 1900), p. 225.

35. Foreman, "Early History of Webbers Falls," p. 469.

36. Grace Steel Woodward, *The Cherokees* (Norman: University of Oklahoma Press, 1963), p. 252.

37. Typewritten copy of the constitution in the NEOSU Cherokee Collection.

38. See Nave Letters, NEOSU Cherokee Collection.

9 _____The Civil War

When the Civil War erupted in the United States, Principal Chief John Ross announced a position of neutrality for the Cherokee Nation. The Civil War polarized the Cherokees in much the same way as it did the United States. The powerful anti-Ross, proslavery faction, which had evolved under the leadership of Stand Watie, was openly Southern in sentiment.

Southern strategists, cognizant that the Indian Territory lying west of Arkansas, north of Texas, and south of Kansas could provide the South with sustenance for troops, bases for raids, and a highway to Texas, diligently sought to win over the Cherokee chiefs. Principal Chief John Ross was pressured by his neighbors to take a pro-Southern position, as the following letter indicates.

> The State of Arkansas, Executive Department,
> Little Rock, January 29, 1861.
>
> To His Excellency John Ross,
>
> Principal Chief Cherokee Nation:
>
> Sir: It may now be regarded as almost certain that the States having slave property within their borders will in consequence of repeated Northern aggression, separate themselves and withdraw from the Federal Government. South Carolina, Alabama, Florida, Mississippi, Georgia, and Louisiana have already, by action of the people, assumed this attitude. Arkansas, Missouri, Tennessee, Kentuckey, Virginia, North Carolina, and Maryland will probably persue the same course by the 4th of March next.
>
> Your people, in their institutions, productions, latitude, and natural sympathies, are allied to the common brotherhood of the slave-holding States.

Our people and yours are natural allies in war and friends in peace.

Your country is salubrious and fertile, and possesses the highest capacity for future progress and development by the application of slave labor.

Besides this, the contiguity of our territory with yours induces relations of so intimate a character as to preclude the idea of discordant or separate action.

It is well established that the Indian country west of Arkansas is looked to by the incoming administration of Mr. Lincoln as fruitful fields ripe for the harvest of abolitionism, freesoilers, and Northern mountebanks.

We hope to find in your people friends willing to co-operate with the South in defense of her institutions, her honor, and her firesides, and with whom the slaveholding States are willing to share a common future, and to afford protection commensurate with your exposed condition and your subsisting monetary interests with the General Government.

As a direct means of expressing to you these sentiments, I have dispatched my aide-de-camp, Lieut. Col. J. J. Gaines, to confer with you confidentially upon these subjects, and to report to me any expressions of kindness and confidence that you may see proper to communicate to the governor of Arkansas, who is your friend and the friend of your people.

Respectfully, your obedient servant,

H. M. Rector,[1]
Governor of Arkansas

John Ross did not reply to Governor Rector's letter for three weeks—then he forwarded the following communication:

Tahlequah, Cherokee Nation
February 22, 1861.

His Excellency Henry M. Rector, Governor of Arkansas:

Sir: I have the honor to acknowledge the receipt of Your

Excellency's communication of the 29th ultimo, per your aide-
de-camp, Lieut. Col. J. J. Gaines.

The Cherokees cannot but feel a deep regret and solicitude
for the unhappy differences which at present disturb the peace
and quietude of the several States, especially when it is understood that some of the slave States have already separated themselves and withdrawn from the Federal Government and that it
is probable others will also persue the same course.

But may we not yet hope and trust in the dispensation of
Divine power to overrule the discordant elements for good,
and that, by the counsel of the wisdom, virtue and patriotism
of the land, measures may happily be adopted for the restoration
of peace and harmony among the brotherhood of States within
the Federal Union.

The relations which the Cherokee people sustain toward their
white brethren have been established by subsisting treaties
with the United States Government, and by them they have
placed themselves under the "protection of the United States
and of no other sovereign power whatever." They are bound
to hold no treaty with any foreign power, or with any individual
state, nor with the citizens of any state. On the other hand, the
faith of the United States is solemnly pledged to the Cherokee
Nation for the protection of the right and title in the lands,
conveyed to them by paten, within their territorial boundaries,
as also for the protection for all other of their national and
individual rights and interests of persons and property. Thus
the Cherokee people are inviolably allied with their white
brethren of the United States in war and friends in peace.
Their institutions, locality, and natural sympathies are
unequivocally with the slave-holding States. And the contiguity
of our territory to your State, in connection with the daily,
social, and commercial intercourse between our respective
citizens, forbids the idea that they should never be otherwise
than steadfast friends.

I am surprised to be informed by Your Excellency that "it is
well established that the Indian country west of Arkansas is
looked to by the incoming administration of Mr. Lincoln as

fruitful fields ripe for the harvest of abolitionism, freesoilers, and Northern mountebanks." As I am sure that the
laborers will be greatly disappointed if they shall expect in the
Cherokee country "fruitful fields ripe for the harvest of
abolitionism," &c., you may rest assured that the Cherokee
people will never tolerate the propagation of any obnoxious
fruit upon their soil.

And in conclusion I have the honor to reciprocate the saluta-
tion of friendship.

I am, sir, very respectfully, Your Excellency's obedient servant,

Jno. Ross, Principal Chief Cherokee Nation.[2]

As the result of pressure at home and from neighboring slave states,
Chief Ross issued an official proclamation on May 17, 1861, restating his
position of strict neutrality. Ross reportedly owned between 70 and 100
black slaves at that time.[3] Nevertheless, there were clashes between the
Keetowahs and Knights during this time. The Nation was wracked by
internal dissension. The Confederate government capitalized on the situation
by promising Stand Watie arms for protection against the Pins. On June 12,
1861, David L. Hubbard, the commissioner of Indian affairs for the Confederate States of America, wrote Chief Ross that if the South succeeded,
Cherokee lands, slaves, and separate nationality would be secure and
perpetual. But:

If the North succeeds you will most certainly lose all. First your
slaves they will take from you; that is one object of the war,
to enable them to abolish slavery in such manner and at such
time as they choose. . . .

If you are obliged to admit the truth of what I say, then join
us and preserve your people, their slaves, their vast possessions
in lands, and their nationality. . . .

As long as your people retain their national character your
country cannot be abolitionized, and it is our interest therefore that you should hold your possessions in perpetuity.[4]

The withdrawal of Federal troops from Indian Territory, the early
military successes of the Confederacy, Confederate treaties with the other

four "Civilized tribes," pressure from Arkansas and Texas, and constant
pressure from prominent slaveowning Cherokees caused Chief Ross to call
a special Council to meet in Tahlequah on August 21, 1861. At this meeting,
which was attended by some 4,000 Cherokees, Ross first urged neutrality,
but, realizing that the Cherokees had been abandoned by Federal forces,
he then capitulated and became convinced that the Confederates would
overrun the Nation unless it joined them. The council passed the following
resolution by acclamation:

> *Resolved,* That among the rights guaranteed by the constitu-
> tion and laws we distinctly recognize that of property in negro
> slaves, and hereby publicly denounce as calumniators those
> who represent us to be Abolitionists, and as a consequence
> hostile to the South, which is both the land of our birth and
> the land of our homes.[5]

Ross then notified Albert Pike, the Confederate commissioner, that the
Cherokee Nation was prepared to form an alliance with the Confederate
States of America. Consequently, the commissioner hastened to Park Hill
and consummated a treaty at Hunters Home Plantation on October 7,
1861.[6] The treaty sanctioned slavery as a legal institution that had "existed
from time immemorial." Property rights in slaves were guaranteed, fugitive
slave laws were declared operative in the Indian country, and mutual return
of fugitives was promised.

Article XXXIV of the treaty stated:

> The provision of all such acts of the Congress of the Confederate
> States as may now be in force, or as may hereafter be enacted,
> for the purpose of carrying into effect the provisions of the
> Constitution in regard to the redelivery or return of fugitive
> slaves, or fugitives from labor and service, shall extend to and
> be in full force within the said Cherokee Nation; and shall also
> apply to all cases of escape of fugitive slaves from the said
> Cherokee Nation into any other Indian nation, or into one of
> the Confederate States; the obligation upon each such nation or
> State to redeliver such slaves being in every case as complete
> as if they had escaped from another State and the mode of
> procedure the same.

Article XXXVII stated:

It is hereby declared and agreed that the institution of slavery
in the said nation is legal and has existed from time immemorial;
that slaves are taken and esteemed to be personal property;
that the title to slaves and other property having its origin in
the said nation shall be determined by the laws and customs
thereof, and that the slaves and other personal property of
every person domiciled in said nation shall pass and be distributed at his or her death in accordance with the laws, usages,
and customs of the said nation, which may be proved like foreign
laws, usages, and customs, and shall everywhere be held binding within the scope of their operations.[7]

The treaty concluded:

[The Cherokee people] accept the issue thus forced upon
them, unite their fortunes now and forever with those of the
Confederate States, and take up arms for the common cause,
and with entire confidence in the justice of that cause and with
a firm reliance upon Divine Providence, will resolutely abide the
consequences.[8]

Subsequently, on October 28, the council issued a declaration that stated:

Whatever causes the Cherokee people may have had in the
past to complain of some of the Southern States, they cannot
but feel that their interests and destiny are inseparately connected with those of the South. The war now waging is a war
of Northern cupidity and fanaticism against the institution
of African servitude; against the commercial freedom of the
South, and against the political freedom of the States, and
its objects are to annihilate the sovereignty of those states
and utterly change the nature of the General Government.

The Cherokee people and their neighbors were warned before
the war commenced that the first object of the party which
now holds the reins of government of the United States would
be to annul the institution of slavery in the whole Indian

country and make it what they term free territory and after a
time a free state: and they have been also warned by the fate
which has befallen those of their race in Kansas, Nebraska and
Oregon that at no distant day they too would be compelled
to surrender their country at the demand of Northern rapacity
and be content with an extinct nationality, and with reserves
of limited extent for individuals of which their people would
soon be despoiled by speculators, if not plundered unscrupu-
lously by the State.[9]

The declaration was signed by Thomas Pegg, president of the National
Committee, and Lacy Mouse, speaker of the council, and approved by Principal
Chief John Ross. Two Cherokee regiments were raised for the Confederate
service. One, the First Regiment Cherokee Mounted Rifles, was under the
command of John Drew. The other, the Second Regiment Cherokee
Mounted Rifles, was under the command of Stand Watie. They participated
in several engagements, including the battle of Pea Ridge on March 7,
1862. During the following summer, Union forces entered the Cherokee
Nation and urged Ross to repudiate the Confederate alliance. Ross declined,
but shortly afterward the men of Drew's regiment, some 2,200 in number,
including some blacks, who were unpaid and neglected, went over—almost
totally—to the Union side. Ross then apparently made an arrangement
with a Union commander, Colonel William Weir.[10] Colonel Weir reported
to his commanding officer that "the negro question is a very difficult one."

Nearly all their [the Cherokees'] negroes are escaping and
are very insolent. I propose to invite the nations to abolish
slavery by a vote and accept compensation from the Government. The President should be telegraphed to recommend
to Congress so to amend the emancipation resolution so to
enable the Indian nations to avail themselves of its benefits.[11]

The early military successes which the Confederates enjoyed in the
Cherokee region proved ephemeral. On July 15, 1862, Principal Chief John
Ross and his family were captured and taken into custody by Captain
H. S. Greeno's detachment of Union forces. Ross and his wife, along with
the Cherokee national records and the Nation's funds, were removed to
Kansas and then to Washington and Philadelphia for safekeeping. The Rosses

were accompanied by two black slaves, John Dedrick Morgan and his wife, Cynthia. John was the property of Margaret Seiver Morgan. His wife, Cynthia, was Mrs. Ross's personal serving maid.[12] With Fort Gibson, Tahlequah, Park Hill, and practically all of the Nation below the Moravian Mission under Confederate control, Stand Watie called for a council at Tahlequah. There, on August 21, 1862, Watie was elected principal chief of the Cherokee Nation.[13] On November 12, 1863, Watie wrote his wife Sarah that he had burned Rose Cottage to the ground and captured some of Ross's slaves.[14]

When hostilities broke out, many Cherokee slaveowners joined the armed service, leaving their families and slaves behind. Many of these slaves were later taken to Fort Gibson for security. At one time more than 7,000 Indians and 500 blacks sought safety at Fort Gibson. The following letter, written by Ross's son, indicates the conditions that both Indians and slaves experienced throughout the war.

> Park Hill
> Aug. 18th 1862

Col Cooper

The negroes, property of my father's, whom you sent in charge Joshua Ross charge, were delivered over to me this morning I'm under many obligations, & thanks to you for their return. As they are the helpless portion of the property, should have been glad if the men had also been sent, their aid will be very much needed, in helping along this very property. For the few who have not gone over to the Federals are either old, infirm or sick. My [father] left ample provisions for the support of these slaves for the year but am sorry to say all has been taken. My brother who has charge of the place being absent for personal safety, the house had been broken open ransacked, & plundered no doubt of many articles. The perpetrators of this outrageous act, I know not, but am told that some of our own people of Col Waties command are the guilty ones. Col Crawford has no doubt reiterated to you all I told him, in reference to the trying position in which my dear father was placed till his removal from this by Federals. Would to God it had been in power to have succored him. Tis a pleasing

reflection that altho he has been forced from his home, &
many endearing ties, and however bitterly his enemies, may
stigmatize his name & say that he went of his own accord,
to know that he left with honor bright and a pure southern
heart.[15]

Some owners took or sent their families and slaves to the Choctaw
Nation, Texas, or elsewhere for the duration of the war. There the slaves
were often hired out. Betsie Merrill Riley owned "a fine, well-improved
farm home" near Park Hill and "had numerous slaves" and "plenty of
fine stock." At the beginning of the war, she took her "property" and went
to Texas.[16] George Starr of Flint District took his slaves to Texas and
started a plantation in Rusk County. Sarah Watie, wife of Stand Watie,
spent part of the Civil War years in Texas with their four younger children
and some of the family slaves.[17] Jane Ross Nave, daughter of Principal
Chief John Ross and the wife of Andrew Nave, fled with her children to
Bethlehem, Pennsylvania.[18] The Whitmires of Peavine Plantation joined
many others and took their slaves south.[19]

Many black slaves remained in the Nation and continued to be faithful
to their absentee masters; sometimes they were the sole occupants of
plantations. Mrs. Ella Coody Robinson related: "Mother took us children
and went to New Hampshire when father died during the war as she had
been educated there and we stayed several months. When she returned
home she found the home affairs in good order, the faithful negroes stay-
ing at their posts of duty."[20] Lydia Keys Taylor explained: "My father
fought with the Confederacy during the Civil War. He left a negro slave to
take care of the plantation near Tahlequah. After the war, on returning
to the plantation, he found the house burned, cattle gone, but the slave
was still there."[21] Major Joseph Lynch Martin, known by many as
"Greenbriar Joe," owned a large plantation at Pensacola, Florida, and
operated three cattle ranches at Ketchum and Greenbriar in the Cherokee
Nation. More than 300 black slaves labored on these properties. When the
war began, Martin placed his black slave driver, Nelson, in charge of his
ranches and gathered a regiment of men for the Confederate army, out-
fitting it at his own expense. He participated in the battle of Cabin Creek,
which was fought on his Pensacola ranch. During the war, Nelson made
two trips to Florida to oversee his master's affairs there.[22] However, during
the confusion of the war years, many Cherokee blacks ran away to safety
and freedom. Some of these who escaped later joined the Union military

and participated in the war. It is estimated that approximately 1,000 blacks served in the Union and Confederate forces, most with the Union.

Guerrillas, bushwhackers, and thieves burned, pillaged, and decimated the Cherokee Nation throughout the war years. Crops, livestock, buildings, homes, household furnishings, and practically everything of value was seized or destroyed by regular and irregular military and night riders who ranged across the country. Organized government virtually ceased to exist. The public school system was closed. The Cherokee National Male Seminary and the National Female Seminary closed. These institutions of higher learning had been the pride of the entire Nation. The Female Seminary had been modeled after Mount Holyoke and enjoyed the distinction of being (1) the first public liberal arts institution of higher learning for women in the trans-Mississippi West, (2) the first public tuition-free institution of higher learning in America, (3) the first public institution of higher learning in America to provide equal salaries for women faculty, (4) the second-oldest public institution of higher learning west of the Mississippi River, and (5) one of the half-dozen oldest liberal arts institutions of higher education for women in America.[23] During the war, munitions were stored in the Female Seminary until it was ransacked. The Male Seminary was occupied for some time by a cavalry unit; troopers were billeted on the second floor and their animals occupied the ground level.

Many Cherokees remained loyal to the Union and had never approved of the treaty with the Confederacy. Accordingly, in February 1863 a pro-Union element made up of many former members of the National Council met in council on Cowskin Prairie, some twenty-two miles southwest of Neosho, Missouri, and repudiated the alliance. They acknowledged their loyalty to Principal Chief John Ross and elected Thomas Pegg acting Principal Chief. Then, following the precedent of President Abraham Lincoln's Emancipation Proclamation, on February 21, 1863, the "Federal Cherokees" passed an act which emancipated slaves and abolished slavery within their Nation. The act read:

ACT OF EMANCIPATION

Be it enacted by the National Council: That all Negroes and other slaves within the lands of the Cherokee Nation be and they are hereby emancipated from slavery, and any person or persons who may have been in slavery are hereby declared to be forever free.

Be it further enacted that this act shall go into effect on the
25th day of June, 1863, and any person who, after that date
shall offend against the provisions of this act, by enslaving
or holding any person in slavery within the limits of the Cherokee
Nation, he or she so offending shall, on conviction thereof before
any courts of this Nation having jurisdiction of the case, forfeit
and pay for each offense, a sum not less than $1,000, nor more
than $5,000, in the discretion of the court.

Two-thirds of said fine shall be paid into the National treasury
and one-third shall be paid, in equal sums, to the solicitor and
sheriff of the district in which the offence shall have been committed. And it is hereby made the duty of the solicitors of
the several districts to see that this law is duly enforced. But in
case any solicitor shall neglect to fail to discharge his duties
herein, and shall be convicted thereof, he shall be deposed
from his office, and shall hereafter be ineligible to hold any
office of trust or honor in this nation. The acting Principal
Chief is hereby required to give due notice of this act.

Be it further enacted that all laws and parts of laws conflicting with the provisions of this act are hereby repealed.

COWSKIN PRAIRIE, C.N. February
21, 1863

J. B. Jones,
    Clerk, National Council

Approved Feb. 21, 1863

Lewis Downing,
    President pro tem.
    School Commissioner

Thos. Pegg,
    Acting Principal [Chief]

George E. Foster.[24]

The Cherokee Nation was the only slaveholding region to abolish slavery
voluntarily during the Civil War. The Federal Cherokees had little to lose,

however. The large slaveowners were practically all Confederate sympa-
thizers and they totally disregarded the law.[25] Throughout the war, Stand
Watie and the Southern wing refused to consider the action at Cowskin
Prairie as tribal action and as legal and binding. From the time of the Act
of Emancipation, there were in reality two Cherokee Nations, the Northern
wing with Principal Chief John Ross as its titular head and the Southern
wing with Stand Watie as its principal chief.[26]

Despite the Act of Emancipation, when the war ended, the United
States claimed that because the Cherokees had aligned themselves with
the Confederacy, all existing treaties between the two nations were void.
During the summer of 1865 the United States government ordered the
Cherokees to send delegates to Fort Smith, Arkansas, to negotiate a peace
treaty. After heated and acrimonious debate in the National Council, two
sets of delegates were dispatched to Fort Smith. One delegation represented
the Northern, or Ross, faction while the other represented the Southern,
or Watie, faction. President Andrew Johnson had appointed a commission
to represent the United States that consisted of Dennis N. Cooley, commissioner of Indian affairs; Elijah Sells, superintendent of the Southern superintendency; Thomas Wistar, a leading member of the Society of Friends;
Brigadier General W. S. Harney, United States Army; and Colonel Ely S.
Parker, an Iroquois Indian, of General Grant's staff. Upon reaching Fort
Smith, the two Cherokee delegations were informed on September 8 that
they had automatically forfeited all annuities and rights of all previous
treaties by joining the Confederacy. Therefore, totally new treaties would
have to be negotiated. In any new agreement, the Cherokees would have
to make peace with the United States and other Indian tribes, free their
slaves, and adopt them into the tribe. The freedmen were to be given
rights to land and annuities. Moreover, the Cherokees would have to grant
rights-of-way to railroads and relinquish their western lands.

The Cherokees pleaded their case by stipulating that they had honored
their allegiance to the Union as soon as it had been possible for them to
receive protection and that they had joined the Confederacy only when
it became necessary to prevent invasion and decimation of their country.
They refused to sign the proffered treaty. With the negotiations stalemated,
it was decided to change the meeting place to Washington, D.C., and resume
deliberations during the summer of 1866.

The Cherokees and the United States proposed four separate plans for
the disposition of the question of Cherokee freedmen. They were:

1. A proposal to establish a segregated district within the Nation for colonization by the freedmen.

2. A plan to remove the freedmen, at the joint expense of the Federal and Cherokee governments, and establish them in colonies outside the Cherokee Nation.

3. A plan for the adoption of the freedmen into the tribe, granting them citizenship, land, and annuities to the same amount as Indian tribal members.

4. A proposal to open the entire Indian Territory to Negro colonization. This proposal was contained in the Harlan Bill, which was introduced in the United States Senate during the special session of 1865.

The Cherokees were willing to make some provisions for their freedmen but were opposed to adoption. Nevertheless, as the ashes of the Civil War were still cooling, a delegation of Cherokees journeyed to Washington to attempt to negotiate a peace treaty. The treaty was formulated and signed on July 19, 1866. Some of its most important provisions treated slavery and freedmen. Article 4 stipulated:

All the Cherokees and freed persons who were formerly slaves to any Cherokee, and all free negroes not having been such slaves, who resided in the Cherokee Nation prior to June first, eighteen hundred and sixty-one, who may within two years elect not to reside northeast of the Arkansas River and southeast of Grand River, shall have the right to settle in and occupy the Canadian District southwest of the Arkansas River, and also all that tract of country lying northwest of Grand River, and bounded on the southeast by Grand River and west by the Creek reservation to the northeast corner thereof; from thence west on the north line of the Creek reservation to the ninty-sixth degree of west longitude; and thence north of said line of longitude so far that a line due east to Grand River will include a quantity of land equal to one hundred and sixty acres for each person who may so elect to reside in the territory above described in this article: *Provided,* That that part of said district north of the Arkansas River shall not be set apart until it shall be found that the Canadian District is not sufficiently large to allow one hundred and sixty acres to each person desiring to obtain settlement under the provisions of this article.[27]

Article 9 stated:

The Cherokee Nation having, voluntarily, in February, eighteen hundred and sixty-three, by an act of the national council, forever abolished slavery, hereby covenant and agree that never hereafter shall either slavery or involuntary servitude exist in their nation otherwise than in the punishment of crime, whereof the party shall have been duly convicted, in accordance with the laws applicable to all the members of said tribe alike.

They further agree that all freedmen who have been liberated by voluntary act of their former owners or by law, as well as all free colored persons who were in the country at the commencement of the rebellion, and are non residents therein, or who may return within six months, and their descendants, shall have all the rights of native Cherokees: *Provided,* That owners of slaves so emancipated in the Cherokee Nation shall never receive any compensation or pay for the slaves so emancipated.[28]

The Nation still faced the necessity of amending its constitution. On November 28, 1866, amendments to Article III of the constitution were approved and adopted by a convention of the Cherokee people at Tahlequah. Section 5 was amended to read:

All native born Cherokees, all Indians, and whites legally members of the Nation by adoption, and all freedmen who have been liberated by voluntary act of their former owners or by law, as well as free colored persons who were in the country at the commencement of the rebellion, and are now residents therein, or who may return within six months from the 19th day of July, 1866, and their descendants, who reside within the limits of the Cherokee Nation, shall be taken, and deemed to be, citizens of the Cherokee Nation.

Section 7 was amended to read:

All male citizens, who have attained the age of eighteen years,
shall be deemed qualified electors of the Cherokee Nation,
and there shall be no restrictions by law, save such as are required for persons convicted of crime, or for such limit as to
residence, not exceeding six months in the district where the
vote is offered, as may be required by census or registration.

Article VII was then appended and Section 1 read:

Neither slavery nor involuntary servitude, shall ever hereafter
exist in the Cherokee Nation, otherwise than in the punishment
of crime, whereof the party shall have been duly convicted;
and any provision of the Constitution of the Cherokee Nation
conflicting with the foregoing section, is hereby annulled.[29]

Cherokee slaves apparently were less cognizant that freedom would be
a result of a Union victory than their southern counterparts. Many Cherokee
slaves had been taken from the Nation to "safety," others had fled to
freedom. Therefore, sizable numbers of freedmen were ignorant of the
treaty clause which provided for their right of incorporation into the tribe
if they returned within six months. Consequently, large numbers either
did not return or returned too late to qualify for the benefits stipulated
in the treaty. Refugee freedmen who returned after January 19, 1867, discovered that they were not citizens, but intruders.

Cherokee freedmen observed August 4 as the anniversary of their freedom.
Emancipation actually occurred during February 1863, but for unknown
reasons August 4 continues to be observed. Picnics, oratory, singing, and
"bountiful repasts" have always been a part of the celebration observed
across the old Cherokee Nation.[30]

NOTES

1. H. M. Rector to John Ross, in *The War of the Rebellion: A Compilation of the Official Records of the Union and Confederate Armies,*
129 vols. (Washington, D.C.: Government Printing Office, 1900), series I,
vol. 13, pp. 490-491. Hereafter cited as *Official Records.*

2. Ibid., pp. 491-492.

3. Albert D. Richardson, *Beyond the Mississippi, 1857-1867* (Hartford: American Publishing Company, 1867), p. 216.

4. David Hubbard to John Ross, in *Official Records,* series I, vol. 13, pp. 497-498.

5. Ibid., pp. 499, 500.

6. Carolyn Thomas Foreman, *Park Hill* (Muskogee, Oklahoma: Star Printery, Inc., 1948), p. 120.

7. *Official Records,* series IV, vol. 1, p. 678.

8. Ibid., series I, vol. 13, p. 505. No treaty more favorable to themselves had ever been signed by the Cherokees.

9. Ibid., pp. 504-505.

10. James Mooney, "Myths of the Cherokees," *Nineteenth Annual Report of the Bureau of Ethnology* (Washington, D.C.: Government Printing Office, 1900), p. 149.

11. Colonel William Weir to Captain Thomas Moonlight in *Official Records,* series I, vol. 13, pp. 487-488.

12. Carolyn Thomas Foreman, "Texana," *Chronicles of Oklahoma* 31, no. 2 (Summer 1953), pp. 187-188. Chief Ross visited with President Abraham Lincoln while he was in Washington before continuing on to Philadelphia where he remained on parole until the end of the war.

13. Grace Steel Woodward, *The Cherokees* (Norman: University of Oklahoma Press, 1963), p. 281.

14. Edward Everett Dale and Gaston Litton, *Cherokee Cavaliers* (Norman: University of Oklahoma Press, 1939), pp. 144-145. Rose Cottage was probably burned on the night of October 23, 1863.

15. Miscellaneous Letters of the NEOSU Cherokee Collection in the John Vaughan Library, Tahlequah, Oklahoma.

16. Foreman Papers, vol. 4, p. 122, found in the Indian Archives of the Oklahoma Historical Society, Oklahoma City, Oklahoma.

17. Dale and Litton, *Cherokee Cavaliers,* p. 125.

18. Edmund Schwarze, *History of the Moravian Missions Among Southern Indian Tribes of the United States* (Bethlehem, Pennsylvania: Times Publishing Company, 1923), p. 293.

19. Foreman Papers, vol. 103, p. 464.

20. Ibid., vol. 17, pp. 374-375.

21. Ibid., vol. 112, p. 56.

22. Foreman Papers, vol. 88, p. 353.

23. R. Halliburton, Jr., "Northeastern's Seminary Hall," *Chronicles of Oklahoma* 51, no. 4 (Winter 1973-1974), p. 391. Also see R. Halliburton, Jr., "The Cherokee National Female Seminary," a bound printed manuscript in NEOSU Cherokee Collection.

24. John D. Benedict, *Muskogee and Northeastern Oklahoma* (Chicago: S. J. Clarke Publishing Company, 1922), vol. 1, p. 204.

25. Morris L. Wardell, *A Political History of the Cherokee Nation* (Norman: University of Oklahoma Press, 1938), p. 173.

26. Dale and Litton, *Cherokee Cavaliers,* p. 125.

27. Charles J. Kappler, ed., *Indian Affairs: Laws and Treaties* (Washington, D.C.: Government Printing Office, 1904), vol. 2, p. 943.

28. Ibid., p. 944.

29. *Constitution and Laws of the Cherokee Nation* (St. Louis: R. & T. A. Ennis Stationers, Printers and Book Binders, 1875), pp. 25-27.

30. Foreman Papers, vol. 61, p. 39.

10 Conclusion

Southern Indians, including the Cherokees, have to a considerable degree been excluded from histories of the Old South. This is demonstrated by a perusal of general histories and other historiographical writing. In numerous works there is no mention of Indians. Where mention is made, it too frequently is only with regard to the colonial struggles among France, Spain, and England for control of the Old Southwest. Consequently, there is a paucity of information about black slavery among the Southern Indians in general and the Cherokees specifically.

A considerable Afro-American historiography exists and some material treating Indian and black relations is readily found. Unfortunately, these materials do not often refer to the institution of black slavery within the tribes. When perfunctory references to black slavery among American Indians in general and Cherokees in particular are found, they all too frequently contain misinformation, unsubstantiated generalizations, and faulty analysis and conclusions. They have provided a distorted image of the subject that has become accepted by most scholars of all races. Consequently, a twisted stereotype has continually been projected.

From earliest times, the Cherokees appear to have been one of the largest and most advanced Indian tribes. They were an ethnocentric people and believed that they were superior to others, regardless of their tribes, races, or origins.

Both the Spanish and French used black slaves on their expeditions of discovery into the Indian country, and when the Cherokees first met these Europeans, they saw black men bearing burdens, performing labor, tending livestock, and acting as body servants. The Cherokees did not at that time or subsequently develop an affinity with blacks as brothers of color, both oppressed by the white man.

Runaway blacks who made their way to the Cherokees seeking sanctuary were usually considered to be intruders and treated accordingly. Later, when the Cherokees came into possession of blacks by marauding and other means, they viewed them as economic commodities to be ransomed, exchanged, sold, or retained as slaves. Although the tribe had employed enforced adoption for as long as their oral history recalled, only other Indians and whites were considered adoptable. Like the colonists, the Cherokees considered Negroes to be an inferior and servile people.

As the Southern colonial population grew in size and affluence, colonists purchased additional black slaves to toil on their plantations. Consequently, they lived in fear of both Indians and blacks and envisioned the possibility of these dark-skinned races joining forces against them. Therefore, they sometimes deliberately attempted to create aversion, distrust, animosity, and fear between black and red men. Indians were sometimes employed to hunt runaway black slaves. Indian atrocities, especially toward runaway blacks, were vividly related to slaves. Colonists also informed Indians that Negroes carried dread diseases such as smallpox and measles. These efforts were consciously made to keep Indians and blacks apart. In the eighteenth century, legislation was enacted to prevent any Negro, slave or free, from going to any Indian tribe. Moreover, white traders were prohibited from taking slaves to the Indians for sale and were required to report Negroes residing among the Indians. Most of the early treaties between the colonial governments and the Cherokees contained provisions for the Indians to return any black slaves in their possession.

Some Cherokees were from time to time enslaved themselves, therefore self-interest encouraged their acceptance of the institution of black slavery among the European colonists. The colonists may have considered Indians and Negroes to be in the same category, but the Cherokees did not. They never considered the Negro to be on the same level with themselves, other Indians, or whites. The Cherokees always viewed blacks from the same perspective that the whites did.

The unrelenting westward movement by colonials was deeply resented by the Cherokees, who opposed the encroachment upon their lands by all means available to them, including force. Finally, tribal leadership reasoned that it was impossible to remain aloof from the white man's civilization and encouraged their brothers to accept those parts of European culture that would be beneficial to them. This acceptance included weapons, tools, clothing, education, Christianity, and a fundamental change in life-style. The Cherokees were forced to curtail hunting as they lost more and more of their land. Subsequently, they began to abandon communal village life and their communal farms for individual farming units.

The loss of hunting lands, acquisition of farm implements from the United States government, and knowledge of new and improved methods of horticulture taught by Indian agents and missionaries all encouraged Cherokees to become black slaveowners. Slavery had become an accepted institution in the Nation before the end of the seventeenth century. Both Cherokee men and women accepted black slavery with alacrity. There was never any effective organized or vocal abolitionist activity in the Nation.

The Cherokee policy of holding all land in common was advantageous to the planter and herdsman. Ample tillable acreage was always available. Land was free and any citizen could gain exclusive usage of any unclaimed acreage if it was not within a quarter-mile of a neighbor's land. If a planter became surrounded by his neighbors, he could start another farming operation at another location. Moreover, there was never any real estate, personal property, or any other regressive tax imposed. From the very beginning, Cherokees, like their American neighbors, gave prestigious names to their homes and plantations.

The first Cherokee plantation owners who exploited slave labor were men of power, prestige, and wealth. They emulated the southern planter's dress, architecture, and agriculture. It is not surprising that they also emulated the southern institution of black slavery. These influential men then served as models for other tribal members. Cherokees became Southerners by birth, marriage, economic ties, and life-style. The political, social, and cultural leadership of the Nation was gravitating toward the more progressive mixed-bloods, who were frequently large slaveholders. The ownership of slaves had become a mark of wealth and status in the tribe.

The Cherokees were already slaveowners when the first missionaries settled in their Nation. The missionaries accepted slavery and periodically borrowed or hired slaves. Some even became slaveowners. Cherokee slaveholders were among the earliest converts, staunchest supporters, and closest friends of the missionaries and the churches. This relationship continued throughout the era of black slavery. As slavery evolved into a moral and political issue that polarized the United States, it became a serious issue among New England supporters of missions in the Cherokee Nation. Governing boards were usually antislavery and opposed to missionaries owning or hiring slaves. Some board members were opposed to the admission of Cherokee slaveowners into their churches. Nevertheless, missionaries knew that to exclude slaveholders and to speak out against slavery would bring on expulsion from the Nation. Consequently, they frequently extolled the benevolence of Cherokee masters to their superiors. They contended that Cherokee slaves were treated much more humanely and performed much less labor than slaves in the southern states or industrial workers in the East.

As the institution of black slavery grew in size and importance, the Cherokees adopted a comprehensive slave code comparable in many respects to the control laws of the southern states. The laws were designed to preserve the slave mentality, protect against insurrection, control or expel free blacks, prevent miscegenation, and control virtually all personal and group activities of slaves. The Cherokees may have exhibited the strongest color prejudice of any Indians. As early as 1793, Little Turkey declared that Spaniards were not "real white people." Moreover, free blacks were always viewed with suspicion and distrust. They suffered social and legal discrimination. In the early 1840s all free blacks, except those manumitted by Cherokee masters, were ordered to leave the Nation.

The work activities of most Cherokee slaves were similar to those of their counterparts in the southern states. Agriculture consumed the time and energy of most slaves. They cleared and improved land, built fences, plowed land, planted, cultivated, and harvested crops of cotton, corn, and other commodities. They also tended livestock, milked, and rendered domestic service by cooking, waiting tables, cleaning, washing, sewing, weaving, gardening, making soap, preserving food, and grooming horses. Female slaves served as "mammies" and frequently taught their mistresses the operation of the card and spinning wheel. A few slaves were highly skilled artisans. These included wheelwrights, blacksmiths, midwives, millwrights, millers, carpenters, tanners, cobblers, masons, and physicians. Domestic manufacture was frequently an important slave activity, especially on the larger plantations. Beginning with raw materials, blacks produced tools, cloth, and other commodities. A small number of blacks was engaged in industrial slavery, including the operation of grist mills, saw mills, tanneries, salt works, ferries, and steam boats.

Living conditions of Cherokee slaves were also similar to those in the southern states. Most lived in windowless log huts with dirt floors and stick-and-mud chimneys. They usually did their own cooking from rations dispensed by the master or overseer. They usually had to carry passes when away from home, and wore the same type of clothing and ate the

same type of food as slaves in the South—although they did eat traditional
Cherokee dishes. Most slaves had no last names and some had never known
their parents. Black women worked in the fields, were whipped, and were
sometimes sold for refusing to become pregnant. Some slaves became
drivers and overseers, but only a very few were ever allowed to purchase
their freedom.

Slave families were sometimes separated by sale. Younger slaves were
called "boy" and "girl," and elderly slaves were known as "uncle" and
"aunt." There was a caste system in operation among the slaves, with the
trusted house servants and bilingual bodyguards and messengers at the
top, followed by the artisans, and then the field hands.

Some Cherokee slaves were treated relatively well while others received
more brutal treatment; some were even killed in fits of anger. Blacks sometimes reacted to their status by running away, exhibiting defiance, stealing,
and malingering. The runaways were frequently hunted with dogs. Punish-
ments usually included whipping, branding, and other disfigurement.
Stripes were the punishment meted out most often, however. Newspapers,
broadsides, and handbills were regularly used to advertise slave sales,
rewards for runaways, and marshalls' sales. Regular patrol companies
operated throughout parts of the Nation.

Virtually all the southern Indian superintendents and Cherokee agents
were proslavery Southerners. Some were slaveowners themselves and
firmly believed slavery to be a divine institution and a blessing to both
master and slave. Some agents brought their blacks to the Indian country.
Cherokee Agent George Butler even wanted to export black slavery to
the "wild" Plains Indians in an effort to "civilize" them. These officials
abhorred abolitionism and worked diligently to prevent its spread into the
Cherokee Nation. They prohibited the teaching of such sentiments among
Indians and often banished those suspected of violating their edicts. These
officials contributed to the myth of lenient treatment of slaves in their
official communications and annual reports.

Some differences between Cherokee slavery and the institution in the
southern states are discernible in the facts that within the Cherokee Nation
an underground railroad never operated, free blacks never owned slaves,
"slave trader" was not a pejorative term, slaves were probably used more
frequently as barter, slaves were used more extensively as interpreters and
business consultants, and many Cherokee slaves did not speak English.
Moreover, Cherokees never experienced the inner conflict between slaveowning and conscience, never felt the need to justify slavery morally,

never claimed slavery was in the best interest of blacks, and never gave voice to the "positive benefits" of Christianizing and civilizing their slaves. Slavery was justified solely on the basis of the benefits which accrued to masters. Yet, unlike the white community, there appears to be little or no feeling of guilt among Cherokees today.

The Keetowah Society, organized just before the Civil War, is often reported to have been antislavery. The society was organized under the direction of the Reverends John B. and Evan Jones, who indeed were abolitionists. The society was also developed to cultivate a nationalistic spirit among the full-bloods, oppose the innovating tendencies of the mixed-bloods, and counteract the influence of the "Blue Lodge," the Knights of the Golden Circle, and other secret secessionist organizations. The Keetowahs were both strongly pro-Union and staunch supporters of Principal Chief John Ross, who was one of the largest slaveowners in the Nation. The abolitionist sentiments of the Joneses did not necessarily transfer to the rank-and-file membership of the Keetowahs. It would probably be more correct to describe the organization as not being proslavery, rather than as being antislavery. Slavery had not been a political issue and there was no particular political base for abolitionism before the Civil War began. All political factions—the Old Settlers, the Treaty Party, and the Ross faction—contained numerous slaveowners in their leadership and in the rank and file.

It appears that the missionaries, Indian superintendents, and Cherokee agents were primarily responsible for creating a distorted image of black slavery within the tribe. Their communications and reports have frequently been cited in the limited literature on the subject. By far the most cited secondary source with regard to the benevolence of Cherokee slavery is Wiley Britton's *The Civil War on the Border,* published in 1891-1904. Britton claimed that Cherokee treatment of black slaves was so lenient that it rendered them undesirable in neighboring slave regions because of resulting discipline problems. Nevertheless, slave dealers from the neighboring slave regions regularly made trips through the Cherokee Nation to purchase slaves. Slave stealing was also a serious problem in the Nation. The kidnapping of slaves became one of the very few capital offences. The stolen slaves were usually taken to a neighboring slave state to be sold.

Black slavery took numerous forms among the different tribes and among individual owners within a tribe. Yet, slavery in the Cherokee Nation evolved into an institution that was a microcosm of slavery in the southern United States.

Appendix A

Very little personal information about Cherokee black slaves was ever recorded and most of that has since been lost or destroyed. There are a few extant sources, however. The following interviews conducted during the 1930s and found among the Foreman Papers in the Indian Archives and the Ex-Slaves File of the Oklahoma Historical Society are the best examples. These reminiscenses were recorded some seventy years after emancipation, however, and faulty memories too frequently tend to smooth the rough edges of history.

PHYLLIS PETITE

AGE 83
FORT GIBSON, OKLA.

I was born in Rusk County, Texas, on a plantation about eight miles east of Belleview. There wasn't no town where I was born, but they had a church.

My mammy and pappy belonged to a part Cherokee named W. P. Thompson when I was born. He had kinfolks in the Cherokee Nation, and we all moved up here to a place on Fourteen-Mile Creek close to where Hulbert now is, 'way before I was big enough to remember anything. Then, so I been told, old master Thompson sell my pappy and mammy and one of my baby brothers and me back to one of his neighbors in Texas name of John Harnage.

Mammy's name was Letitia Thompson and pappy's was Riley Thompson. My little brother was named Johnson Thompson, but I had another brother

sold to a Vann and he always call hisself Harry Vann. His Cherokee master
lived on the Arkansas River close to Webbers Falls and I never did know
him until we was both grown. My only sister was Patsy and she was borned
after slavery and died at Wagoner, Oklahoma.

I can just remember when Master John Harnage took us to Texas. We
went in a covered wagon with oxen and camped out all along the way.
Mammy done the cooking in big wash kettles and pappy done the driving
of the oxen. I would set in a wagon and listen to him pop his whip and
holler.

Master John took us to his plantation and it was a big one, too. You
could look from the field up to the Big House and any grown body in
the yard look like a little body, it was so far away.

We negroes lived in quarters not far from the Big House and ours was
a single log house with a stick and dirt chimney. We cooked over the hot
coals in the fireplace.

I just played around until I was about six years old I reckon, and then
they put me up at the Big House with my mammy to work. She done all
the cording and spinning and weaving, and I done a whole lot of sweeping
and minding the baby. The baby was only about six months old I reckon.
I used to stand by the cradle and rock it all day, and when I quit I would
go to sleep right by the cradle sometimes before mammy would come and
get me.

The Big House had great big rooms in front, and they was fixed up nice,
too. I remember when old Mistress Harnage tried me out sweeping up
the front rooms. They had two or three great big pictures of some old
people hanging on the wall. They was full blood Indians it look like, and
I was sure scared of them pictures! I would go here and there and every
which-a-way, and anywheres I go them big pictures always looking straight
at me and watching me sweep! I kept my eyes right on them so I could
run if they moved, and old Mistress take me back to the kitchen and say
I can't sweep because I miss all the dirt.

We always have good eating, like turnip greens cooked in a kettle with
hog skins and crackling grease, and skinned corn, and rabbit or possum
stew. I liked big fish tolerable well too, but I was afraid of the bones in
the little ones.

That skinned corn aint like the boiled hominy we have today. To make
it you boil some wood ashes, or have some drip lye from the hopper to
put in the hot water. Let the corn boil in the lye water until the skin drops
off and the eyes drop out and then wash that corn in fresh water about

a dozen times, or just keep carrying water from the spring until you are wore out, like I did. Then you put the corn in a crock and set it in the spring, and you got good skinned corn as long as it last, all ready to warm up a little batch at a time.

Master had a big, long log kitchen setting away from the house, and we set a big table for the family first, and when they was gone we negroes at the house eat at that table too, but we don't use the china dishes.

The negro cook was Tilda Chisholm. She and my mammy didn't do no outwork. Aunt Tilda sure could make them corn-dodgers. Us children would catch her eating her dinner first out of the kettles and when we say something she say: 'Go on child, I jest tasting that dinner.'

In the summer we had cotton homespun clothes, and in winter it had wool mixed in. They was dyed with copperas and wild indigo.

My brother, Johnson Thompson, would get up behind old Master Harnage on his horse and go with him to hunt squirrels so they would go 'round on Master's side so's he could shoot them. Master's old mare was named 'Old Willow', and she knowed when to stop and stand real still so he could shoot.

His children was just all over the place! He had two houses full of them! I only remember Bell, Ida, Maley, Mary and Will, but they was plenty more I don't remember.

That old horn blowed 'way before daylight, and all the field negroes had to be out in the row by the time of sun up. House negroes got up too, because old Master always up to see everybody get out to work.

Old Master Harnage bought and sold slaves most all the time, and some of the new negroes always acted up and needed a licking. The worst ones got beat up good, too! They didn't have no jail to put slaves in because when the Masters got done licking them they didn't need no jail.

My husband was George Petite. He tell me his mammy was sold away from him when he was a little boy. He looked down a long lane after her just as long as he could see her, and cried after her. He went down to the big road and set down by his mammy's barefooted tracks in the sand and set there until it got dark, and then he come on back to the quarters.

I just saw one slave try to get away right in hand. They caught him with bloodhounds and brung him back in. The hounds had nearly tore him up, and he was sick a long time. I don't remember his name, but he wasn't one of the old regular negroes.

In Texas we had a church where we could go. I think it was a white church and they just let the negroes have it when they got a preacher sometimes. My mammy took me sometimes, and she loved to sing them salvation songs.

We used to carry news from one plantation to the other I reckon, 'cause mammy would tell about things going on some other plantation and I know she never been there.

Christmas morning we always got some brown sugar candy or some molasses to pull, and we children was up bright and early to get that 'lasses pull. I tell you! And in the winter we played skeeting on the ice when the water frose over. No, I don't mean skating. That's when you got iron skates, and we didn't have them things. We just got a running start and jump on the ice and skeet as far as we could go, and then run some more.

I nearly busted my head open, and brother Johnson said: 'Try it again,' but after that I was scared to skeet any more.

Mammy say we was down in Texas to get away from the War, but I didn't see any war and any soldiers. But one day old Master stay after he eat breakfast and when us negroes come in to eat he say: 'After today I ain't your master any more. You all as free as I am.' We just stand look and don't know what to say about it.

After while pappy got a wagon and some oxen to drive for a white man who was coming to the Cherokee Nation because he had folks here. His name was Dave Mounts and he had a boy named John.

We come with them and stopped at Fort Gibson where my own grand mammy was cooking for the soldiers at the garrison. Her name was Phyllis Brewer and I was named after her. She had a good Cherokee master. My mammy was born on his place.

We stayed with her about a week and then we moved out on Four Mile Creek to live. She died on Fourteen-Mile Creek about a year later.

When we first went to Four Mile Creek I seen negro women chopping wood and ask them who they work for and I found out they didn't know they was free yet.

After a while my pappy and mammy both died, and I was took care of by my aunt Elsie Vann. She took my brother Johnson too, but I don't know who took Harry Vann.

I was married to George Petite, and I had on a white underdress and black high-top shoes, and a large cream colored hat, and on top of all I had a blue wool dress with tassels all around the bottom of it. That dress was for me to eat the terrible supper in. That what we called the wedding supper because we eat too much of it. Just dances all night, too! I was at Mandy Foster's house in Fort Gibson, and the preacher was Reverend Barrows. I had that dress a long time, but it is gone now. I still got the little sun bonnet I wore to church in Texas.

We had six children, but all are dead but George, Tish, and Annie now.

Yes, they tell me Abraham Lincoln set me free, and I love to look at his picture on the wall in the school house at Four Mile branch where they have church. My grand mammy kind of help start that church, and I think everybody ought to belong to some church.

I want to say again my Master Harnage was Indian, but he was a good man and mighty good to us slaves, and you can see I am more than six feet high and they say I weighs over a hundred and sixty, even if my hair is snow white.

NANCY ROGERS BEAN

AGE ABOUT 82
HULBERT, OKLA.

I'm getting old and it's easy to forget most of the happenings of slave days: anyway I was too little to know much about them, for my mammy told me I was born about six years before the War. My folks was on their way to Fort Gibson, and on the trip I was born at Boggy Depot, down in southern Oklahoma.

There was a lot of us children; I got their names somewhere here. Yes, there was George, Sarah, Emma, Stella, Sylvia, Lucinda, Rose, Dan, Pamp, Jeff, Austin, Jessie, Isaac and Andrew; we all lived in a one-room log cabin on Master Rogers' place not far from the old military road near Choteau. Mammy was raised around the Cherokee town of Tahlequah.

I got my name from the Rogers', but I was loaned around to their relatives most of the time. I helped around the house for Bill McCracken, then I was with Cornelius and Carline Wright, and when I was freed my Mistress was a Mrs. O'Neal, wife of a officer at Fort Gibson. She treated me the best of all and gave me the first doll I ever had. It was a rag doll with charcoal eyes and red thread worked in for the mouth. She allowed me one hour every day to play with it. When the War ended Mistress O'Neal wanted to take me with her to Richmond, Virginia, but my people wouldn't let me go. I wanted to stay with her, she was so good, and she promised to come back for me when I get older, but she never did.

All the time I was at the Fort I hear the bugles and see the soldiers marching around, but never did I see any battles. The fighting must have been too far away.

Master Rogers kept all our family together, but my folks have told me about how the slaves was sold. One of my aunts was a mean, fighting woman. She was to be sold and when the bidding started she grabbed a hatchet, laid her hand on a log and chopped it off. Then she throwed the bleeding hand right in her master's face. Not long ago I hear she is still living in the country around Nowata, Oklahoma.

Sometimes I would try to get mean, but always I got me a whipping for it. When I was a little girl, moving around from one family to another, I done housework, ironing, peeling potatoes and helping the main cook. I went barefoot most of my life, but the Master would get his shoes from the government at Fort Gibson.

I wore cotton dresses, and the Mistress wore long dresses, with different colors for Sunday clothes, but we slaves didn't know much about Sunday in a religious way. The Master had a brother who used to preach to the negroes on the sly. One time he was caught and the Master whipped him something awful.

Years ago I married Joe Bean. Our children died as babies. Twenty years ago Joe Bean and I separated for good and all.

The good Lord knows I'm glad slavery is over. Now I can stay peaceful in one place—that's all I aim to do.

VICTORIA TAYLOR THOMPSON

AGE 80
MUSKÓGEE, OKLAHOMA

My mother, Judy Taylor, named for her mistress, told me that I was born about three year before the war; that make me about 80 year old, so they say down at the Indian Agency where my name is on the Cherokee rolls since all the land was give to the Indian families a long time ago.

Father kept the name of 'Doc' Hayes, and my brother Coose was a Hayes too, but mother Jude, Patsy, Bonaparte (Boney, we always called him), Lewis and me was always Taylors. Daddy was bought by the Taylors (Cherokee Indians); they made a trade for him with some hilly land, but he kept the name of Hayes even then.

Like my mother, I was born on the Taylor place. They lived in Flint District, around the Caney settlement on Caney Creek. Lots of the Arkansas Cherokees come here from the east, my mother said.

The farm wasn't very big, we was the only slaves on the place, and it was just a little ways from a hill everybody called Sugar Mountain, because it was covered with maple sugar trees, an old Indian lived on the hillside, making maple sugar candy to sell and trade.

Master Taylor's house had three big rooms and a room for the loom, all made of logs, with a long front porch high off the ground. The spring house set to the east, in the corner like. Spring water boiled up all the time, and the water run down the branch which we crossed on a log bridge.

On the north side of the front porch, under a window in the mistress' room, was the grave of her little boy who was found drowned in the spring. The mistress set a heap of store by that child; said she wanted him buried right where she could always see his grave. She was mighty good.

So was the master good, too. None of us was ever beat or whipped like I hear about other slaves. They fix up a log cabin for us close by the big house. The yard fenced high with five or six rails, and there was an apple orchard that set off the place with its blooming in the spring days.

Mother worked in the fields and in the house. She would hoe and plow, milk and do the cooking. She was a good cook and made the best corn bread I ever eat. Cook it in a skillet in the fireplace—I likes a piece of it right now! Grub these days don't taste the same. Sometime after the war she cook for the prisoners in the jail at Tahlequah.

That was the first jail I ever saw; they had hangings there. Always on a Friday, but I never see one, for it scare me and I run and hide.

Well, mother leave us children in the cabin while she gets breakfast for the master. We'd be nearly starved before she get back to tend us. And we slept on the floor, but the big house had wood beds, with high boards on the head and foot.

Mother took me with her to weaving room, and the mistress learn me how to weave in the stripes and colors and shades. She ask me the color and I never miss telling her. That's one thing my sister Patsy can't learn when she was a little girl. I try the knitting, but I drop the stitches and lay it down.

Some of the things mother made was cloth socks and fringe for the hunting shirt that daddy always wore. The mistress made long tail shirts for the boys; we wore cotton all the year, and the first shoes I ever saw was brass toed brogans.

For sickness daddy give us tea and herbs. He was a herb doctor, that's how come he have the name 'Doc.' He made us wear charms, made out of shiny buttons and Indian rock beads. They cured lots of things and the misery too.

I hear mother tell about the slaves running away from mean masters, and how she help hide them at night from the dogs that come trailing them. The high fence keep out the dogs from the yard, and soon's they leave the runoffs would break for the river (Illinois), cross over and get away from the dogs.

The master had a mill run by oxen, the same oxen used in the fields. They stepped on the pedals and turn the rollers, that how it was done.

There was another mill in the hills run by a white man name of Uncle Mosie. One day he stole me to live in a cabin with him. He branded a circle on my cheek, but in two days I got away and run back to the Taylors where I was safe.

When the war broke out my daddy went on the side of the South with Master Taylor. They was gone a long time and when they come back he told of fighting the Federals north of Fort Gibson (it may have been the battle of Locust Grove), and how the Federals drove them off like dogs. He said most of the time the soldiers starved and suffered, some of them freezing to death. After the war I was stole again. I was hired to Judge Wolfe and his wife Mary took good care of me and I helped her around the big two-story house. She didn't like my father and kept him off the place. One day an Indian, John Prichett, told me my daddy wanted to see me down by the old barn, to follow him. He grabbed me when we got back of the barn and took me away to his place where my daddy was waiting for me. We worked for that Indian to pay for him getting me away from Judge Wolfe. That was around Fort Gibson.

That's where I married William Thompson, an uncle of Johnson Thompson, who was born a slave and lives now on Four Mile Branch (near Hulbert, Okla.) There was seven boys; where they is I don't know, except for my boy George Lewis Thompson, who lives in this four-room house he builds for us, and stays unmarried so's he can take care of his old mammy.

I been belonging to church ever since there was a colored church, and I thinks everybody should obey the Master. He died, and I wants to go where Jesus lives. Like the poor Indian I saw one time waiting to be hung. There he was, setting on his own coffin box, singing over and over the words I just said: 'I wants to go where Jesus lived!'

There's one things before I go. My time is short and I wants to go back to the Taylor place, to my old mistress' place, and just see the ground where she use to walk—that's what I most want, but time is short.

JOHNSON THOMPSON

AGE 84
FORT GIBSON, OKLAHOMA

Just about two weeks before the coming of Christmas Day in 1835, I was born on a plantation somewheres eight miles east of Bellview, Rusk County, Texas. One year later my sister Phyllis was born on the same place and we been together pretty much of the time ever since, and I reckon there's only one thing that could separate us slave born children.

Mammy and pappy belong to W. P. Thompson, mixed-blood Cherokee Indian, but before that pappy had been owned by three different masters; one was the rich Joe Vann who lived down at Webbers Falls and another was Chief Lowrey of the Cherokees. I had a brother named Harry who belonged to the Vann family at Tahlequah. There was a sister named Patsy; she died at Wagoner, Oklahoma. My mother was born 'way back in the hills of the old Flint District of the Cherokee Nation; just about where Scraper, Okla., is now.

My parents are both dead now—seems like fifty, maybe sixty year ago. Mammy died in Texas, and when we left Rusk County after the Civil War, pappy took us children to the graveyard. We patted her grave and kissed the ground . . . telling her goodbye. Pappy is buried in the church yard on Four Mile Branch.

I don't remember much about my pappy's mother; but I remember she would milk for a man named Columbus Balredge, and she went to prayer meeting every Wednesday night. Sometimes us children would try to follow her, but she'd turn us around pretty quick and chase us back with: 'Go on back to the house or the wolves'll get you.'

Master Thompson brought us from Texas when I was too little to remember about it, and I don't know how long it was before we was all sold to John Harnage; 'Marse John' was his pet name and he liked to be called that-a-way. He took us back to Texas, right down near where I was born at Bellview.

The master's house was a big log building setting east and west, with a porch on the north side of the house. The slave cabins was in a row, and we lived in one of them. It had no windows, but it had a wood floor that was kept clean with plenty of brushings, and a fireplace where mammy'd cook the turnip greens and peas and corn—I still likes the cornbread with finger-prints baked on it, like in the old days when it was cooked in a skillet over the hot wood ashes. I eat from a big pan and set on the floor—there was no chairs—and I slept in a trundle bed that was pushed under the big bed in the daytime.

I spent happy days on the Harnage Plantation; going squirrel hunting with the master—he always riding, while I run along and throw rocks in the trees to scare the squirrels so's Marse John could get the aim on them; pick a little cotton and put it in somebody's hamper (basket), and run races with other colored boys to see who would get to saddle the master's horse, while the master would stand laughing by the gate to see which boy won the race.

Our clothes was home-made—cotton in the summer, mostly just a long-tailed shirt and no shoes, and wool goods in the winter. Mammy was the house girl and she weaved the cloth and my Aunt 'Tilda dyed the cloth with wild indigo, leaving her hands blue looking most of the time. Mammy work late in the night, and I hear the loom making noises while I try to sleep in the cabin. Pappy was the shoe-maker and he used wooden pegs of maple to fashion the shoes.

The master had a bell to ring every morning at four o'clock for the folks to turn out. Sometimes the sleep was too deep and somebody would be late, but the master never punish anybody, and I never see anybody whipped and only one slave sold.

Pappy wanted to go back to his mother when the War was over and the slaves was freed. He made a deal with Dave Mounts, a white man, who was moving into the Indian country, to drive for him. A four-mule team was hitched to the wagon, and for five weeks we was on the road from Texas, finally getting to grandmaw Brewers at Fort Gibson. Pappy worked around the farms and fiddled for the Cherokee dances.

Then I went to a subscription school for a little while, but didn't get much learning. Lots of the slave children didn't ever learn to read or write. And we learned something about religion from an old colored preacher named Tom Vann. He would sing for us, and I'd like to hear them old songs again!

The first time I married was to Clara Nevens, and I wore checked wool pants and a blue striped cotton shirt. There come six children; Charley, Alec, Laura, Harry, Richard and Jeffy, who was named after Jefferson Davis. The second time I married a cousin, Rela Brewer.

Jefferson Davis was a great man, but I think Roosevelt is greater than Davis or Abraham Lincoln.

ROCHELLE ALLRED WARD

AGE 91
FORT GIBSON, OKLA.

My maw, Lottie Beck, was belonging to old master Joe Beck when I was born, about 1847, on the Beck farm in Flint District of the old Cherokee Nation. That is a mighty long time ago and lots of things my old mind won't remember, but I never forget the old Beck mill place because I done many a cooking there and watch the mill grind up the corn and wheat for the Indians' meal and flour.

Before I tell about the mill I want to tell about paw; Jim, he was named, and belong to Sarah Eaton, who must have stole him when he about eight or nine year old from his folks in Georgia and brought him out here, maybe to Fort Gibson near as he could tell. That make paw born about 1827 because he was a young man grown to full grown when he meet my maw.

He come to the mill place for his mistress, that the way he always tell about it, and the only girl he see right off was Lottie, one of the Beck slave girls, but they was lots more on the place, only he could see no one but Lottie and fall in love with her. She feel the same way about him; she asked old Master Joe to buy Jim Eaton so's they can marry, and build a cabin.

Master Joe want to know if the young slave a good worker, and when Jim Eaton say, 'I is the best cane stripper and field man in the whole country,' the master offer Sarah Eaton $500 for her slave boy and that done bought him. So he come to the Becks, change his name to Jim Beck and keept it ever since.

My paw always told me he was part Indian account of his mamma was a Cherokee Indian girl name Downing; that make my paw some kin to Chief Downing who was a big man among the Cherokees after the Civil War when the Indians stop fighting amongst themselves.

Two of my sisters, Sabra and Celia, was both real light in color, but my brothers was all dark. They was named Milton, Nelson and Dennis.

Well, the old mill had done been built by some of the Becks when they first come out to this country a long time before I was born. Some of Master Joe's kin they was; all over this country was Beck families, but other folks come in here too, and one of them new settlers run the old mill for awhile until he died. I hear his name when I was a young girl, seem like it was Hildebrand; different from all them Indian names anyways.

We all done move away from the mill place during the war, but bad things happen around the old place after the war and I hear it the way folks tell about it then.

When the old miller die his wife marry one of the men who work in the mill, but an Indian name Zeke Proctor work up a grudge for the woman's husband and fix up to kill him. When the Indian come to the mill and start a ruckus with the man, his wife mix in and get shot. Seem like she jump in front of the Indian when he try to shoot and get the bullet herself. She died and that cause lots more trouble, and it was a long time before it was settled and folks stop killing each other.

After my paw come with the Becks they make him a kind of overseer. There was several families living in the little log cabins on the farm, and all these slave families look to my paw for the way to do things. The mistress say, 'whatever Jim do is all right.' She trusted him cause she saw he was a good worker and would do the right thing.

None of the Beck slaves was sold, but paw said he seen slaves sold off. He told us children, that was after the war, "we was all good Negroes, and that's why the Becks keep us. And we ought to be glad, because I see sorrow at the auctions, and crying, when the mother sold off from her child, or when the child is took away from her."

The mistress always get us anything we need, even after the war, and she come down to where we live around Fort Gibson, and bring cloth for our dresses and help make them, and one time she said she was going to bring her old Bible down for paw to get all the children's ages, but she died before she could get back the next spring.

Some of the slaves work around and get money and pay this money to their master for freedom, so there was some freed before the close of the war. Some others try to run away after the war start, and maybe they get caught, like the one man who hide in a house around the old mill. Some said he was a freedman, too, but anyways some of the Confederates

find him in the old house, take him off to Texas and sell him. They got
a big price for him, $5,000 they said, but it was Confederate money and
that kind of money got worthless as a cotton patch without no hoeing.

But the patrollers didn't bother nobody with a pass and when anybody
leave the Beck place it was with a pass. But lots of slaves was stole and
the masters fix up to get their slaves out of the hills and take them to
Fort Gibson for safety. The Confederate soldiers was there then (1862).

The mistress was getting old and she cried terrible when all the slaves
leave in the night for the fort. Everybody loaded in the ox wagons, hating
to leave the mistress, but they all have to go.

We camped around the garrison place at Fort Gibson and there was no
buildings there like there is now. The soldiers was all camped there in
tents. They was all Confederate soldiers and I mean there was lots of
soldiers camped in the tents.

The Negroes piled in there from everywheres, and I mean there was
lots of them, too. Cooking in the open, sleeping most anywhere, making
shelter places out of cloth scraps and brush, digging caves along the river
bank to live in. There was no way to keep the place clean for there was
too many folks living all in one place and if you walk around in the night-
time most likely you stumble over some Negro rolled up in a dirty blanket
and sleeping under a bush.

I never was where the fighting went on, but I heard the cannon go
"Bum! Bum!" and the little guns go "Bang!" in all directions. I seen the
soldiers come in after the fights; they be all shot up with blood soaking
through the clothes, trying to help each other tie on a bannage—the
awfulest sights I ever see.

The generals have some young boys, I guess they was soldiers, herding
the horses a little way south of the fort. Then one day a scout come riding
in and yell, "The Federals is coming!" All the soldiers run for the horses
and gallop out for the mountain south from the fort. I hear that fighting,
gun speaking in the hills, and the Federals was whipped. Lots of them
killed and some of them captured and brought back to the fort, and
some got away.

Some folks say that while the war is on the Federals take charge of the
old Beck mill. Guess they stole the grain too, for to make meal, anyway
they kept the soldiers in food when the other folks was starving. They
captured one of the Confederate boys and made him run the mill.

Master Joe Beck died during the war by a horse kick, and after the war everything so upsettled that folks don't know what to do. For awhile we lived on Carroll Branch near Fort Gibson and I nursed around first one family and another.

Then come a time of cholera; people die all that season, and the dead— seem like they pass and pass all the time—was carried on little two-wheeled wagons pulled by a mule to a burying place out near the National Cemetery. Slaves was buried back in the woods to the north.

The Federals tried to catch the cholera germs. They kill beefs, hung the pieces high up in the air, leave the meat for days and days out in the open—say it catch the germs, but I don't know.

Mostly in my coming-up time we didn't know what doctering was. Some of the older men and women use to dig roots and get different herbs for medicine; them medicines cure the chill fever and such.

When I married Amos Allred, a State man from Freeport, Texas, more than seventy year ago, we had to get signers before old Judge Walker at Fort Gibson could say the words. I get seven signers, all of them Cherokee Indians who know I was a good slave woman. We divorced a long time later and I married a State man from Mississippi, Nelson Ward. There was thirteen children, but I done forget all the names; some was, Amos, Susie, Jess, Will, Frank, Lottie, Cora.

CHARLOTTE JOHNSON WHITE

AGE 88
FORT GIBSON, OKLAHOMA

Near as I ever know, I was born in the year of 1850, away back in the hills east of Tahlequah; the Cherokee folks called it the Flint District and old master Ben Johnson lived somewheres about ten miles east of the big Indian town, Tahlequah. Never did know just where his farm was, and when the new towns of the country spring up it make it that much harder for me to figure out just where he lived and where at I was born.

Don't know much about own folks either, 'ceptin' that my mother's name was Elasey Johnson and my pappy's name was Banjo Lastley, who one time lived 'round where Lenapah now is. There was one brother name of Turner Whitmire Johnson, and a half sister name of Jennie Miller

Lastley, who is still living down in Muskogee, but brother Turner been dead most 40 year ago I guess. Pappy was belonging to another master, that's how come my folks' name was different, but I kept the old Johnson name, even though the old master was the meanest kind of a man.

His wife, Mistress Anna, died when one of the children was born; maybe that's why he was so mean, just worried all the time. The master lived in a double log house, with a double fireplace in the middle of two rooms, and I was one of the girls who stayed in the house to take care of the children. How many children they had I never remember and I don't remember the names, but they was all pretty mean, like the master and the overseer that drive the folks who work in the field.

The cabin where I live with my mother was a two-room log house having two doors that open right into the yard. There was no gallery on the slave cabins and no windows, so the corners of the rooms get dark early and sometime I get pretty scared before mother got in from the fields in the evening. She be gone all the day and always leave me a big baked sweet potato on the board above the fireplace and then I eat about noon for my dinner.

That was before I got big enough to work in the master's house and take care of the children. She always work in the fields; she was sick all the time, but that didn't keep her out of the fields or the garden work. Sometimes she be so sick she could barely get out of the old wood bunk when the morning work call sound on the farm.

One day my mother couldn't get up and the old master come around to see about it, and he yelled, 'Get out of here and get yourself in the fields.' She tried to go but was too sick to work. She got to the door alright; couldn't hurry fast enough for the old master though, so he pushed her in a little ditch that was by the cabin and whipped her back with the lash, then he reached down and rolled her over so's he could beat her face and neck. She didn't live long after that and I guess the whippings helped to kill her, but she better off dead than just living for the whip.

Time I was twelve year old I was tendin' the master's children like what they tell me to do, and then one day somehow I drop one of them right by where the old master was burning some brush in the yard. 'What you do that for?' he yelled, and while I was stopping to pick up the baby he grabbed me and shoved me into the fire! I went into that fire head first, but I never know how I got out. See this old scarred face? That's what I got from the fire, and inside my lips is burned off, and my back is scarred with lashings that'll be with me when I meet my Jesus!

Them things help me remember about the slave days and how once when I got sick of being treated mean by everybody after mother died, I slipped off in the woods to get away and wandered 'round 'till I come to a place folks said was Scullyville. On the way I eat berries and chew bark from the trees, and one feed I got from some colored people on the way.

But the old master track me down and there I is back at the old farm for more whippings. Then I was give away to my Aunt Easter Johnson, but she was a mean woman—mean to everybody. She had a boy six year old. That boy got to crying one day and she grabbed up a big club and beat her own child to death. Then she laughed about it! Like she was crazy, I guess. And the only thing was done to her was a locking up in the chicken house, ending up with a salt and pepper whipping.

All the slaves wore cotton clothes in the summer, wool jackets in the winter and brass-toed shoes made from the hide of some old cow that wasn't no good milker anymore. I lost the first pair of shoes they give me and had to go barefoot all the winter. Out in a thicket I had seen a rabbit so I started after it, but took my shoes and set them down so's I could sneak up without making noise. Then I miss the rabbit and go back for the shoes but they was nowhere I could find them. When Master Johnson find out the shoes was lost I got another whipping.

I hear about the slaves being free when maybe a hundred soldiers come to the house. They was a pretty sight settin' on the horses, and the men had on blue uniforms with little caps. 'All the slaves is free' one of the men said, and after that I just told everybody, 'I is a free Negro now and I ain't goin' to work for nobody!'

A long time after the war is over and everybody is free of the masters, I get down to Muldrow, Okla., and that's where I join the church. For 58 year I belong to the colored Baptists and I learn that everybody ought to be good while they is living so's they will have a better restin' place when they die.

In 1891, I met a good man, Randolph White, and we got married. I still got some of the pieces or scraps of my weddin' dress, a cotton dress it was, with lots of colors printed on it—with colors like the Indians use to wear.

SARAH WILSON

AGE 87
FORT GIBSON, OKLA.

I was a Cherokee slave and now I am a Cherokee freedwoman, and besides that I am a quarter Cherokee my own self. And this is the way it is.

I was born in 1850 along the Arkansas river about half way between Fort Smith and old Fort Coffee and the Skullyville boat landing on the river. The farm place was on the north side of the river on the old wagon road what run from Fort Smith out to Fort Gibson, and that old road was like you couldn't hardly call a road when I first remember seeing it. The ox teams bog down to they bellies in some places, and the wagon wheel mighty nigh bust on the big rocks in some places.

I remember seeing soldiers coming along that old road lots of times, and freighting wagons, and wagons what we all know carry whiskey, and that was breaking the law, too! Them soldiers catch the man with the whiskey they sure put him up for a long time, less'n he put some silver in they hands. That's what my Uncle Nick say. That Uncle Nick a mean Negro, and he ought to know about that.

Like I tell you, I am a quarter Cherokee. My mammy was named Adeline and she belong to old Master Ben Johnson. Old Master Ben bring my grandmammy out to that Sequoyah district way back when they call it Arkansas, mammy tell me, and God only know who my mammy's pa is, but mine was Old Master Ben's boy, Ned Johnson.

Old Master Ben come from Tennessee when he was still a young man, and he bring a whole passel of slaves and my mammy say they all was kin to one another, all the slaves I mean. He was a white man that married a Cherokee woman, and he was a devil on this earth. I don't want to talk about him none.

White folks was mean to us like the devil, and so I just let them pass. When I say my brothers and sisters I mean my half brothers and sisters, you know, but maybe some of them was my whole kin anyways, I don't know. They was Lottie that was sold off to a Starr because she wouldn't have a baby, and Ed, Dave, Ben, Jim and Ned.

My name is Sarah now but it was Annie until I was eight years old. My old Mistress' name was Annie and she name me that, and Mammy was afraid to change it until old Mistress died, then she change it. She hate old Mistress and that name too.

Lottie's name was Annie, too, but Mammy changed it in her own mind but she was afraid to say it out loud, a-feared she would get a whipping. When sister was sold off Mammy tell her to call herself Annie when she was leaving but call herself Lottie when she get over to the Starrs. And she done it too. I seen her after that and she was called Lottie all right.

The Negroes lived all huddled up in a bunch in little one-room log cabins with stick and mud chimneys. We lived in one, and it had beds for us children like shelves in the wall. Mammy used to help us up into them.

Grandmammy was mighty old and mistress was old too. Grandmammy set on the Master's porch and minded the baby mostly. I think it was Young Master's. He was married to a Cherokee girl. They was several of the boys but only one girl, Nicie. The old Master's boys were Aaron, John, Ned, Cy and Nathan. They lived in a double log house made out of square hewed logs, and with a double fireplace out of rock where they warmed theirselves on one side and cooked on the other. They had a long front porch where they set most of the time in the summer, and slept on it too.

There was over a hundred acres in the Master's farm, and it was all bottom land too, and maybe you think he let them slaves off easy! Work from daylight to dark! They all hated him and the overseer too, and before slavery ended my grandmammy was dead and old Mistress was dead and old Master was might feeble and Uncle Nick had run away to the North soldiers and they never got him back. He run away once before, about ten years before I was born, Mammy say, but the Cherokees went over in the Creek Nation and got him back that time.

The way he made the Negroes work so hard, old Master must have been trying to get rich. When they wouldn't stand for a whipping he would sell them.

I saw him sell a old woman and her son. Must have been my aunt. She was always pestering around trying to get something for herself, and one day she was cleaning the yard he seen her pick up something and put it inside her apron. He flew at her and cussed her, and started like he was going to hit her but she just stood right up to him and never budged, and when he come close she just screamed out loud and run at him with her fingers stuck out straight and jabbed him in the belly. He had a big soft belly, too, and it hurt him. He seen she wasn't going to be afraid, and he set out to sell her. He went off on his horse to get some men to come and bid on her and her boy, and all us children was mighty scared about it.

They would have hangings at Fort Smith courthouse, and old Master would take a slave there sometimes to see the hangings, and that slave would come back and tell us all scary stories about the hanging.

One time he whipped a whole bunch of the men on account of a fight in the quarters, and then he took them all to Fort Smith to see a hanging. He tied them all in the wagon, and when they had seen the hanging he asked them if they was scared of them dead men hanging up there. They all said yes, of course, but my old uncle Nick was a bad Negro and he said, 'No, I aint a-feared of them nor nothing else in this world', and old Master jumped on him while he was tied and beat him with a rope, and then when they got home he tied old Nick to a tree and took his shirt off and poured the cat-o-nine tails to him until he fainted away and fell over like he was dead.

I never forget seeing all that blood all over my uncle, and if I could hate that old Indian any more I guess I would, but I hated him all I could already I reckon.

Old Master wasn't the only hellion neither. Old Mistress just as bad, and she took most of her wrath out hitting us children all the time. She was afraid of the grown Negroes. Afraid of what they might do while old Master was away, but she beat us children all the time.

She would call me, 'Come here Annie!' and I wouldn't know what to do. If I went when she called 'Annie' my mammy would beat me for answering to that name, and if I didn't go old Mistress would beat me for that. That made me hate both of them, and I got the devil in me and I wouldn't come to either one. My grandmammy minded the Master's yard, and she set on the front porch all the time, and when I was called I would run to her and she wouldn't let anybody touch me.

When I was eight years old Mistress died, and Grandmammy told me why old Mistress picked on me so. She told me about me being half Mister Ned's blood. Then I knowed why Mister Ned would say, 'Let her along, she got big big blood in her', and then laugh.

Young Mister Ned was a devil, too. When his mammy died he went out and 'blanket married.' I mean he brung in a half white and half Indian woman and just lived with her.

The slaves would get rations every Monday morning to do them all week. The overseer would weigh and measure according to how many in the family, and if you run out you just starve till you get some more. We all know the overseer steal some of it for his own self but we can't do anything, so we get it from the old Master some other way.

One day I was carrying water from the spring and I run up on Grandmammy and Uncle Nick skinning a cow. 'What you-all doing?', I say, and they say keep my mouth shut or they kill me. They was stealing from the Master to piece out down at the quarters with. Old Master had so many cows he never did count the difference.

I guess I wasn't any worse than any the rest of the Negroes, but I was bad to tell little lies. I carry scars on my legs to this day where Old Master whip me for lying, with a raw hide quirt he carry all the time for his horse. When I lie to him he just jump down off'n his horse and whip me good right there.

In slavery days we all ate sweet potatoes all the time. When they didn't measure out enough of the tame kind we would go out in the woods and get the wild kind. They growed along the river sand between where we lived and Wilson's Rock, out west of our place.

Then we had boiled sheep and goat, mostly goat, and milk and wild greens and corn pone. I think the goat meat was the best, but I ain had no teeth for forty years now, and a chunk of meat hurts my stomach. So I just eats grits mostly. Besides hoeing in the field, chopping sprouts, shearing sheep, carrying water, cutting firewood, picking cotton and sewing I was the one they picked to work Mistress' little garden where she raised things from seed they got in Fort Smith. Green peas and beans and radishes and things like that. If we raised a good garden she give me a little of it, and if we had a poor one I got a little anyhow even when she didn't give it.

For clothes we had homespun cotton all the year round, but in winter we had a sheep skin jacket with the wool left on the inside. Sometimes sheep skin shoes with the wool on the inside and sometimes real cow leather shoes with wood peggings for winter, but always barefooted in summer, all the men and women too.

Lord, I never earned a dime of money in slave days for myself but plenty for the old Master. He would send us out to work the neighbors field and he got paid for it, but we never did see any money.

I remember the first money I ever did see. It was a little while after we was free, and I found a greenback in the road at Fort Gibson and I didn't know what it was. Mammy said it was money and grabbed for it, but I was still a hell cat and I run with it. I went to the little sutler store and laid it down and pointed to a pitcher I been wanting. The man took the money and give me the pitcher, but I don't know to this day how much money it was and how much was the pitcher, but I still got that pitcher put away. It's all blue and white stripedy.

Most of the work I done off the plantation was sewing. I learned from my Granny and I loved to sew. That was about the only thing I was industrious in. When I was just a little bitsy girl I found a steel needle in the yard that belong to old Mistress. My mammy took it and I cried. She put it in her dress and started for the field. I cried so old Mistress found out why and made Mammy give me the needle for my own.

We had some neighbor Indians named Starr, and Mrs. Starr used me sometimes to sew. She had nine boys and one girl, and she would sew up all they clothes at once to do for a year. She would cut out the cloth for about a week, and then send the word around to all the neighbors, and old Mistress would send me because she couldn't see good to sew. They would have stacks of drawers, shirts, pants and some dresses all cut out to sew up.

I was the only Negro that would set there and sew in that bunch of women, and they always talked to me nice and when they eat I get part of it too, out in the kitchen.

One Negro girl, Eula Davis, had a mistress sent her too, one time, but she wouldn't sew. She didn't like me because she said I was too white and she played off to spite the white people. She got sent home, too.

When old Mistress die I done all the sewing for the family almost. I could sew good enough to go out before I was eight years old, and when I got to be about ten I was better than any other girl on the place for sewing.

I can still quilt without my glasses, and I have sewed all night long many a time while I was watching young Master's baby after old Mistress died.

They was over a hundred acres in the plantation, and I don't know how many slaves, but before the War ended lots of the men had run away. Uncle Nick went to the North and never come home, and Grandmammy died about that time.

We was way down across the Red River in Texas at that time, close to Shawneetown of the Choctaw Nation but just across the river on the other side in Texas bottoms. Old Master took us there in covered wagons when the Yankee soldiers got too close by in the first part of the War. He hired the slaves out to Texas people because he didn't make any crops down there, and we all lived in kind of camps. That's how some of the men and my uncle Nick got to slip off to the north that way.

Old Master just rent and rave all the time we was in Texas. That's the first time I ever saw a doctor. Before that when a slave sick the old woman give them herbs, but down there one day old Master whip a Negro girl and she fall in the fire, and he had a doctor come out to fix her up where she was burnt. I remember Granny giving me clabber milk when I was sick, and when I was grown I found out it had had medicine in it.

Before freedom we didn't have no church, but slipped around to the other cabins and had a little singing sometimes. Couldn't have anybody show us the letters either, and you better not let them catch you pick up a book even to look at the pictures, for it was against a Cherokee law to have a Negro read and write or to teach a Negro.

Some Negroes believed in buckeyes and charms but I never did. Old Master had some good boys, named Aaron, John, Ned, Cy and Nat and they told me the charms was no good. Their sister Nicie told me too, and said when I was sick just come and tell her.

They didn't tell us anything about Christmas and New Year though, and all we done was work.

When the War was ended we was still in Texas, and when old Master got a letter from Fort Smith telling him the slaves was free he couldn't read, and young Miss read it to him. He went wild and jumped on her and beat the devil out of her. Said she was lying to him. It near about killed him to let us loose, but he cooled down after awhile and said he would help us all get back home if we wanted to come.

Mammy told him she could bear her own expenses. I remember I didn't know what 'expenses' was, and I thought it was something I was going to have to help carry all the way back.

It was a long time after he knew we was free before he told us. He tried to keep us, I reckon, but had to let us go. He died pretty soon after he told us, and some said his heart just broke and some said some Negroes poisoned him. I didn't know which.

Anyways we had to straggle back the best way we could, and me and mammy just got along one way and another till we got to a ferry over the Red River and into Arkansas. Then we got some rides and walked some until we got to Fort Smith. They was a lot of Negro camps there and we stayed awhile and then started out to Fort Gibson because we heard they was giving rations out there. Mammy knew we was Cherokee anyway, I guess.

That trip was hell on earth. Nobody let us ride and it took us nearly two weeks to walk all that ways, and we nearly starved all the time. We was skin and bones and feet all bloody when we got to the Fort.

We come here to Four Mile Branch to where the Negroes was all setting down, and pretty soon Mammy died.

I married Oliver Wilson on January second, 1878. He used to belong to Mr. DeWitt Wilson of Tahlequah, and I think the old people used to live down at Wilson Rock because my husband used to know all about that place and the place where I was borned. Old Mister DeWitt Wilson give me a pear tree the next year after I was married, and it is still out in my yard and bears every year.

I was married in a white and black checkedy calico apron that I washed for Mr. Tim Walker's mother Lizzie all day for, over close to Ft. Gibson, and I was sure a happy woman when I married that day. Him and me both got our land on our Cherokee freedman blood and I have lived to bury my husband and see two great grandchildren so far.

I bless God about Abraham Lincoln. I remember when my mammy sold pictures of him in Fort Smith for a Jew. If he give me my freedom I know he is in Heaven now.

I heard a lot about Jefferson Davis in my life. During the War we hear the Negroes singing the soldier song about hang Jeff Davis to a apple tree, and old Master tell about the time we know Jeff Davis. Old Master say Jeff Davis was just a dragoon soldier out of Fort Gibson when he bring his family out here from Tennessee, and while they was on the road from Fort Smith to where they settled young Jeff Davis and some more dragoon soldiers rid up and talked to him a long time. He say my grandmammy had a bundle on her head, and Jeff Davis say, 'Where you going Aunty?' and she was tired and mad and she said, 'I don't know, to Hell I reckon', and all the white soldiers laughed at her and made her that much mader.

I joined the Four Mile Branch church in 1879 and Sam Solomon was a Creek Negro and the first preacher I ever heard preach. Everybody ought to be in the church and ready for that better home on the other side.

All the old slaves I know are dead excepting two, and I will be going pretty soon I reckon, but I'm glad to lived to see the day the Negroes get the right treatment if they work good and behave themselves right. They don't have to have no pass to walk abroad no more, and they can all read and write now, but it's a tarnation shame some of them go and read the wrong kind of things anyways.

CHANEY RICHARDSON

AGE 90
FORT GIBSON, OKLA.

I was born in the old Caney settlement southeast of Tahlequah on the banks of Caney Creek. Off to the north we could see the big old ridge of Sugar Mountain when the sun shine on him first thing in the morning when we all getting up.

I didn't know nothing else but some kind of war until I was a grown woman, because when I first can remember my old Master, Charley Rogers, was always on the lookout for somebody or other he was lined up against in the big feud.

My master and all the rest of the folks was Cherokees, and they'd been killing each other off in the feud ever since long before I was borned, and jest because old Master have a big farm and three-four families of Negroes them other Cherokees keep on pestering his stuff all the time. Us children was always afeared to go any place less'n some of the grown folks was along.

We didn't know what we was a-feared of, but we heard the Master and Mistress talking 'bout 'another Party killing' and we stuck close to the place.

Old Mistress' name was Nancy Rogers, but I was a orphan after I was a big girl and I called her 'Aunt' and 'Mama' like I did when I was little. You see my own mammy was the house woman and I was raised in the house, and I heard the little children call old mistress 'mama' and so I did too. She never did make me stop.

My pappy and mammy and us children lived in a one-room log cabin close to the creek bank and just a little piece from old Master's house.

My pappy's name was Joe Tucker and my mammy's name was Ruth Tucker. They belonged to a man named Tucker before I was born and he sold them to Master Charley Rogers and he just let them go on by the same name if they wanted to, because last name didn't mean nothing to a slave anyways. The folks jest called my pappy 'Charley Rogers' boy Joe.'

I already had two sisters, Mary and Mandy, when I was born, and purty soon I had a baby brother, Louis. Mammy worked at the Big House and took me along every day. When I was a little bigger I would help hold the hank when she done the spinning and old Mistress done a lot of the weaving and some knitting. She jest set by the window and knit most all of the time.

When we weave the cloth we had a big loom out on the gallery, and Miss Nancy tell us how to do it.

Mammy eat at our own cabin, and we had lots of game meat and fish the boys get in the Caney Creek. Mammy bring down deer meat and wild turkey sometimes, that the Indian boys git on Sugar Mountain.

Then we had corn bread, dried bean bread and green stuff out'n Master's patch. Mammy make the bean bread when we git short of corn meal and nobody going to the mill right away. She take and bile the beans and mash them up in some meal and that make it go a long ways.

The slaves didn't have no garden 'cause they work in old Master's garden and make enough for everybody to have some anyway.

When I was about 10 years old that feud got so bad the Indians was always talking about getting their horses and cattle killed and their slaves harmed. I was too little to know how bad it was until one morning my own mammy went off somewhere down the road to git some stuff to dye cloth and she didn't come back.

Lots of the young Indian bucks on both sides of the feud would ride around the woods at night, and old Master got powerful oneasy about my mammy and had all the neighbors and slaves out looking for her, but nobody find her.

It was about a week later that two Indian men rid up and ast old master wasn't his gal Ruth gone. He says yes, and they take one of the slaves along with a wagon to show where they seen her.

They find her in some bushes where she'd been getting bark to set the dyes, and she been dead all the time. Somebody done hit her in the head with a club and shot her through and through with a bullet too. She was so swole up they couldn't lift her up and jest had to make a deep hole right along side of her and roll her in it she was so bad mortified.

Old Master nearly go crazy he was so mad, and the young Cherokee men ride the woods every night for about a month, but they never catch on to who done it.

I think old Master sell the children or give them out to somebody then, because I never see my sisters and brother for a long time after the Civil War, and for me, I have to go live with a new mistress that was a Cherokee neighbor. Her name was Hannah Ross, and she raised me until I was grown.

I was her home girl, and she and me did a lot of spinning and weaving too. I helped the cook and carried water and milked. I carried the water in a home-made pegging set on my head. Them peggings was kind of buckets made out of staves set around a bottom and didn't have no handle.

I can remember weaving with Miss Hannah Ross. She would weave a strip of white and one of yellow and one of brown to make it pretty. She had a reel that would pop every time it got to half skein so she would know to stop and fill it up again. We used copperas and some kind of bark she bought at the store to dye with. It was cotton clothes winter and summer for the slaves, too, I'll tell you.

When the Civil War come along we seen lots of white soldiers in them brown butternut suits all over the place, and about all the Indian men was in it too. Old master Charley Rogers' boy Charley went along too. Then pretty soon—it seem like about a year—a lot of the Cherokee men come back home and say they not going back to the War with that General Cooper and some of them go off the Federal side because the captain go to the Federal side too.

Somebody come along and tell me my own pappy have to go in the war and I think they say he on the Copper side, and then after while Miss Hannah tell me he git kilt over in Arkansas.

I was so grieved all the time I don't remember much what went on, but I know pretty soon my Cherokee folks had all the stuff they had et up by the soldiers and they was jest a few wagons and mules left.

All the slaves was piled in together and some of the grown ones walking, and they took us way down across the big river and kept us in the bottoms a long time until the War was over.

We lived in a kind of a camp, but I was too little to know where they got the grub to feed us with. Most all the Negro men was off somewhere in the War.

Then one day they had to bust up the camp and some Federal soldiers go with us and we all start back home. We git to a place where all the houses is burned down and I ask what is that place. Miss Hannah say: 'Skullyville, child. That's where they had part of the War.'

All the slaves was set out when we git to Fort Gibson, and the soldiers say we all free now. They give us grub and clothes to the Negroes at that place. It wasn't no town but a fort place and a patch of big trees.

Miss Hannah take me to her place and I work there until I was grown. I didn't git any money that I seen, but I got a good place to stay.

Pretty soon I married Ran Lovely and we lived in a double log house here at Fort Gibson. Then my second husband was Henry Richardson, but he's been dead for years, too. We had six children, but they all dead but one.

I didn't want slavery to be over with, mostly because we had the War I reckon. All that trouble made me the loss of my mammy and pappy, and I was always treated good when I was a slave. When it was over I had rather be at home like I was. None of the Cherokees ever whipped us, and my mistress give me some mighty fine rules to live by to git along in the world, too.

The Cherokees didn't have no jail for Negroes and no jail for themselves either. If a man done a crime he come back to take his punishment without being locked up.

None of the Negroes ran away when I was a child that I know of. We all had plenty to eat. The Negroes didn't have no school and so I can't read and write, but they did have a school after the War, I hear. But we had a church made out of a brush arbor and we would sing good songs in Cherokee sometimes.

I always got Sunday off to play, and at night I could go git a piece of sugar or something to eat before I went to bed and Mistress didn't care.

We played bread-and-butter and the boys played hide the switch. The one found the switch got to whip the one he wanted to.

When I got sick they give me some kind of tea from weeds, and if I et too many roasting ears and swole up they biled gourds and give me the liquor off'n them to make me throw up.

I've been a good church-goer all my life until I git too feeble, and I still understand and talk Cherokee language and love to hear songs and parts of the Bible in it because it make me think about the time I was a little girl before my mammy and pappy leave me.

BETTY ROBERTSON

AGE 93
FORT GIBSON, OKLAHOMA

I was born close to Webbers Falls, in the Canadian District of the Cherokee Nation, in the same year that my pappy was blowed up and killed in the big boat accident that killed my old Master.

I never did see my daddy excepting when I was a baby and I only know what my mammy told me about him. He come from across the water when he was a little boy, and was grown when old Master Joseph Vann bought him, so he never did learn to talk much Cherokee. My mammy was a Cherokee slave, and talked it good. My husband was Cherokee born negro, too, and when he got mad he forgit all the English he knowed.

Old Master Joe had a mighty big farm and several families of negroes, and he was a powerful rich man. Pappy's name was Kalet Vann, and mammy's name was Sally. My brothers was name Sone and Frank. I had one brother and one sister sold when I was little and I don't remember the names. My other sisters was Polly, Ruth and Liddie. I had to work in the kitchen when I was a gal, and they was ten or twelve children smaller than me for me to look after, too. Sometime Young Master Joe and the other boys give me a piece of money and say I worked for it, and I reckon I did for I have to cook five or six times a day. Some of the Master's family was always going down to the river and back, and every time they come in I have to fix something to eat. Old Mistress had a good cookin' stove, but most Cherokees had only a big fireplace and pot hooks. We had meat, bread, rice, potatoes and plenty of fish and chicken. The spring time give us plenty of green corn and beans too. I couldn't buy anything in slavery time, so I jest give the piece of money to the Vann children. I got all the clothes I need from old Mistress, and in winter I had high top shoes with brass caps on the toe. In the summer I wear them on Sunday, too. I wore loom cloth clothes, dyed in copperas what the old negro women and the old Cherokee women made.

The slaves had a pretty easy time I think. Young Master Vann never very hard on us and he never whupped us, and old Mistress was a widow woman and a good Christian and always kind. I sure did love her. Maybe old Master Joe Vann was harder, I don't know, but that was before my time. Young Master never whip his slaves, but if they don't mind good he sell them off sometimes. He sold one of my brothers and one sister because they kept running off. They wasn't very big either, but one day two Cherokees rode up and talked a long time, then young Master came to the cabin and said they were sold because mammy couldn't make them mind him. They got on the horses behind the men and went off.

Old Master Joe had a big steam boat he called the Lucy Walker, and he run it up and down the Arkansas and the Mississippi and the Ohio river, old Mistress say. He went clean to Louisville, Kentucky, and back. My pappy was a kind of a boss of the negroes that run the boat, and they all belong to old Master Joe. Some had been in a big run-away and had been brung back, and wasn't so good, so he keep them on the boat all the time mostly. Mistress say old Master and my pappy on the boat somewhere close to Louisville and the boiler bust and tear the boat up. Some niggers say my pappy kept hollering, 'Run it to the bank! Run it to the bank!' but it sink and him and old Master died.

Old Master Joe was a big man in the Cherokees, I hear, and was good to his negroes before I was born. My pappy run away one time, four or five years before I was born, mammy tell me, and at that time a whole lot of Cherokee slaves run off at once. They got over in the Creek country and stood off the Cherokee officers that went to git them, but pretty soon they give up and come home. Mammy say they was lots of excitement on old Master's place and all the negroes mighty scared, but he didn't sell my pappy off. He jest kept him and he was a good negro after that. He had to work on the boat, though, and never got to come home but once in a long while.

Young Master Joe let us have singing and be baptized if we want to, but I wasn't baptized till after the War. But we couldn't learn to read or have a book, and the Cherokee folks was afraid to tell us about the letters and figgers because they have a law you go to jail and a big fine if you show a slave about the letters.

When the War come they have a big battle away west of us, but I never see any battles. Lots of soldiers around all the time though.

One day young Master come to the cabins and say we all free and can't stay there less'n we want to go on working for him just like we'd been for our feed and clothes. Mammy got a wagon and we traveled around a few days and go to Fort Gibson. When we git to Fort Gibson they was a lot of negroes there, and they had a camp meeting and I was baptized. It was in the Grand River close to the ford, and winter time. Snow on the ground and the water was muddy and all full of pieces of ice. The place was all woods, and the Cherokees and the soldiers all come down to see the baptizing.

We settled down a little ways above Fort Gibson. Mammy had the wagon and two oxen, and we worked a good size patch there until she died, and then I git married to Cal Robertson to have some body to take care of me. Cal Robertson was eighty-nine years old when I married him forty years ago, right on this porch. I had on my old clothes for the wedding, and I ain't had any good clothes since I was a little slave girl. Then I had clean warm clothes and I had to keep them clean, too!

I got my allotment as a Cherokee Freedman, and so did Cal, but we lived here at this place because we was too old to work the land ourselves. In slavery time the Cherokee negroes do like anybody else when they is a death—jest listen to a chapter in the Bible and all cry. We had a good song I remember. It was "Don't Call the Roll, Jesus, Because I'm Coming Home." The only song I remember from the soldiers was "Hang Jeff Davis to a Sour Apple Tree," and I remember that because they said he used to be at Fort Gibson one time. I don't know what he done after that.

I don't know about Robert Lee, but I know about Lee's Creek.

I been a good Christian ever since I was baptized, but I keep a little charm here on my neck anyways, to keep me from having the nose bleed. Its got a buckeye and a lead bullet in it. I had a silver dime on it, too, for a long time, but I took it off and got me a box of snuff. I'm glad the War's over and I am free to meet God like anybody else, and my grandchildren can learn to read and write.

MORRIS SHEPPARD

AGE 85 YRS.
FORT GIBSON, OKLA.

Old Master tell me I was borned in November 1852, at de old home place about five miles east of Webbers Falls, mebbe kind of northeast, not far from de east bank of de Illinois River.

Master's name was Joe Sheppard, and he was a Cherokee Indian. Tall and slim and handsome. He had black eyes and mustache but his hair was iron gray, and everybody liked him because he was so good-natured and kind.

I don't remember old Mistress' name. My mammy was a Crossland negro before she come to belong to Master Joe and marry my pappy, and I think she come wid old Mistress and belong to her. Old Mistress was small and mighty pretty too, and she was only half Cherokee. She inherit about half a dozen slaves, and say dey was her own and old Master can't sell one unless she give him leave to do it.

Dey only had two families of slaves wid about twenty in all, and dey only worked about fifty acres, so we sure did work every foot of it good. We git three or four crops of different things out of dat farm every year, and something growing on dat place winter and summer.

Pappy's name was Caesar Sheppard and Mammy's name was Easter. Dey was both raised 'round Webber's Falls somewhere. I had two brothers, Silas and George, dat belong to Mr. George Holt in Webber's Falls town. I got a pass and went to see dem sometimes, and dey was both treated mighty fine.

The Big House was a double log wid a big hall and a stone chimney but no porches, wid two rooms at each end, one top side of de other. I thought it was mighty big and fine.

Us slaves lived in log cabins dat only had one room and no windows so we kept de doors open most of de time. We had home-made wooden beds wid rope springs, and de little ones slept on trundle beds dat was home-made too.

At night dem trundles was jest all over de floor, and in de morning we shove dem back under de big beds to git dem out'n de way. No nails in none of dem nor in de chairs and tables. Nails cost big money and old Master's blacksmith wouldn't make none 'cepting a few for old Master now and den, so we used wooden dowels to put things together.

They was so many of us for dat little field we never did have to work hard. Up at five o'clock and back in sometimes about de middle of de evening, long before sundown, unless they was a crop to git in before it rain or something like dat.

When crop was laid by de slaves jest work 'round at dis and dat and keep tol'able busy. I never did have much of a job, jest tending de calves mostly. We had about twenty calves and I would take dem out and graze 'em while some grown-up negro was grazing de cows so as to keep de cows milk. I had me a good blaze-faced horse for dat.

One time old Master and another man come and took some calves off and Pappy say old Master taking dem off to sell. I didn't know what 'sell' meant and I ast Pappy, 'Is he going to bring 'em back when he git through selling them?' I never did see no money neither, until time of de War or a little before.

Master Joe was sure a good provider, and we always had plenty of corn pone, sow belly and greens, sweet potatoes, cow peas and cane molasses. We even had brown sugar and cane molasses most of de time before de War. Sometimes coffee, too.

De clothes wasn't no worry neither. Everything we had was made by my folks. My aunt done de carding and spinning and my mammy done de weaving and cutting and sewing, and my pappy could make cowhide shoes wid wooden pegs. Dey was for bad winter only.

Old Master bought de cotton in Ft. Smith because he didn't raise no cotton, but he had a few sheep and we had wool-mix for winter.

Everything was stripedy 'cause Mammy like to make it fancy. She dye wid copperas and walnut and wild indigo and things like dat and make pretty cloth. I wore a stripedy shirt till I was about eleven years old, and den one day while we was down in de Choctaw Country old Mistress see me and nearly fall off'n her horse! She holler, 'Easter, you go right now and make dat big buck of a boy some britches!'

We never put on de shoes until about late November when de frost begin to hit regular and split our feet up, and den when it git good and cold and de crop all gather in any ways, they is nothing to do 'cepting hog killing and a lot of wood chopping, and you don't git cold doing dem two things.

De hog killing mean we gits lots of spare-ribs and chitlings, and somebody always git sick eating too much of dat fresh pork. I always pick a whole passel of muskatines for old Master and he make up sour wine, and dat helps out when we git the bowel complaint from eating dat fresh pork.

If somebody bad sick he git de doctor right quick, and he don't let no negroes mess around wid no poultices and teas and sech things like cupping-horns neither!

Us Cherokee slaves seen lots of green corn shootings and de like of dat, but we never had no games of our own. We was too tired when we come in to play any games. We had to have a pass to go any place to have singing or praying, and den they was always a bunch of patrollers around to watch everything we done. Dey would come up in a bunch of about nine men on horses, and look at all our passes, and if a negro didn't have no pass dey wore him out good and made him go home. Dey didn't let us have much enjoyment.

Right after de War de Cherokees that had been wid the South kind of pestered the freedmen some, but I was so small dey never bothered me; jest de grown ones. Old Master and Mistress kept on asking me did de night riders persecute me any but dey never did. Dey told me some of dem was bad on negroes but I never did see none of dem night riding like some said dey did.

Old Master had some kind of business in Fort Smith, I think, 'cause he used to ride in to dat town 'bout every day on his horse. He would start at de crack of daylight and not git home till way after dark. When he get home he call my uncle in and ask about what we done all day and tell him what we beter do de next day. My uncle Joe was de slave boss and he tell us what de Master say do.

When dat Civil War come along I was a pretty big boy and I 'member it good as anybody. Uncle Joe tell us all to lay low and work hard and nobody bother us, and he would look after us. He sure stood good with de Cherokee neighbors we had, and dey all liked him. There was Mr. Jim Collins, and Mr. Bell, and Mr. Dave Franklin, and Mr. Jim Sutton and Mr. Blackburn that lived around close to us and de all had slaves. Dey was all wid the South, but dey was a lot of dem Pin Indians all up on de Illinois River and dey was wid de North and dey taken it out on de slave owners a lot before de War and during it too.

Dey would come in de night and hamstring de horses and maybe set fire to de barn, and two of 'em named Joab Scarrel and Tom Starr killed my pappy one night just before de War broke out.

I don't know what dey done it for, only to be mean, and I guess they was drunk.

Them Pins was after Master all de time for a while at de first of de War, and he was afraid to ride into Fort Smith much. Dey come to de house one time when he was gone to Fort Smith and us children told dem he was at Honey Springs, but they knowed better and when he got home he said somebody shot at him and bushwhacked him all the way from Wilson's Rock to dem Wildhorse Mountains, but he run his horse like de devil was setting on his tail and dey never did hit him. He never seen dem either. We told him 'bout de Pins coming for him and he just laughed.

When de War come old Master seen he was going into trouble and he sold off most of de slaves. In de second year of de War he sold my mammy and my aunt dat was Uncle Joe's wife and my two brothers and my little sister. Mammy went to a mean old man named Peper Goodman and he took her off down de river, and pretty soon Mistress tell me she died 'cause she can't stand de rough treatment.

When Mammy went old Mistress took me to de Big House to help her, and she was kind to me like I was part of her own family. I never forget when they sold off some more negroes at de same time, too, and put dem all in a pen for de trader to come and look at.

He never come until the next day, so dey had to sleep in dat pen in a pile like hogs.

It wasn't my Master done dat. He done already sold 'em to a man and it was dat man was waiting for de trader. It made my Master mad, but dey didn't belong to him no more and he couldn't say nothing.

The man put dem on block and sold 'em to a man dat had come in on a steamboat, and he took dem off on it when de freshet come down and de boat could go back to Fort Smith. It was tied up at de dock at Webbers Falls about a week and we went down and talked to my aunt and brothers and sister. De brothers was Sam and Eli. Old Mistress cried jest like any of de rest of us when de boat pull out with dem on it.

Pretty soon all de young Cherokee menfolks all gone off to de War, and de Pins was riding 'round all de time, and it ain't safe to be in dat part around Webber's Falls, so old Master take us all to Fort Smith where they was a lot of Confederate soldiers.

We camp at dat place a while and old Mistress stay in de town wid some kinfolks. Den old Master get three wagons and ox teams and take us all way down on Red River in de Choctaw Nation.

We went by Webber's Falls and filled de wagons. We left de furniture and only took grub and tools and bedding and clothes, 'cause they wasn't very big wagons and was only single-yoke.

We went on a place in de Red River bottoms close to Shawneetown and not far from de place where all de wagons crossed over to go into Texas. We was at dat place two years and made two little crops.

One night a runaway negro come across from Texas and he had de blood hounds after him. His britches was all muddy and tore where de hounds had cut him up in de legs when he clumb a tree in de bottoms. He come to our house and Mistress said for us negroes to give him something to eat and we did.

Then up come de man from Texas with de hounds and wid him was young Mr. Joe Vann and my uncle that belong to young Joe. Dey called young Mr. Joe "Little Joe Vann" even after he was grown on account of when he was a little boy before his pappy was killed. His pappy was old Captain "Rich Joe" Vann, and he been dead ever since long before de War. My uncle belong to old Captain Joe nearly all his life.

Mistress try to get de man to tell her who de negro belong to so she can buy him, but de man say he can't sell him and he take him on back to Texas wid a chain around his two ankles. Dat was one poor negro dat never got away to de North, and I was sorry for him 'cause I know he must have had a mean master, but none of us Sheppard negroes, I mean the grown ones, tried to git away.

I never seen any fighting in de War, but I seen soldiers in de South army doing a lot of blacksmithing 'long side de road one day. Dey was fixing wagons and shoeing horses.

After de War was over, old Master tell me I am free but he will look out after me 'cause I am just a little negro and I ain't got no sense. I know he is right, too.

Well, I go ahead and make me a crop of corn all by myself and then I don't know what to do wid it. I was afraid I would get cheated out of it 'cause I can't figure and read, so I tell old Master about it and he bought it off'n me.

We never had no school in slavery and it was agin the law for anybody to even show a negro de letters and figures, so no Cherokee slave could read.

We all come back to de negro cabins and barns burned down and de fences all gone and de field in crab grass and cockleburrs. But de Big House aint hurt 'cepting it need a new roof. De furniture is all gone, and some said de soldiers burned it up for firewood. Some officers stayed in de house for a while and tore everything up or took it off.

Master give me over to de National Freedmen's Bureau and I was bound out to a Cherokee woman name Lizzie McGee. Then one day one of my uncles named Wash Sheppard come and tried to git me to live wid him. He say he wanted to git de family all together agin.

He had run off after he was sold and joined de North army and discharged at Fort Scott in Kansas, and he said lots of freedmen was living close to each other up by Coffeyville in de Coo-ee-scoo-ee District.

I wouldn't go, so he sent Isaac and Joe Vann dat had been two of old Captain Joe's negroes to talk to me. Isaac had been Young Joe's driver, and he told me all about how rich Master Joe was and how he would look after us negroes. Dey kept after me 'bout a year, but I didn't go anyways.

But later on I got a freedman's allotment up in dat part close to Coffeyville, and I lived in Coffeyville a while but I didn't like it in Kansas.

I lost my land trying to live honest and pay my debts. I raised eleven children just on de sweat of my hands and none of dem ever tasted anything dat was stole.

When I left Mrs. McGee's I worked about three years for Mr. Sterling Scott and Mr. Roddy Reese. Mr. Reese had a big flock of peafowls dat had belonged to Mr. Scott and I had to take care of dem.

White folks, I would have to tromp seven miles to Mr. Scott's house two or three times a week to bring back some old peafowl dat had got out and gone back to de old place!

Poor old Master and Mistress only lived a few years after de War. Master went plumb blind after he move back to Webber's Falls and so he move up on de Illinois River 'bout three miles from de Arkansas, and there old Mistress take de white swelling and die and den he die pretty soon. I went to see dem lots of times and they was always glad to see me.

I would stay around about a week and help 'em, and dey would try to git me to take something but I never would. Dey didn't have much and couldn't make anymore and dem so old. Old Mistress had inherited some property from her pappy and dey had de slave money and when dey turned everything into good money after de War dat stuff only come to about six thousand dollars in good money, she told me. Dat just about lasted 'em through until dey died, I reckon.

By and by I married Nancy Hildebrand what lived on Greenleaf Creek, 'bout four miles northwest of Gore. She had belonged to Joe Hildebrand and he was kin to old Steve Hildebrand dat owned de mill on Flint Creek up in de Going Snake District. She was raised up at dat mill, but she was borned in Tennessee before dey come out to de Nation. Her master was white but he had married into de Nation and so she got a freedman's allotment too. She had some land close to Catoosa and some down on Greenleaf Creek.

We was married at my home in Coffeyville, and she bore me eleven children and then went on to her reward. A long time ago I came to live wid my daughter Emma here at dis place, but my wife just died last year. She was eighty three.

I reckon I wasn't cut out on de church pattern, but I raised my children right. We never had no church in slavery, and no schooling, and you had better not be caught wid a book in your hand even, so I never did go to church hardly any.

Wife belong to de church and all de children too, and I think all should look after saving their souls so as to drive de nail in, and den go about de earth spreading kindness and hoeing de row clean so as to clinch dat nail and make dem safe for Glory.

Of course I hear about Abraham Lincoln and he was a great man, but I was told mostly by my children when dey come home from school about him. I always think of my old Master as de one dat freed me, and anyways Abraham Lincoln and none of his North people didn't look after me and buy my crop right after I was free like old Master did. Dat was de time dat was de hardest and everything was dark and confusion.

Appendix B

Table I

CHEROKEE SLAVEOWNERS IN TENNESSEE IN 1835

Total Number of Owners	Name of Owner	Number of Male Slaves Owned	Number of Female Slaves Owned	Total Number of Slaves Owned	Occupation of Slaveowner
			Hamilton County		
1	John Brown	9	3	12	Farmer
2	Alexander Knave	7	7	14	Farmer
3	Levi Timberlake	1	1	2	Farmer
4	Dick Timberlake	4	2	6	Not listed
5	The Walker	1	4	5	Farmer
6	Daniel Griffin	0	1	1	Farmer
			Chickamauga County		
7	Dennis Wolf	0	1	1	Farmer
8	James Starr	4	1	5	Not listed
9	A. McCoy	0	1	1	Farmer, 1 ferry
10	Thomas Cairy	0	1	1	Farmer
11	Ezekiel McLaughlin	1	1	2	Farmer
12	Andrew McLaughlin	1	1	2	Farmer
13	James Brown	14	14	28	Farmer
14	George Candy	1	1	2	Farmer
15	William Williams	6	5	11	Farmer
16	Hair Conrad	1	6	7	Farmer

Table I (Continued)

Total Number of Owners	Name of Owner	Number of Male Slaves Owned	Number of Female Slaves Owned	Total Number of Slaves Owned	Occupation of Slaveowner
		McMinn County			
17	Samuel Candy, Sr.	1	3	4	Farmer
18	Maxwell	4	2	6	Farmer
19	John Gothard	0	1	1	Farmer
20	Franklin Adair	0	1	1	Farmer
21	Ailsey Eldridge	8	13	21	Farmer
22	John Bullard	0	1	1	Farmer
23	William Blyth	9	4	13	Farmer, 1 mill, 2 ferries
24	William Blyth, Jr.	0	1	1	Not listed
		Hamilton County			
25	Moses Fields	2	3	5	Farmer
26	John L. Garnell			3	Farmer
27	Joseph Vann	55	55	110	Farmer, 1 mill, 1 ferry
28	William Read	1	1	2	Farmer
29	John Blythe	0	1	1	Farmer
30	James Vann	5	9	14	Farmer
31	Adam Seabolt	0	1	1	Farmer
32	Wilson Nivins	0	1	1	Farmer
		McMinn County			
33	Samuel Parks	7	5	12	Farmer
34	Betsey Walker**	1	2	3	Farmer
35	Jessee Mayfield	8	7	15	Farmer
36	Jessee Bushyhead	0	4	4	Farmer

Table I (Continued)

Total Number of Owners	Name of Owner	Number of Male Slaves Owned	Number of Female Slaves Owned	Total Number of Slaves Owned	Occupation of Slaveowner
			McMinn County		
37	Alexander Clingen	0	1	1	Farmer
38	Susy Otterlifter**	2	1	3	Farmer
39	Jonathan Mulkey	0	3	3	Farmer, 1 ferry
40	John Ross	13	6	19	Farmer, 2 ferries
41	G. M. Muncell	2	2	4	Farmer
42	Lewis Ross	24	17	41	Farmer, 1 mill, 3 ferries
43	James Foreman*	0	1	1	Farmer
44	Peter Helderbrand	2	6	8	Farmer, 1 mill, 1 ferry
45	Lewis Helderbrand	1	0	1	Farmer
46	Pigeon	0	1	1	Farmer
47	J. V. Helderbrand	1	1	2	Farmer
48	Nich. B. McNair	2	2	4	Farmer, 1 ferry
49	John Helderbrand	2	1	3	Farmer, 1 ferry
50	James V. McNair	2	1	3	Farmer
51	(Name indistinguishable)	11	10	21	Not listed
52	George Hicks	1	2	3	Farmer
53	James Petit	17	11	28	Farmer
54	Lewis Tiner	2	2	4	Farmer
55	Michl. Hilderbrand	3	2	5	Farmer, 2 mills, 1 ferry
56	Levi Baley	2	1	3	Farmer
57	George Stair	2	1	3	Farmer

* Full-blood
** Female

ADDITIONAL NOTES:

427 Cherokee heads of families were listed in Tennessee, of whom 57 were listed as slaveowners; thus approximately 0.13 percent of heads of families were slaveowners.

The slaveowners possessed 480 black slaves, averaging 8.42 slaves each.

1 full-blood slaveowner was listed; he owned 1 slave.

2 female slaveowners were listed; they possessed a total of 6 slaves.

There were 56 mixed-blood Cherokees who were slaveowners.

Table II

CHEROKEE SLAVEOWNERS IN ALABAMA IN 1835

Total Number of Owners	Name of Owner	Number of Male Slaves Owned	Number of Female Slaves Owned	Total Number of Slaves Owned	Occupation of Slaveowner
58	Geo. Lowry, Sr.	7	13	20	Farmer

Jackson County

59	Geo. Lowery, Jr.	1	0	1	Farmer
60	Anderson Lowery	2	1	3	Farmer
61	Rachel Brown**	3	4	7	Not listed
62	Elizabeth Pack**	16	13	29	Farmer
63	John Cowart	0	2	2	Not listed
64	James Lowry	4	1	5	Farmer
65	Martin Benge	1	1	2	Farmer
66	Sam'l. Keys	0	1	1	Farmer
67	Doctor Wm. Davis	2	2	4	Farmer
68	Arch Campbell	0	2	2	Farmer
69	George Gunter	3	4	7	Farmer
70	Charles Melton	4	10	14	Farmer
71	Sam'l Gunter	11	11	22	Farmer
72	Edward Gunter	17	13	30	Farmer, 2 farms, 2 ferries
73	Rich. Blackburn	1	3	4	Farmer
74	John Gunter	14	16	30	Farmer

Table II (Continued)

Total Number of Owners	Name of Owner	Number of Male Slaves Owned	Number of Female Slaves Owned	Total Number of Slaves Owned	Occupation of Slaveowner
		Blount County			
75	Corn Silk	1	2	3	Farmer, 3 farms
76	David Carter	3	2	5	Farmer
77	Alexr. Gilbreath	11	11	22	Farmer
78	Martin Scrimsher	1	1	2	Farmer, 2 farms
79	John G. Ross	3	3	6	Not listed
80	John Bell	5	4	9	Farmer, 5 farms
81	James Lamar	1	1	2	Farmer
82	George Baldridge	2	3	5	Farmer
83	Jas. Crutchfield	5	3	8	Farmer
84	James Orr	0	1	1	Farmer
		Wills County			
85	Betsey Broom***	2	2	4	Farmer
86	Scraper*	0	1	1	Farmer
87	Wm. Grimmett	3	4	7	Farmer, 2 farms, 1 ferry
88	Wm. Lasley	1	1	2	Farmer
89	Nelson R. Harlin	0	1	1	Not listed
90	John Nicholson	1	0	1	Farmer
91	Richd. Ratliff, Jr.	6	7	13	Farmer
92	Richd. Ratliff, Sr.*	4	3	7	Farmer
93	James Lassley	1	1	2	Farmer, 2 farms, 1 ferry
94	John Ratliff	2	0	2	Farmer
95	George Campbell	1	6	7	Farmer
96	Chas Vann	1	3	4	Farmer
97	Geo. Fields	1	1	2	Farmer

* Full-blood
** Female
*** Female Full-blood

ADDITIONAL NOTES:

244 Cherokee heads of families were listed in Alabama, of whom 40 were listed as slaveowners; thus approximately 0.16 percent of heads of families were slaveowners.

The slaveowners possessed 299 black slaves, averaging 7.48 slaves each.

3 full-blood slaveowners were listed; they possessed a total of 12 slaves.

3 female slaveowners were listed; they possessed a total of 40 slaves.

There were 36 mixed-blood Cherokees who were slaveowners.

Table III

CHEROKEE SLAVEOWNERS IN NORTH CAROLINA IN 1835

Total Number of Owners	Name of Owner	Number of Male Slaves Owned	Number of Female Slaves Owned	Total Number of Slaves Owned	Occupation of Slaveowner
98	Charles Buffington	1	0	1	Farmer
99	Oolaohee*	1	5	6	Farmer
100	John Timpson	1	0	1	Farmer
101	David England	0	1	1	Farmer, 1 mill
102	Autheeskey*	1	0	1	Farmer, 2 farms
103	Robert Muskrat*	1	2	3	Farmer
104	George Blair	1	3	4	Farmer
105	Ned Christey	2	1	3	Farmer, 2 farms
106	John Welch	2	4	6	Farmer, 3 farms, 2 mills
107	Gideon Morris	1	1	2	Farmer
108	David Taylor	0	2	2	Farmer
109	Catey***	0	1	1	Not listed
110	Chicksuttehe*	0	1	1	Farmer
111	Dick Downing	0	1	1	Farmer, 2 farms
112	(Name indistinguishable)	1	1	2	Not listed
113	Jessee Rayper	1	1	2	Farmer

* Full-blood
** Female
*** Female Full-blood

ADDITIONAL NOTES:
  644 Cherokee heads of families were listed in North Carolina, of whom 16 were listed as slaveowners; thus approximately 0.02 percent of heads of families were slaveowners.
  The slaveowners possessed 37 black slaves, averaging 2.31 slaves each.
  5 full-blood slaveowners were listed; they possessed a total of 12 slaves.
  1 female slaveowner was listed; she possessed 1 slave.
  There were 11 mixed-blood Cherokees who were slaveowners.

Table IV

CHEROKEE SLAVEOWNERS IN GEORGIA IN 1835

Total Number of Owners	Name of Owner	Number of Male Slaves Owned	Number of Female Slaves Owned	Total Number of Slaves Owned	Occupation of Slaveowner
		Cherokee County			
114	Moses Downing	3	2	5	Farmer, 5 farms, 1 ferry
115	George Still	5	5	10	Farmer, 3 farms
116	Jack Still	1	2	3	Farmer, 4 farms
117	Laughing Girl***	0	2	2	Farmer, 4 farms
118	Jenny Harnage**	0	1	1	Not listed
119	Joseph Beck	2	1	3	Farmer
120	Surry Eaton	1	4	5	Farmer
121	James Daniel	21	16	37	Farmer, 4 farms
122	Robert Berry	0	3	3	Not listed
123	Sam Sanders	0	2	2	Farmer
124	John Sanders	2	7	9	Farmer, 5 farms
125	George Sanders	6	7	13	Farmer, 3 farms
126	Charley Tahe*	1	0	1	Farmer
127	Betsy Wolf***	2	5	7	Farmer
128	Big Chickistahe*	3	0	3	Farmer, 2 farms
		Lumpkin County			
129	Daniel Davis	9	14	23	Farmer, 5 farms, 2 mills
130	James Landrum	1	7	8	Farmer, 6 farms
131	Charles Landrum	0	1	1	Farmer
132	Silus Palmer	0	1	1	Farmer, 2 mills
133	James Crittenton*	0	1	1	Farmer
134	Sam Downing*	1	1	2	Not listed
135	Nelly Downing***	2	5	7	Farmer, 2 farms

Table IV (Continued)

Total Number of Owners	Name of Owner	Number of Male Slaves Owned	Number of Female Slaves Owned	Total Number of Slaves Owned	Occupation of Slaveowner
		Forsyth County			
136	Alford Hatson	7	3	10	Farmer
137	George Welch	0	1	1	Farmer
138	George Waters	50	50	100	Farmer, 2 farms 1 ferry
139	T. J. Charlton	15	15	30	Not listed
140	James Cleland	1	4	5	Farmer
141	John Rogers	8	8	16	Ferry boat
142	Master Brannon	6	8	14	Farmer, 2 farms, 1 ferry
143	Charles Harriss	1	2	3	Not listed
144	William Rogers	3	5	8	Farmer, 1 ferry
145	Robert Rogers	0	3	3	Farmer
146	Alford Scudder	3	3	6	Farmer, 1 mill
147	Lewis Blackburn	11	10	21	Farmer, 1 mill 1 ferry
148	Joshua Buffington	6	4	10	Farmer
149	Mosses Daniel	3	1	4	Farmer
		Floyd County			
150	Cornsilk*	2	1	3	Not listed
151	John Fields*	0	1	1	Farmer
152	Buffalo Fish*	2	1	3	Farmer
153	Water Hunter*	0	1	1	Farmer
154	Sawney Vann*	1	1	2	Farmer
155	Jacob West	8	5	13	Farmer
156	David Vann	7	6	13	Farmer
157	(Name indistinguishable)	4	1	5	Not listed
158	Rain Crow*	0	3	3	Farmer
159	Watie*	1	1	2	Farmer
160	John Ridge	11	10	21	Farmer, 2 farms, 1 ferry
161	Alexander Brown	5	2	7	Farmer
162	Tom Woodard	2	6	8	Farmer
163	Major Ridge*	6	9	15	Farmer, 4 farms, 2 ferries

Table IV (Continued)

Total Number of Owners	Name of Owner	Number of Male Slaves Owned	Number of Female Slaves Owned	Total Number of Slaves Owned	Occupation of Slaveowner

Cass County

Total Number of Owners	Name of Owner	Number of Male Slaves Owned	Number of Female Slaves Owned	Total Number of Slaves Owned	Occupation of Slaveowner
164	Lila Conacene***	1	1	2	Not listed
165	Samuel Mays	3	2	5	Farmer
166	Sally Hughes***	2	0	2	Not listed
167	Sokeeney Smith*	0	2	2	Not listed
168	Thomas Pettit	4	5	9	Not listed
169	Rachel Adair**	3	2	5	Not listed
170	Joseph Lynch	3	4	7	Farmer, 2 farms
171	James A. Thompson	3	4	7	Farmer, 2 farms
172	Lowry Williams	4	2	6	Farmer
173	Johnson Thompson	3	4	7	Farmer
174	Benjamin F. Thompson	8	5	13	Farmer
175	Baldridge*	1	1	2	Farmer
176	George W. Adair	2	3	5	Not listed
177	David Sanders	0	2	2	Farmer
178	Lucy Martin**	7	13	20	Not listed
179	Jeremiah C. Towers	5	5	10	Farmer, 2 farms
180	Edward Adair	4	3	7	Farmer
181	Samuel Adair	0	3	3	Farmer
182	Walter T. Adair	1	1	2	Farmer, 2 farms
183	Catherine Gann**	4	2	6	Not listed
184	Collins McDaniel	1	0	1	Farmer
185	Elias Boudinot	1	0	1	Not listed
186	Elijah Hicks	2	5	7	Farmer
187	John Martin	33	36	69	Not listed
188	Polly Euker***	2	2	4	Farmer
189	Jack Bell	4	3	7	Farmer
190	Wot Sanders*	1	1	2	Farmer
191	John Williams	0	2	2	Farmer
192	Daniel McCoy	1	2	3	Farmer, 1 mill
193	Arch Fields	6	1	7	Not listed
194	Polly Ratlingoard*	2	1	3	Not listed
195	Betsey Thompson**	1	1	2	Farmer
196	John Young	0	3	3	Farmer

Table IV (Continued)

Total Number of Owners	Name of Owner	Number of Male Slaves Owned	Number of Female Slaves Owned	Total Number of Slaves Owned	Occupation of Slaveowner
		Walker County			
197	John Benge	4	1	5	Farmer
198	Fox Baldridge	2	3	5	Farmer
199	Gwen (or Gwin) Baldridge**	1	0	1	Farmer
200	Suaky Smith	1	3	4	Farmer
201	Henry Nave	4	4	8	Farmer
202	Little Meat*	0	1	1	Farmer
203	Charley Fought	2	3	5	Farmer
204	Dick Taylor	10	6	16	Farmer
205	Tom Brewer*	1	0	1	Farmer
206	Tom Taylor	6	3	9	Farmer
207	John Brewer	2	1	3	Farmer, 2 farms
208	Nancy Hicks**	2	6	8	Farmer
209	Jim Sanders	0	2	2	Farmer

* Full-blood
** Female
*** Female fullblood

ADDITIONAL NOTES:

1,461 Cherokee heads of families were listed in Georgia, of whom 96 were listed as slaveowners; thus approximately 0.06 percent of heads of families were slaveowners.

The slaveowners possessed 776 black slaves, averaging 8.08 slaves each.

23 full-blood slaveowners were listed; they possessed a total of 69 slaves.

14 female slaveowners were listed; they possessed a total of 70 slaves.

There were 73 mixed-blood Cherokees who were slaveowners.

Table V

	State				Total
	Alabama	Tennessee	North Carolina	Georgia	
Number of Cherokees	11,424	2,528	3,644	8,946	26,542
Number of Cherokee Heads of Families	244	427	644	1,461	2,776
Cherokee Slaveowning Heads of Families	40	57	16	96	209
Percentage of Heads of Families Who Were Slaveowners	0.16	0.13	0.02	0.06	
Number of Male Slaves Owned	141	242	13	370	766
Number of Female Slaves Owned	158	238	24	406	826
Total Number of Slaves Owned	299	480	37	776	1,592
Average Number of Slaves Owned	7.47	8.42	2.31	8.08	
Cherokee Female Slaveowners	3	2	1	14	20
Number of Slaves Owned by Cherokee Females	40	6	6	70	129
Average Number of Slaves Owned by Cherokee Females	13.3	3	6	5	
Cherokee Full-blood Slaveowners	3	1	5	23	31
Number of Slaves Owned by Full-bloods	12	1	12	69	85
Average Number of Slaves Owned by Full-bloods	4	1	2.4	3	
Average Number of Slaves Owned by all Cherokees	7.47	8.42	2.31	8.08	
Total Acres Tilled	7,252	10,692	6,906	19,216	44,066

Table VI

EASTERN CHEROKEES WHO OWNED TWENTY OR MORE
BLACK SLAVES IN 1835

George Lowrey, Sr.	20
Lucy Martin	20
Ailsey Eldridge	21
Lewis Blackburn	21
John Ridge	21
(Name indistinguishable)	21
Samuel Gunter	22
Alexander Gilbreath	22
Daniel Davis	23
James Brown	28
James Petit	28
Elizabeth Pack	29
Edward Gunter	30
John Gunter	30
T. J. Charlton	30
James Daniel	37
Lewis Ross	41
John Martin	69
George Waters	100
Joseph Vann	110

Appendix C

A CHEROKEE ADOPTION RITE

I was adopted as a brother by a savage who bought me of my master, which he did by promising him a quantity of merchandise, and giving me what at that time I needed, such as bed-coverings, shirts, and mittens, and from that time I had the same treatment as himself. My companions were adopted by other savages, either as nephews or as cousins, and treated in the same manner by their liberators and all their families.[1]

Our clothes were taken off, and a stock was made for each of us, without, however, putting us in it; they merely put on us our slaves-collar. Then the savages, putting in each one's hand a white stick and a rattle, told us that we must sing, which we did for the space of more than three hours, at different times, singing both French and Indian songs, after which they gave us to eat of all that the women had brought from the village, bread of different sorts, sagamite (corn porridge), buffalo meat, bear meat, rabbit, sweet potatoes, and graumons. We passed the night at this place. The next day, February 8, in the morning the savages having matache [decorated] themselves according to their custom. Matacherent our whole bodies, having left us nothing but breeches, made the entry into their village in the order of a troop of infantry, marching four in each rank, half of them in front of us, who were placed two and two after being tied together, and having our collars dragging. . . . They made us march in this order, singing, and having, as we had had the evening before, a white stick and a rattle in our hands, to the chief square of the village and march three or four times around a great tree which is in the middle of that place. Then they burried at the foot of the tree a parcel of hair from each one of us, which the savages had preserved for that purpose from the time when they cut our hair off. After the march was finished they brought us into the council-house, where we were each obliged to sing four songs. Then the savages who had adopted us came and took away our collars. I followed my adopted brother who, on entering into his cabin, washed me, then after he had told me that the way was free before me, I ate with him, and there I remained two months, dressed and treated like himself, without other occupation than to go hunting twice with him. We were about thirteen days the first time and nine days the last.[2]

The savage who adopts a captive promises a quantity of merchandise to the one to whom he belongs at the moment when he buys him. This merchandise is collected from all the family of the one who makes the purchase, and is delivered in an assembly of all the relatives, each one of whom brings what he is to give and delivers it, piece by piece, to him who sold the slave, and at the receipt of each piece, he makes the rounds of the assembly, constantly carrying what has been given him, it being forbidden to lay down any piece on the ground, for then it would belong to whoever touched it first. The collection of my ransom was made on the 9th and 10th and the ceremony on the 11th.[3]

NOTES

1. *Journal of Antoine Bonnefoy,* in Samuel Cole Williams, *Early Travels in the Tennessee Country, 1540-1800* (Johnson City, Tennessee: The Watauga Press, 1928), p. 152.
2. Ibid., p. 153.
3. Ibid., p. 155.

Bibliography

MANUSCRIPTS

CHEROKEE COLLECTION, NORTHEASTERN OKLAHOMA STATE UNIVERSITY

Cherokee Documents, Vol. 27, "Missions 1849-1873"
John Ross Letters
Miscellaneous Letters
Miscellaneous Letters and Manuscripts Relating to Cherokee History
    Andrew Nave Letters
    Business Accounts
    Business Letters and Accounts
    Civil War
    Social Correspondence

GEORGIA STATE DEPARTMENT OF ARCHIVES

Cherokee Letters

GILCREASE INSTITUTE OF AMERICAN HISTORY AND ART, TULSA, OKLAHOMA

Cherokee Documents
Diary of Hannah Hicks
Foreman Papers
Hicks Papers
Hitchcock Papers
John Drew Papers
John Ross Papers
Worcester-Robertson Papers

HOUGHTON LIBRARY, HARVARD UNIVERSITY

American Board of Commissioners for Foreign Missions Archives

NATIONAL ARCHIVES, WASHINGTON, D.C.

Arbuckle to Fulton, June 26, 1839, Record Group 393, Records of the United States Continental Commands, 1821-1920, 2d Military Department, Letters Sent, November 1834-June 1841.

Smith to Dearborn, 1805, Record Group 393, Records of the United States Army Continental Commands, 1821-1920, Secretary of War Files, Indian Division, No. 484, 1805.

OKLAHOMA HISTORICAL SOCIETY

Ex-Slaves File
Foreman Collection
Foreman Papers
John Drew Papers

TENNESSEE STATE LIBRARY AND ARCHIVES

Cherokee Collection

UNIVERSITY OF TULSA LIBRARY

Alice Robertson Collection

WESTERN HISTORY COLLECTIONS, UNIVERSITY OF OKLAHOMA LIBRARY

Cherokee Nation Collection
Documents Relating to the Five Civilized Tribes
John Ross Manuscripts and Papers

CHEROKEE NATIONAL DOCUMENTS

Constitution and Laws of the Cherokee Nation. St. Louis, 1875.
Constitution of the Knights of the Golden Circle.
Eastern Cherokee Census of 1835.
Laws of the Cherokee Nation: Adopted by the Council at Various Periods. Tahlequah, 1852.

*Laws of the Cherokee Nation: Adopted by the Council at Various Periods.
The Constitution and Laws of the Cherokee Nation: Passed at Tahlequah,
Cherokee Nation, 1839-51.* Tahlequah, 1852.
*Laws of the Cherokee Nation, Passed During the Years 1839-1867, Com-
piled by Authority of the National Council.* St. Louis, 1868.

GOVERNMENT DOCUMENTS AND PUBLICATIONS

American State Papers: Indian Affairs. Vol. I. Washington, 1832.
Annual Reports of the Commissioner of Indian Affairs.
Carter, Clarence E., comp. and ed. *The Territorial Papers of the United
States.* Vols. XIX, XX. Washington, 1936-1954.
Kappler, Charles J., comp. and ed. *Indian Affairs: Laws and Treaties.*
Vols. I-III. Washington, 1904.
Mooney, James. "Myths of the Cherokees," *Nineteenth Annual Report
of the Bureau of American Ethnology.* Washington, 1900.
Royce, Charles C. "Indian Land Cessions In The United States."
Eighteenth Annual Report of The Bureau of American Ethnology.
Washington, 1899.
U.S. Congress, House. *Executive Document* No. 116. 37th Cong., 2d.
Sess. Washington, 1862.
*War of the Rebellion: A Compilation of the Official Records of the
Union and Confederate Armies, The.* Series I, Vol. XIII; Series IV,
Vol. I. Washington, 1880-1900.

THESES AND DISSERTATIONS

Ballenger, Thomas Lee. "The Development of Law and Legal Institutions
Among the Cherokees." Ph.D. dissertation, University of Oklahoma,
1938.
Foster, Lawrence. "Negro-Indian Relationships in the Southeast."
Printed Ph.D. dissertation, University of Pennsylvania, 1935.
Malone, Henry Thompson. "Cherokee Civilization in the Lower Appalachians,
Especially in North Georgia, Before 1830." M.A. thesis, Emory University,
1949.

Moffitt, James W. "A History of Early Baptist Missions among the Five
    Civilized Tribes." Ph.D. dissertation, University of Oklahoma, 1946.
Moulton, Gary Evan. "John Ross, Cherokee Chief." Ph.D. dissertation,
    Oklahoma State University, 1974.
Roethler, Michael. "Negro Slavery among the Cherokee Indians, 1540-1866."
    Ph.D. dissertation, Fordham University, 1964.

RESEARCH PAPERS

Halliburton, Janet D. "Black Slavery Among the Creek Indians." A paper
    read at the 1973 Annual Convention of the Oklahoma College History
    Professors Association at Ada, Oklahoma.
Lambert, Paul F. "The Cherokee Reconstruction Treaty of 1866." A paper
    read at the 1973 Annual Convention of the Oklahoma College History
    Professors Association at Ada, Oklahoma.
Wilms, Douglas C. "Cherokee Slave Ownership prior to the Removal."
    A paper read at the Ninth Annual Meeting of the Southern Anthropol-
    ogical Society, Blacksburg, Virginia, 1974.

PERSONAL CORRESPONDENCE

Charles E. Farris to Author, February 15, 1973.

NEWSPAPERS

Arkansas Gazette, October 14, 1823; November 24, 1826; January 20,
    1829; January 27, 1829.
Chattanooga Times, February 2, 1938; April 27, 1948.
Cherokee Advocate, May 15, 1845; October 23, 1845; December 18,
    1845; October 7, 1847; February 12, 1849; April 16, 1849.

Cherokee Phoenix, June 18, 1828; June 24, 1829; July 15, 1829;
  October 14, 1829; June 5, 1830; December 26, 1830; October 1,
  1831; October 12, 1831; February 4, 1832.
Christian Observer (London), November 1811.
Daily Oklahoman (Oklahoma City), October 30, 1932.
Missionary Herald, Vol. XLIX, 1853.
Muskogee Sunday Phoenix & Times-Democrat, August 5, 1973; December
  30, 1973.
Tulsa Daily World, November 11, 1925.
Tulsa Tribune, July 13, 1973.

ARTICLES

Abel, Annie H. "The History of Events Resulting in Indian Consolidation
  West of the Mississippi." *Annual Report of the American Historical
  Association for 1906.* Washington, 1908.
Ashcraft, Allan C. "Confederate Indian Department Conditions in August,
  1864." *Chronicles of Oklahoma* 41, no. 3 (Autumn 1963): 270-285.
_____. "Confederate Indian Territory Conditions in 1865." *Chronicles
  of Oklahoma* 42, no. 4 (Winter 1964-1965): 421-428.
_____. "Confederate Indian Troop Conditions in 1864." *Chronicles of
  Oklahoma* 41, no. 4 (Winter 1963-1964): 442-449.
Aycock, Roger. "Historic 'Chieftains.' " *State Mutual Anchor* 35, no. 3
  (Third Quarter, 1971): 1-17.
Baillow, Clemens de. "The Chief Vann House at Spring Place Georgia."
  Early Georgia 2, no. 2 (Spring 1957): 3-11.
Ballenger, T. L. "The Andrew Nave Letters: New Cherokee Source
  Materials at Northeastern State College." *Chronicles of Oklahoma*
  30, no. 1 (Spring 1952): 2-5.
_____. "The Death and Burial of Major Ridge." *Chronicles of Oklahoma*
  51, no. 1 (Spring 1973): 100-105.
Beeson, Leola Selman. "Homes of Distinguished Cherokee Indians."
  Chronicles of Oklahoma 11, no. 3 (September 1933): 927-941.
Broemeling, Carol B. "Cherokee Indian Agents, 1830-1874." *Chronicles
  of Oklahoma* 50, no. 4 (Winter 1974): 437-457.
Dale, Edward Everett. "Letters of John Rollin Ridge." *Chronicles of
  Oklahoma* 4, no. 4 (December 1926): 312-321.

_____. "The Cherokees in the Confederacy." *Journal of Southern History* 13, no. 2 (May 1947): 159-185.

Davis, J. B. "Slavery in the Cherokee Nation." *Chronicles of Oklahoma* 11, no. 4 (December 1933): 1056-1072.

Delly, Lillian. "Episode at Cornwall." *Chronicles of Oklahoma* 51, no. 4 (Winter 1973-1974): 444-450.

Downes, Randolph C. "Cherokee-American Relations in the Upper Tennessee Valley, 1776-1791." *East Tennessee Historical Society Publications* (1936): 35-53.

Downing, A. "The Cherokee Indians and Their Neighbors." *American Antiquarian* 17, no. 6 (November 1895): 307-316.

Forbes, Gerald. "The Part Played by the Enslavement of the Indians in the Removal of the Tribes to Oklahoma." *Chronicles of Oklahoma* 16, no. 2 (June 1938): 163-170.

Foreman, Carolyn Thomas. "The Foreign Mission School at Cornwall, Connecticut." *Chronicles of Oklahoma* 7, no. 3 (September 1929): 242-259.

_____. "Alice Ross Howard." *Chronicles of Oklahoma* 23, no. 3 (Autumn 1945): 249-253.

_____. "Captain David McNair and His Descendants." *Chronicles of Oklahoma* 36, no. 1 (Autumn 1958): 270-281.

_____. "Early History of Webbers Falls." *Chronicles of Oklahoma* 29, no. 4 (Winter 1951-1952): 444-483.

_____. "Miss Sophia Sawyer and Her School." *Chronicles of Oklahoma* 32, no. 4 (Winter 1954-1955): 395-413.

_____. "Pierce Mason Butler." *Chronicles of Oklahoma* 30, no. 1 (Spring 1952): 6-28.

_____. "Texana." *Chronicles of Oklahoma* 31, no. 2 (Summer 1953): 178-188.

Foreman, Grant. "Notes of a Missionary among the Cherokees." *Chronicles of Oklahoma* 16, no. 2 (June 1938): 171-189.

_____. "Some New Light on Houston's Life among the Cherokee Indians." *Chronicles of Oklahoma* 9, no. 2 (June 1931): 139-152.

Good, Mary Elizabeth. "The Diary of Hannah Hicks." *American Scene* 13, no. 3: 2-21.

Graebner, Norman Arthur. "Pioneer Indian Agriculture in Oklahoma." *Chronicles of Oklahoma* 23, no. 3 (Autumn 1945): 232-248.

_____. "Provincial Indian Society in Eastern Oklahoma." *Chronicles of Oklahoma* 23, no. 4 (Winter 1945-1946): 323-337.

Grant, Ludovick. "Historical Relation of Facts Delivered by Ludovick Grant, Indian Trader, to his Excellency, the Governor of South Carolina," *South Carolina Historical and Genealogical Magazine* 10, no. 1 (January 1909): 54-69.

Hafen, LeRoy R. "Cherokee Goldseekers in Colorado, 1849-50." *Colorado Magazine* 15, no. 3 (May 1938): 101-109.

Halliburton, R., Jr. "Black Slave Control in the Cherokee Nation." *Journal of Ethnic Studies* 3, no. 2 (Summer 1975): 23-35.

_____. "Free Black Owners of Slaves: A Reappraisal of the Woodson Thesis." *South Carolina Historical Magazine* 76, no. 3 (July 1975): 129-142.

_____. "Northeastern's Seminary Hall." *Chronicles of Oklahoma* 51, no. 4 (Winter 1973-1974): 391-398.

_____. "Origins of Black Slavery among the Cherokees." *Chronicles of Oklahoma* 52, no. 4 (Winter 1974-1975): 483-496.

Hamer, Philip M. "The Wataugans and the Cherokee Indians in 1776." *East Tennessee Historical Society Publications* (1931), 108-126.

Holland, Reid A. "Life in the Cherokee Nation." *Chronicles of Oklahoma* 49, no. 3 (Autumn 1971): 284-301.

Jeltz, Wyatt F. "The Relations of Negroes and Choctaw and Chickasaw Indians." *Journal of Negro History* 33, no. 1 (January 1948): 24-37.

Johnson, J. H. "Documentary Evidence of the Relations of Negroes and Indians." *Journal of Negro History* 14, no. 1 (January 1929): 21-43.

Knight, Oliver. "History of the Cherokees, 1830-1846." *Chronicles of Oklahoma* 34, no. 2 (Summer 1956): 159-182.

Lewit, Robert T. "Indian Missions and Antislavery Sentiment: A Conflict of Evangelical and Humanitarian Ideals." *Mississippi Valley Historical Review* 50, no. 1 (June 1963): 39-55.

Malone, Henry Thompson. "The Early Nineteenth Century Missionaries in the Cherokee Country." *Tennessee Historical Quarterly* 10, no. 2 (June 1951): 127-139.

Moore, Cherrie Adair. "William Penn Adair." *Chronicles of Oklahoma* 29, no. 1 (Spring 1951): 32-41.

Porter, Kenneth W. "Negroes on the Southern Frontier." *Journal of Negro History* 33, no. 1 (January 1948): 53-78.

_____. "Notes Supplementary to Relations between Negroes and Indians." *Journal of Negro History* 18, no. 3 (July 1933): 282-321.

_____. "Relations between Negroes and Indians within the Present
Limits of the United States." *Journal of Negro History* 17, no. 3
(July 1932): 287-367.

Rothrock, Mary U. "Carolina Traders among the Overhill Cherokees,
1690-1760." *East Tennessee Historical Society Publications,*
no. 1 (1929): 3-18.

"Samuel Houston Mayes," *Chronicles of Oklahoma* 6, no. 2 (June 1928):
228-331.

Shadburn, Don L. "Cherokee Statesmen: The John Rogers Family of
Chattahoochee." *Chronicles of Oklahoma* 50, no. 1 (Spring 1972):
12-40.

Springston, John L. "Lynch's Mill Was Spavinaw's Name in Early Day
History." *Chronicles of Oklahoma* 5, no. 3 (September 1927):
322-327.

Swanton, John R. "Aboriginal Culture of the Southeast." Bureau of
American Ethnology, Forty-second Annual Report (1928): 673-
726.

_____. "De Soto's Line of March from the Viewpoint of an Ethnologist."
Proceedings of the Mississippi Valley Historical Association 5 (1911):
147-157.

Torrey, Charles Cutler. "Autobiography of Mr. Torrey." Ed. by Grant
Foreman. *Chronicles of Oklahoma* 16, no. 2 (June 1938): 171-189.

Vann, R. P. "Reminiscences of Mr. R. P. Vann East of Webbers Falls,
Oklahoma." Ed. by Grant Foreman. *Chronicles of Oklahoma* 11,
no. 2 (June 1933): 838-844.

Westbrook, Harriette Johnson. "The Chouteaus." *Chronicles of Oklahoma*
11, no. 2 (September 1933): 786-797.

Willis, William P. "Divide and Rule: Red, White and Black in the Southeast." *Journal of Negro History* 48, no. 3 (July 1963): 157-176.

Willston, Walt. "Freedmen in Indian Territory during Reconstruction."
Chronicles of Oklahoma 49, no. 2 (Summer 1971-1972): 230-344.

Wilms, Douglas C. "A Note on the District Boundaries of the Cherokee
Nation, 1820." *Appalachian Journal* 2: 284-285.

_____. "Cherokee Settlement Patterns in Nineteenth Century Georgia."
Southeastern Geographer 14, no. 1 (May 1974): 46-53.

Wright, Muriel H. "Early Navigation and Commerce along the Arkansas
and Red Rivers in Oklahoma." *Chronicles of Oklahoma* 8, no. 1
(March 1930): 64-88.

_____. "The Journal of John Lowery Brown of the Cherokee Nation En Route to California in 1850." *Chronicles of Oklahoma* 12, no. 2 (June 1934): 177-213.

BOOKS

Abel, Annie H. *The American Indian as a Participant in the Civil War.* Cleveland, 1919.
_____. *The American Indian as Slaveholder and Secessionist.* Cleveland, 1915.
_____. *The American Indian under Reconstruction.* Cleveland, 1925.
Adair, James. *The History of the American Indians.* Ed. with an introduction by Samuel C. Williams. Johnson City, Tennessee, 1930.
Alden, John R. *John Stuart and the Southern Colonial Frontier.* Ann Arbor, 1944.
Armstrong, Zella. *The History of Hamilton County and Chattanooga Tennessee.* Vols. 1 and 2. Chattanooga, 1931.
Ballenger, T. L. *Around Tahlequah Council Fires.* Oklahoma City, 1945.
Bartram, William. *Travels through North and South Carolina, Georgia, East and West Florida, the Cherokee Country, the Extensive Territory of the Muscolgulges or Creek Confederacy and the Country of the Choctaws.* Philadelphia, 1791.
Bass, Althea. *Cherokee Messenger.* Norman, 1936.
Battey, George M., Jr. *A History of Rome and Floyd County.* Atlanta, 1922.
Bearss, Ed, and Arrell M. Gibson. *Fort Smith: Little Gibraltar on the Arkansas.* Norman, 1969.
Bell, George Morrison, Sr. *Genealogy of "Old & New Cherokee Indian Families."* Bartlesville, Oklahoma, 1972.
Benedict, John D. *Muskogee and Northeastern Oklahoma.* Vol. 1. Chicago, 1922.
Bourne, Edward G., ed. *Narratives of the Career of Hernando de Soto.* Vols. 1 and 2. New York, 1922.
Britton, Wiley. *Civil War on the Border.* New York, 1891-1904.
_____. *The Union Indian Brigade in the Civil War.* Kansas City, 1922.

Brown, Catherine. *Memoir of Catherine Brown, A Christian Indian of the Cherokee Nation.* Ed. by Rufus Anderson. Boston, 1928.

Brown, John P. *Old Frontiers: The Story of the Cherokee Indians from Earliest Times to the Date of Their Removal to the West, 1838.* Kingsport, Tennessee, 1938.

Cain, Andrew V. *History of Lumpkin County for the First Hundred Years 1832-1932.* Atlanta, 1932.

Corkran, David H. *The Cherokee Frontier: Conflict and Survival, 1740-62.* Norman, 1962.

Corry, John Pitts. *Indian Affairs in Georgia 1732-1756.* Philadelphia, 1936.

Cotterill, Robert S. *The Southern Indians: The Story of the Civilized Tribes before Removal.* Norman, 1954.

Couch, Nevada. *Pages from Cherokee Indian History.* St. Louis, 1884.

Crane, Verner W. *The Southern Frontier, 1670-1732.* Philadelphia, 1929.

Cunningham, Frank. *General Stand Watie's Confederate Indians.* San Antonio, 1959.

Dale, Edward Everett. *Cherokee Cavaliers.* Norman, 1939.

Dennis, Henry C., comp. and ed. *The American Indian 1492-1970: A Chronology and Fact Book.* Dobbs Ferry, New York, 1971.

Dixon, William H. *White Conquest.* Vols. 1 and 2. London, 1876.

Drago, Harry Sinclair. *The Steamboaters.* New York, 1960.

Eaton, Rachel Carolyn. *John Ross and the Cherokee Indians.* Menasha, Wisconsin, 1914.

Faux, William. *Faux's Memorable Days in America, November 27, 1818-July 21, 1820.* In Thwaites, Reuben Gold, *Early Western Travels, 1748-1846,* Vol. 11. Cleveland, 1904-1907.

Fleischmann, Glen. *The Cherokee Removal, 1838.* New York, 1971.

Foreman, Carolyn Thomas. *Indians Abroad.* Norman, 1936.

_____. *Indian Women Chiefs.* Muskogee, Oklahoma, 1954.

_____. *Oklahoma Imprints.* Norman, 1936.

_____. *Park Hill.* Muskogee, Oklahoma, 1948.

Foreman, Grant. *Advancing the Frontier 1830-1860.* Norman, 1933.

_____. *A History of Oklahoma.* Norman, 1942.

_____. *The Five Civilized Tribes.* Norman, 1934.

_____. *Fort Gibson, A Brief History.* Norman, 1936.

_____. *Indian Removal: The Emigration of the Five Civilized Tribes of Indians.* Norman, 1932.

_____. *Indians and Pioneers: The Story of the American Southwest before 1830.* New Haven, 1930.

_____. *Sequoyah.* Norman, 1938.

Foster, George Everett. *Se-quo-yah, The American Cadmus and Modern Moses.* Philadelphia, 1885.

Franklin, John Hope. *From Slavery to Freedom: A History of Negro Americans.* New York, 1967.

Fries, Adelaide L., ed. *Records of the Moravians in North Carolina, 1752-1820.* Raleigh, North Carolina, 1922.

Gabriel, Henry Ralph. *Elias Boudinot & His America.* Norman, 1941.

Gibson, Arrell M. *Oklahoma: A History of Five Centuries.* Norman, 1965.

Gideon, D. C. *History of Indian Territory.* New York, 1901.

Govan, Gilbert E. *The Chattanooga Country (1540-1951).* New York, 1951.

Gregg, Josiah. *Commerce of the Prairies.* Ed. by Max L. Moorhead. Norman, 1954.

Gregory, Jack. *Sam Houston with the Cherokees 1829-1833.* Austin, 1967.

Hafen, LeRoy R. *Pike's Peak Gold Rush Guidebooks of 1859.* Glendale, 1941.

Hagan, William T. *American Indians.* Chicago, 1961.

Harrington, Mark R. *Cherokee and Earlier Remains on Upper Tennessee River.* New York, 1922.

Harris, Phil. *This Is Three Forks Country.* Muskogee, Oklahoma, 1965.

Hawkins, Benjamin. *A Sketch of Creek Country in 1788-1789.* New York, 1848.

_____. *Letters of Benjamin Hawkins, 1796-1806. Collections of the Georgia Historical Society* 9. Savannah, 1916.

Haywood, John. *The Natural and Aboriginal History of Tennessee up to the First Settlement Therein by the White People in the Year 1768.* Nashville, 1823.

Herskovits, Melville J. *The American Negro.* Bloomington, Indiana, 1928.

Hitchcock, Ethan A. *A Traveler in Indian Territory: The Journal of Ethan Allen Hitchcock.* Ed. by Grant Foreman. Cedar Rapids, 1930.

Hodge, Frederick W. *Handbook of American Indians North of Mexico.* Vols. 1 and 2. Washington, D.C., 1907-1910.

_____, ed. *Spanish Explorers in the Southern United States.* New York, 1907.

Houston, Sam. *The Autobiography of Sam Houston.* Ed. by Donald Day and Harry Herbert Ullom. Norman, 1954.

James, Marquis. *The Life of Andrew Jackson: Border Captain–Portrait of a President.* New York, 1938.

Josephy, Alvin M., Jr. *The Indian Heritage of America.* New York, 1968.

Ketchum, Richard M. *Will Rogers: His Life and Times.* New York, 1973.

Latrobe, Charles Joseph. *The Rambler in North America.* London, 1836.

Lauber, Almon W. *Indian Slavery in Colonial Times within the Present Limits of the United States.* New York, 1913.

Litton, Gaston. *History of Oklahoma.* Vol. 1. New York, 1957.

Lumpkin, Wilson. *The Removal of the Cherokee Indians from Georgia.* Vols. 1 and 2. New York, 1907.

McCoy, Isaac. *Annual Register of Indian Affairs within the Indian Territory.* Washington, D.C., 1838.

_____. *History of Baptist Indian Missions.* Washington, D.C., 1840.

McDowell, W. L., ed. *Documents Relating to Indian Affairs.* Columbia, South Carolina, 1955.

_____. *Journals of the Commissioners of the Indian Trade.* Columbia, South Carolina, 1955.

McGee, G. B. *A History of Tennessee from 1663-1900.* New York, 1899.

McKenney, Thomas L. *History of the Indian Tribes of North America with Biographical Sketches and Anecdotes of the Principal Chiefs.* Vols. 1-3. Philadelphia, 1870.

McReynolds, Edwin C. *Oklahoma: A History of the Sooner State.* Norman, 1954.

_____. *Oklahoma: The Story of Its Past and Present.* Norman, 1967.

Malone, Henry Thompson. *Cherokees of the Old South: A People in Transition.* Athens, Georgia, 1956.

Maynard, Theodore. *De Soto and the Conquistadores.* New York, 1930.

Michaux, F. A. "Travels to the West of the Allegheney Mountains in the States of Ohio, Kentucky and Tennessee." In Thwaites, Reuben Gold, *Early Western Travels, 1748-1846.* Vol. 18. Cleveland, 1904-1907.

Milling, Chapman J. *Red Carolinians.* Chapel Hill, 1940.

Mohr, Walter H. *Federal Indian Relations, 1774-1778.* Philadelphia, 1933.

Mooney, James. *The Cherokee Ball Play.* Washington, 1890.

Murrell, Mrs. George. *Mrs. Murrell's Cook Book.* Walnut Hill, Montgomery, Maryland, 1846.

Nuttall, Thomas. *Journals Of Travels Into The Arkansa[s] Territory During The Year 1819, With Occasional Observations on the Manners of the*

Aborigines. In Thwaites, Reuben Gold, *Early Western Travels, 1748-1846.* Vol. 13. Cleveland, 1904-1907.

O'Beirne, H. F. *The Indian Territory: Its Chiefs, Legislators and Leading Men.* Saint Louis, 1892.

Owen, Narcissa. *Memoirs of Narcissa Owen.* Washington, D.C., 1907.

Parker, Thomas Valentine. *The Cherokee Indians.* New York, 1907.

Payne, Betty. *Dwight Presbyterian Mission.* Tulsa, 1954.

Pickett, Albert J. *History of Alabama.* Vols. 1 and 2. Charleston, 1851.

Pound, Merritt B. *Benjamin Hawkins—Indian Agent.* Athens, Georgia, 1951.

Preston, Thomas W. *Historical Sketches of the Holston Valleys.* Kingsport, Tennessee, 1926.

Richardson, Albert D. *Beyond the Mississippi, 1857-1867.* Hartford, 1867.

Rights, Douglas L. *The American Indian in North Carolina.* Winston-Salem, 1957.

Rister, Carl C. *Baptist Missions among the American Indians.* Atlanta, 1944.

Ross, Mrs. William P., ed. *The Life and Times of Honorable William P. Ross of the Cherokee Nation.* Fort Smith, Arkansas. 1893.

Ruskin, Gertrude McDaris. *John Ross: Chief of an Eagle Race.* Chattanooga, 1963.

Schwarze, Edmund. *History of the Moravian Missions among Southern Indian Tribes of the United States.* Bethlehem, Pennsylvania, 1923.

Shaw, Hellen L. *British Administration of the Southern Indians, 1756-1783.* Lancaster, Pennsylvania, 1931.

Shirk, George H. *Oklahoma Place Names.* Norman, 1965.

Smith, W. R. L. *The Story of the Cherokees.* Cleveland, Tennessee, 1928.

Stambaugh, Samuel C. *A History of the Cherokee from the Period of Our First Intercourse with Them Down to the Present Time—1846.* Washington, D.C., 1849.

Starkey, Marion L. *The Cherokee Nation.* New York, 1946.

Starr, Emmet. *Cherokees "West," 1794-1839.* Claremore, Oklahoma, 1910.

_____. *Early History of the Cherokees.* n.p., 1917.

Taylor, Orville W. *Negro Slavery in Arkansas.* Durham, North Carolina, 1958.

Teall, Kaye M., ed. *Black History in Oklahoma: A Resource Book.* n.p., 1971.

Thomas, Cyrus. *The Cherokees in Pre-Columbian Times.* New York, 1890.

Thwaites, Reuben Gold, ed. *Account of an Expedition from Pittsburg to the Rocky Mountains, Compiled from the Notes of Major Long and Other Gentlemen of the Party by Edwin James.* Vol. 4. Cleveland, 1905.
_____. *Early Western Travels, 1748-1846. . . .* 32 vols. Cleveland, 1904-1907.

Timberlake, Henry. *Lieut. Henry Timberlake's Memoirs.* Ed. by Samuel Cole Williams. Johnson City, Tennessee, 1927.

Tolson, Arthur L. *The Black Oklahomans, A History: 1541-1972.* New Orleans, 1974.

Tracy, Joseph. *History of the American Board of Commissioners for Foreign Missions.* Worcester, Massachusetts, 1840.

Underhill, Ruth Murray. *Red Man's America: A History of Indians in the United States.* Chicago, 1953.

Underwood, Thomas Bryan. *Cherokee Legends and the Trail of Tears.* Knoxville, 1956.

Van Every, Dale. *Disinherited: The Lost Birthright of the American Indian.* New York, 1966.

Walker, Robert Sparks. *Torchlight to the Cherokees.* New York, 1931.

Wardell, Morris L. *A Political History of the Cherokee Nation.* New York, 1931.

Washburn, Ceipas. *Reminiscences of the Indians.* Richmond, Virginia, 1869.

West, Anson. *A History of Methodism in Alabama.* Nashville, 1893.

Whipple, Charles K. *Relations of the American Board of Commissioners for Foreign Missions to Slavery.* Boston, 1861.

Wilkins, Thurman. *Cherokee Tragedy: The Story of the Ridge Family and the Decimation of a People.* London, 1970.

Williams, Samuel Cole. *Early Travels in the Tennessee Country, 1540-1800.* Johnson City, Tennessee, 1928.

Woodward, Grace Steel. *The Cherokees.* Norman, 1963.

Wright, Muriel H. *A Guide to the Indian Tribes of Oklahoma.* Norman, 1951.

_____. *Springplace, Moravian Mission, Cherokee Nation.* Guthrie, Oklahoma, 1940.

Young, Mary E. *Redskins, Ruffleshirts, and Rednecks: Indian Allotments in Alabama and Mississippi, 1830-1860.* Norman, 1961.

Index

ABOUT THE AUTHOR

R. Halliburton Jr. is the coordinator for the Department of History, Northeastern Oklahoma State University. His previous publications include *The Tulsa Race "War" of 1921* and articles written for *Journal of Ethnic Studies, American History Illustrated,* and *Agricultural History.*